WHEN NO ONE PURSUES

WHEN NO ONE PURSUES
Inside an FBI Investigation

Len Burton

TO: LEE NEWELL — FELLOW F-84
PILOT AND AN OLD FRIEND.

Len Burton

Golden Shield Press

WHEN NO ONE PURSUES
This is a work of fiction. All the characters and events
portrayed in this book are fictional, and any similarity to
real people or incidents is strictly coincidental.
This book was submitted to the FBI for prepublication review
and was found to contain no information of a sensitive or
classified nature. The review process does not indicate an
endorsement of the book.

Published 1999 by Golden Shield Press
Post Office Box 8115
Hot Springs, AR 71910-8115

ISBN: 0-9675510-0-5
Library of Congress Catalog Card Number: 99-75481

Cover art by Byron Taylor
Editorial team: Joy Freeman, Sally Crisp, April McGee

10 9 8 7 6 5 4 3 2 1

Printed in the United States of America

This book is dedicated, with love…

to Patsy
*who has given me forty-four years of happiness
and who gave us Weldon and Lisa*

to Weldon and Paula
who gave us Zachery and Alexander

to Lisa and Ali
who gave us Brittney

to Zach, Alex, and Brittney
who have already made us proud—and they've only just begun.

ACKNOWLEDGMENTS

Bill Ausman and Nancy Donaldson of my Hot Springs Village fiction writers' critique group were largely responsible for my finishing this project. They accepted me when I started, prodded me when I faltered, corrected me with kid gloves, and encouraged me all the way. Both of them are gifted writers and, of more importance, my good friends.

There are many others who gave me technical assistance and advice. Among them are: Wayne Bennett, Hot Springs, Arkansas; Bruce Burton, Tulsa, Oklahoma; Taylor Eubank, Pine Bluff, Arkansas; Ruth Raupe, Orlando, Oklahoma; Alex Finger, Little Rock, Arkansas; and Sue Coffey, Lisa Burton, and Kathy Karriker, Springfield, Missouri.

Both my brothers, Paul and Ben, are published writers. Not only did I benefit directly from their knowledge and experience, but their "status" provided me with an underlying motivation to succeed.

I am grateful to all.

The wicked flee when no one pursues,
but the righteous are bold as a lion.
—Proverbs 28:1, Holy Bible, RSV

THE ABDUCTION

(a)Whoever unlawfully seizes, confines, inveigles, decoys, kidnaps, abducts, or carries away and holds for ransom or reward or otherwise any person…when: (1) the person is willfully transported in interstate or foreign commerce; shall be punished by imprisonment for any term of years or for life.

—18 U.S. Code, Section 1201 (a)(1)

Charles Kogan hadn't threatened to fire anyone all day. Bookkeeper Amy Coates, not daring to look up, whispered, "If he makes it until five, he'll set a new record."

Charles Kogan was having a good day. He didn't have many. Occasionally a new employee made the mistake of suggesting to Kogan that he "have a good day." Kogan's patented reply was, "When you are surrounded by dumbshits and lazy incompetents, it is hard to have a good day." That was vintage Kogan.

Kogan had started out as a line boy at the airport in Olathe, Kansas, washing airplanes and carrying luggage. From that humble beginning, with little formal education, he clawed and scratched his way to the top of his own company. Along the way he didn't make a single friend. He made a lot of enemies.

Kogan knew every employee's job better than they did and was not shy about telling them so. His leadership tools were intimidation and fear. He was despised by most employees but grudgingly respected by those who recognized his drive and knowledge. No, Charles Kogan didn't have many good days but today he hadn't had a single occasion to ream out one of his flight instructors. Not one of his charter flights was late.

Kogan Aviation was making money, a lot of money. Kogan smiled at the thought. He was close to signing a major contract with a sprawling electronics firm to provide all their executive air travel.

He had outbid his major competitor, South County Charter, by a razor-thin margin. As usual Kogan left defeated rivals and hard feelings in his wake. The fight between Kogan Aviation and South County Charter had been played up in the local press for months. Not even the news media could exaggerate the animosity that developed between Kogan and his South County counterpart, James Kline. But now the contract seemed to be in Kogan's bag.

Today, for the first time in any employee's memory, Kogan left work early.

Sixteen-year-old Jenny Kogan had checked the clock in her red Mustang every thirty seconds since leaving cheerleader trials early. She pulled into the driveway at her Springfield, Missouri, home at exactly 4:39. She was crestfallen to see her father's Cadillac already in the garage. Her father did not tolerate tardiness. She was already nine minutes late for a conference her father had scheduled at the end of their heated discussion last night. Jenny knew what this conference would be about. It would be about grades in general, algebra in particular, and Jason Yeager. She now added punctuality to the agenda as she parked in the drive and hurried in.

In spite of the gravity of the situation, there was a spring in Jenny's step, and she barely suppressed a whistle as she bounded up the walk toward her father's office. She dreaded the upcoming lecture and the restrictions that would follow, but she knew the session would end with her father being a little less severe than he intended. Her brother Michael, twenty-five and married, and her twenty-year-old sister Kerry, a sophomore in college, both had gone through a stage of semi-rebellion against the strict rule of their father before leaving home. Jenny's mother had long ago wilted under her father's domination and now rarely spoke in his presence. But Jenny—beautiful, vivacious, energetic Jennifer Marie Kogan—knew how to handle her father.

As Jenny entered, her father was standing by his desk. He was wearing his usual business suit and stern expression. No matter how recently Jenny had seen him, she was always a little surprised at how small he was. At five feet four inches she felt she was almost eye-to-eye with him. She knew he wore elevator shoes. Her mother once warned her never to mention that fact to anyone, especially to him. A thought of Jason Yeager, six foot two in his bare feet, flashed through Jenny's mind as she turned on her best smile and reached to hug her father.

Jenny heard a noise behind her. A look of horror spread across her father's face. He yelled, "What the hell do you think you're doing?"

Jenny turned, then screamed as she saw two masked men rushing toward her. She smelled a clinic-like odor as a strong, gloved hand pressed a cloth to her mouth and nose, and a muscular arm pulled her backward toward the door. She reached up to try to free herself and felt her car keys ripped from her hand. Charles Kogan lunged toward his daughter and was intercepted by the second intruder. The man pressed a gun against Kogan's chest and pushed him violently backward across his desk. Jenny and the first man were already out the door. The second man recovered his balance and said in a high-pitched voice, "You'll hear from us." He then turned and ran behind his accomplice down the hall toward the garage.

Kogan was too shocked to feel fear. He scrambled to his feet and followed the man. Entering the garage he saw the larger man pushing Jenny into the back seat of her own car. The second man jumped into the driver's seat. Kogan stood paralyzed in disbelief as they backed down the drive and burned rubber southbound toward Battlefield Road. He made several pitiful strides in that direction before collapsing on his neighbor's lawn. He pounded the grass. "What in hell is going on?" He looked toward the corner and vowed, "I'll get you, you lousy bastards!" He then rose, straightened his tie, looked around, stretched himself to his full height and strode back toward his garage.

Police Officer Don Vickers was dispatched to the Kogan residence in response to Charles Kogan's 911 call. Vickers looked younger than his thirty-five years. He never wore his uniform hat. His blond hair was parted in the middle and hung evenly on each side of his forehead. He also had a blond mustache, much to the chagrin of his captain. When out of uniform, Vickers looked more like a small-time drug pusher than a policeman. His appearance and his "street smarts" had been largely responsible for his tremendous success as an undercover officer during his first three years on the force. He was responsible for more drug busts and the resulting convictions than any other police officer in the history of the force. In a city as small as Springfield however, the identity of an undercover officer was soon compromised through having to testify. For the past two and a half years, Vickers had been assigned to regular uniformed patrol in southeast Springfield, working the four to midnight shift, a low-crime shift in a low-crime area. Vickers was still enthusiastic about his job but recently admitted to his sergeant that he was bored with working traffic accidents and barking dogs. He requested re-assignment to northwest Springfield where there were some burglaries and convenience store holdups, and where he could keep his eyes on some of his old drug hangouts. His request was under consideration.

Vickers cut his lights and siren as he rolled into the drive at the Kogan residence on Martin Avenue. The time was 5:03 P.M. Vickers could not know he was about to enter the biggest case he would ever work.

Jenny Kogan started to regain consciousness. Her first thought was that she was floating, the same feeling as when Michael taught her how to get a high on gasoline fumes from the lawn mower.

A passing car startled Jenny. She jerked upward in fear that she had gone to sleep while driving. She screamed and reached for the steering wheel. A heavy hand pressed down on her shoulder. She couldn't see. Her hands were tied together. The memory of the incident in her father's office came crashing into her consciousness and she screamed again.

"Whoa there, baby. Just take it easy and you'll be all right. We're just taking you for a little ride."

The high-pitched voice was from in front of her. Jenny fought against panic as she tried to make sense of the situation. *I'm in the back seat of a car. My hands are tied! I'm blindfolded! Why?*

The sickening odor she smelled before was still there. It reminded her of biology lab.

"Please, please, who are you? What do you want? Please let me go."

A commanding voice directly in her left ear said, "Just shut up, and that goes for you in the front seat, too. Remember what I told you about your mouth?" The voice was stern and cruel.

For several minutes there was only the sound of the automobile and Jenny crying softly. She raised her hands to her face. The blindfold was very tight and seemed to be made of tape. It stuck to her hair at the sides of her head.

Suddenly the "boss" voice said, "Get your hands back down in your lap or I'll tie them down."

Jenny obeyed immediately. The car slowed. The driver, voice quivering, said, "There's more traffic than there ought to be. I don't like it. Maybe we ought to keep…"

"Shut your goddamn mouth and pull over! We'll do it just like we planned!" The "Boss" was shouting.

Jenny felt the car slow. She could hear the tires on the left crunching on the gravel shoulder. They stopped. She heard the driver-side door open. The Boss took her arm and pulled her past the tilted seat and out the left side. *This is my car!* She now vaguely recalled being pushed into the back seat at home. *How long ago was that? Ten minutes? Twenty minutes?* She couldn't remember. She could hear cars going by at high speed just to the right of her car.

Why are we stopping here? Jenny struggled with her sanity as these questions flew, unanswered, through her mind.

The men were on either side of her, holding her arms as they walked her down an incline. The sound of passing cars diminished behind them. Jenny felt bushes and vines pulling at her skirt and legs as the men rushed her through the underbrush. She experienced the natural fear of running into something. She attempted to slow the pace, but the two men continued to pull her forward. She caught her foot on a vine and almost fell, but the men were strong. Their grip on her arms supported her.

Do these men live in the woods? Are they going to rape me? Are they going to kill me? What have I done? Driver said they were just taking me for a little ride. That's absurd. What would be the purpose of that? Jenny sobbed quietly and contemplated the possibilities. She heard cars again. *How long have we been walking? Five minutes, at most. Are we going back to my car? What was the purpose of the walk in the woods if we are going back to the car?*

The two pulled Jenny up an incline and again the sound of traffic was very close. Boss said, "Step over the cable." Jenny stepped high when she felt the rough metal against her thigh.

Are we back to my car? It's a divided highway. Are we on the interstate?

Driver turned loose of her arm. She heard keys rattle and the opening and then the closing of a car door in front of her. Boss was still holding her left arm in a strong grip as she felt him lean forward. She heard a door open, and he pushed her into a car. *This is not my car! There's too much room.* Boss pushed her across the seat and then forced her shoulder down and away until her head was on the seat against the door. She felt the car accelerate.

The word "kidnapping" jumped unsummoned into her mind. Brief scenes from numerous TV and movie kidnappings scrolled by, but she couldn't recall the details of any of them. Some involved children.

What did the kids do? What should they have done? What do these men want? Where are we going? Will I ever see my mother again? What will Jason do? Jenny Kogan had many questions. She had no answers.

At the Kogan residence Corporal Vickers rang the doorbell.

Charles Kogan jerked the door open, "It's about, by god, time you got here."

Vickers thought, *Who is this little jerk. I made the quickest response in the history of the force and this guy jumps me about it.*

He bit his tongue to avoid saying what he felt. "What's happened here?"

"Two niggers busted in here and took my daughter. That's what has happened here," Kogan mocked. "You better get your ass in gear and get her back here, or I'll go straight to the mayor."

Vickers's reply was deceptively calm, "May I come in, sir?" He could not believe how much restraint he had learned since transferring to his new beat.

Kogan turned and walked ahead to his office. Vickers thought, *If I weren't a member of the "Thin Blue Line" I'd drop-kick this little turd from here to Branson.*

Kogan took a seat in a large padded chair behind an enormous mahogany desk. Scowling, he motioned Vickers to a chair on the other side.

Vickers said, "Now, sir, tell me what happened."

Kogan, face flushed, recited in clipped sentences the events since he arrived home.

Vickers, through questioning, pinpointed the time of the abduction as approximately 4:40 P.M. Kogan's description of the two subjects was meager. He could only say that one was big and the other was smaller. The big one was the one that took Jenny. The little one had the gun and was the one who spoke. He had a high-pitched voice. They were both dressed in dark coveralls like mechanics wear. Both were wearing full ski masks and leather gloves.

Vickers said, "You earlier referred to the subjects as African-Americans. Is that correct?"

"No, I referred to them as niggers, and that is what they were."

"How did you determine that, sir?"

"Well, you can bet your ass they were."

"Did you see that they were dark skinned? There are so few blacks in this area…"

Kogan interrupted, "Look, officer, you wanted to know what their race was, and I told you. I can't tell you how I determined that but that was my impression. I saw them for about fifteen seconds."

"And they were wearing gloves."

"Yes, I remember when the big one grabbed Jenny he had on a black glove, and he had something in his hand that he slapped over her mouth."

"Okay, I'm not trying to put words in your mouth. I just want you to be sure. I want to have our radio dispatcher get out a look-out message for your daughter, the subjects, and the car. A good description of the subjects is important now and could be even more important later."

"Well, that's all I can tell you about them, but they ought to be easy to spot, dressed like they were."

Vickers restrained himself. *I doubt, you little smartass, that they'll be driving around town in their ski masks and coveralls.* "You mentioned earlier that one of them said…What was it he said?"

Kogan replied, "It was the little one. The big one didn't say a word. The little one shoved me across my desk with his gun and said, 'You'll hear from us.' That's all that was said."

"Was there anything unusual about his voice or accent?"

"Yeah, he had a sort of high, squeaky voice."

"Did he sound like a black man?" Vickers asked with care. He didn't mean to sound sarcastic but it lit Kogan's fuse.

"How the hell should I know? I know that damn Kline has

several working for him, and I'll bet you will find out he is behind this. Why don't you ask him what one sounds like? He's probably an expert."

"Sir, I'm just trying to get a good description. I don't mean to argue with you. I realize you don't have much to go on, but we better stick with what you actually saw. If they were covered from hand to foot and wearing gloves and masks, and you didn't recognize any unusual accents or speech patterns, we better go with race unknown."

Vickers had seen cases lost on eyewitness identifications that were so far off they established reasonable doubt for the jury in spite of other overwhelming evidence. In a stressful situation, the mind can do strange things.

Kogan said, "That's one of the problems with you guys. You bend over backward to protect the minorities; but go ahead and put down what you want."

Vickers couldn't follow the logic of that statement, but it was a different slant from what he usually heard.

"Now, about the car. What can you tell me about it?"

"It's Jenny's car. A red Mustang, 1991. I don't know the tag number offhand. Two-door of course."

"Is it registered to Jenny? We need to get that tag number."

"No, she's only sixteen. It's registered to me."

"All right, sir. Now let me get a description of your daughter."

Kogan seemed stumped for a second and could only say, "Well…she's a white girl. I don't know what you need. She's about this high," holding out his hand, "blond hair. I don't know what she weighs. She's slender. She's sixteen. What else do you need?"

Vickers paused, *This guy doesn't even know his daughter. I know more about the Dairy Queen waitress who served me at lunch than he knows about his daughter.* "How was she dressed?"

"She had on her cheerleader outfit. White sweater, red skirt. It has Glendale High School or maybe just GHS on it."

Vickers called in the description of the subjects and Jenny. He asked the dispatcher to look up a 1991 Mustang registered to Charles Kogan at 2868 South Martin and include the description of the car and the tag in an all-points bulletin for a stop on the vehicle. He advised the dispatcher that the subjects were armed and the female was a hostage.

"And, Linda, make sure you get it out to the sheriff's office and the highway patrol as well."

Vickers then asked the dispatcher to contact the FBI and advise them that there had been an abduction at gunpoint and it looked like a kidnapping. "Give them Mr. Kogan's address and this telephone number, 922-3075. And advise the shift commander that I will stay on the scene pending further orders."

Jenny decided the best thing she could do was try to remember as much as she could about what was happening to her. That would keep her mind off all the unanswered questions.

Their speed had slowed to a crawl. Driver said, "We couldn't have picked a worse time. You think we ought to take the bypass?"

Boss had relaxed some, "We're not in any hurry now. Do it like we planned. We've got some waiting to do anyway."

After what Jenny judged to be twenty to twenty-five minutes in the stop-and-go traffic, their pace started to pick up again. They were almost up to their previous speed when Boss said, "This is the turn—up ahead."

Jenny felt the right turn. This was the first turn she had felt since they changed cars. The traffic sounds diminished. Jenny's panic started to return as she realized they were on a country road. "Please tell me why you are doing this. What do you want? Please don't hurt me."

Boss said, "We're gonna see how much your daddy loves you." Driver laughed.

Boss continued, "Yeah, it's gonna cost the little man a pretty penny if he wants to see your cute ass again. He might have to sell one of his airplanes."

Driver laughed even louder and started to comment, but Boss brought the merriment to an end. "Keep your eyes on the road and slow down. This would be a helluva time to get pulled over by the cops."

Driver couldn't stifle another laugh, then squeaked, "Boy, wouldn't that be the shits? I can just hear it, 'Yes sir, officer, I know we were a little fast, but we are rushing our little blind sister here to the hospital…'"

Boss exploded, "Keep your eyes on the road and your mouth shut! You're the silliest ass I've ever known."

In the silence Jenny's mind went back to that question of how much her Daddy loved her. She had never even considered that before. He didn't attend any of her school activities as many of her friends' fathers did. Her mother always defended him when that subject came up. Her mother's stock answer to any criticism of her father was, "Yes, but he is a good provider."

Her father had only recently showed any interest in her grades. He had also shown a great deal of interest in her relationship with Jason Yeager. Jason was a senior and a football player. Her father scoffed at the idea that Jason might go to college on a football scholarship. He had said, "I can't believe anyone is going to pay for his college education because he plays a silly game. Anyway, I didn't play football or go to college either and I've done all right."

Jenny couldn't argue with that nor could she see any other similarities between Jason and her father.

As for her grades, Jenny was pleased that her father was showing some interest. He never had before. She had often wondered if her father cared about her schooling. He sometimes asked how her car was running, though.

When she was eleven, her father gave her a telephone and her own private line. She didn't ask for it. She hadn't even started using the phone a lot. She later heard her mother tell a friend, "Charles heard one of his pilots talking about getting his teenage daughter her own phone. Charles ordered one for Jenny that very day."

It had been much the same with her car. She had not asked for it. None of her girlfriends had their own car even now, but on her sixteenth birthday, there it was—even before she got her driver's license. Her dad seemed to be in competition with everyone over everything. He gave her a generous allowance and sometimes asked if she had enough spending money...But did he truly love her? Some of her friends were real pals with their dads. She had never felt that way. She couldn't remember ever sharing a joke with her dad. She seemed to be more of a responsibility to him than a pal.

Some of her classmates were already reading catalogues from colleges and starting to narrow down their choices. When she tried to broach this subject with her father, he usually said, "We have plenty of time to think about that."

Jenny's thoughts were interrupted. She realized the car was coming to a stop. She could hear the turn signal, and then she felt the car make a left turn. It accelerated again. *How long has it been since that right turn? Fifteen minutes? Twenty at the most.* They seemed to be on a two-lane road again. They had only met a couple of cars.

In what Jenny judged to be ten minutes the car slowed, turned left onto a gravel road and stopped. Driver got out. Jenny heard dogs barking. She heard a chain rattle and a gate open. It sounded like one of those gates where you slide one pipe out of another to open it. Driver got back in, drove through the gate, and stopped. Boss said, "Just leave it open. We won't be here long."

Driver squeaked, "Hell no. Her goats will get out." He got out and Jenny heard the gate close. The sound was like the gate at their cabin on the Jack's Fork River.

They drove on the gravel for a short distance and stopped. The dogs were close now. She heard Driver trying to calm them. Boss pulled her upright and across the seat with him as he went out the far side of the car. When she stood up she felt dizzy and nauseated from the long ride in the awkward position and the lingering effects of the chemical. As Boss led her away from the car, one of the dogs reared up on her, causing her to stumble backward. Boss, who was behind her, caught her. Both his hands went directly onto her breasts. He yelled obscenities at the dog. She hoped his grasp was accidental, but he held her a little longer than was necessary. He then led her up three steps and onto what seemed to be a narrow porch. She heard a door open right in front of her. A woman asked, "Any trouble?"

Boss's reply was, "Do you have the place ready?"

"Yes, it's ready." The woman's voice was soft. Jenny, searching for any kind of hope on which to anchor her sanity, was comforted by that.

The Boss led her through a room, maybe two, that were carpeted; then through a room with vinyl or linoleum on the floor. They paused. She heard keys rattle and the sound of a door being unlocked and opened. Boss guided her down two steps into an area with a concrete floor. *Could this be the garage?* They stopped. "Did you get the sleeping bag put in?"

"Yes, it's in there." It was the woman, close behind her.

Jenny heard a creaking sound to her right. Boss said, "Step over the side. This will be your bed until the little man does what he is told to do."

Jenny bumped into what seemed to be a low wall or partition. It was on the floor and reached up to just above her knees. She reached out with her tied hands and felt the edge of it. It felt like wood. Boss was nudging her arm and shoulder, forcing her to step over the side with one leg and then the other. She felt the other side. It was a box! A picture of a pine coffin and a funeral flashed before her sealed eyes. She stiffened and cried out,

"Please don't do this. Please." She was still standing.

Boss turned her halfway around and pushed down on her shoulders. "Lay down. Lay down."

Jenny dropped down to her knees, sobbing from the pain and the fear of what was happening.

Boss pushed her backward. She was able to get one leg out straight before falling onto her back. With her hands still tied in front, she could not break her fall and she fell heavily onto her elbows. Her upper arms jammed hard into her shoulders. She was startled to hear a scream—her own. The sobs came harder.

"For God's sake be careful with her." It was the lady. "Don't cry, honey. We're not going to hurt you."

"I'm going to untie your hands, but you better not touch that blindfold. You understand?" It was Boss in his commanding voice.

Jenny was able to control her sobs enough to ask, "Won't you please tell me what is going on?"

Boss said, "I told you we are going to see how much your daddy loves you." With that he untied her hands and she heard the squeaking hinges. She realized they were closing the box over her. Jenny had a moment of panic. She reached up and pushed against the box. It was already solidly in place, but she was relieved to find there was some distance between her face and the lid. She remembered her grandfather's funeral. When the viewing was over, and the attendants closed the coffin, she had gasped at how close the coffin lid was to his face. *Is this to be my coffin?*

Jenny heard a car start and tires on the gravel driveway. *Are they leaving me locked up here all alone? Can I stand it here in the dark?* She started to sob but then heard footsteps. She heard the creaking lid and felt a hand on her cheek. She reached up to protect herself.

"I'll make you as comfortable as I can, honey." It was the lady. "I can't let you out except to go to the bathroom. You must stay in the box and I have to keep the lid closed and locked unless I'm here in the room. They will be here part of the time, but when they're not, I'll come and be with you when I can. It will help pass the time…for you and for me."

Mercifully, Jenny Kogan didn't know how much time she would have to pass.

THE RESPONSE

(b) With respect to subsection (a)(1) above, (18 U.S. Code, Section 1201) the failure to release the victim within twenty-four hours after he shall have been unlawfully seized, confined, inveigled, decoyed, kidnapped, abducted, or carried away shall create a rebuttable presumption that such person has been transported in interstate or foreign commerce.

—18 U.S. Code, Section 1201(b)

There was an unwritten rule in the Springfield Resident Agency of the FBI that after-hours calls were rotated among the agents still on the book. There was also a strong belief among agents that the biggest cases always surfaced after 5:30 in the afternoon and usually on Friday when they had big plans for the evening and the weekend. It wasn't Friday, but it was after 5:30, and it was Lance Barron's turn. "FBI, Barron."

"Sir, this is the dispatcher at the Springfield Police Department. Corporal Don Vickers asked that I contact you regarding a kidnapping in southeast Springfield. He responded to a 911 call and took a preliminary report from a Mr. Charles Kogan. According to the complainant, two masked males, one of them armed, took Mr. Kogan's sixteen-year-old daughter and fled the scene in the daughter's car. They were last seen going east on Battlefield Road. At 1725 hours, Officer Vickers put out an all-points bulletin with descriptions of the subjects, the victim and the automobile." The dispatcher rattled off details, including Kogan's address and telephone number.

As Barron took down the information, he motioned for the other two agents to pick up their extensions.

"Just a moment, ma'am; I'm writing as fast as I can. What time did you say the abduction occurred?"

"According to the father, 4:40 this afternoon."

"Okay and what is the name of the girl?"

"Sorry, sir." Papers rattled before the dispatcher replied, "Jennifer Marie Kogan, age sixteen."

"Did the subjects make any demands?"

"I don't know about that, sir. I've given you everything Corporal Vickers gave me."

"Okay. I will call Vickers at that number—922-3075 wasn't it?—and see what else has developed."

"Yes, sir, that's right, and what is your name, sir?"

"Barron—Lance Barron, FBI."

Most agents would have given their name and added, "Special Agent, FBI." Barron had always felt that title, Special Agent, sounded a little pretentious. Most agents were special people. He hoped he was special. He knew he was fortunate. He loved his work. He met at lot of people who didn't.

Barron repeated the information the other two agents had missed.

"Ben, how about going over to the telephone company and start the ball rolling on a trap-and-trace on Kogan's phone. Maybe you can get there before all their technicians leave. After I get all the facts and talk to the boss in Kansas City, I'll give you a call there and let you know if we are in or out. We need to get a jump if we're in. Also run it by the U.S. Attorney. Try to get the head guy if you can." They both knew why. The other assistant might want to do legal research or even consult with the judge. Both agents had had investigations delayed and opportunities lost because of an overly cautious AUSA who always seemed to be more interested in covering his rear than solving crimes. Paul Trammel wasn't afraid to make a decision even if it meant sticking his neck out a little. He knew the law and wasn't afraid to use it. The trap-and-trace did not require a court order, but FBI regulations required that the U.S. Attorney's office be advised that the Bureau was using one. It was standard procedure in a kidnapping case to obtain a release from the telephone subscriber and get the trap on the line as soon as possible in case of an early call.

Barron had retrieved a checklist labeled "Kidnapping, Title 18, Section 1201, United States Code" from his desk and was following it as he planned his response.

"Ben, also mention to the phone people that we want to piggy-back in another line for our use so we can keep the victim's published number open."

Castle asked, "Can't that second line wait until tomorrow even if we take the case tonight? I don't want to overload them."

"Yeah, you're right. But we want that trap on as soon as we can get it."

Castle moaned, "There goes my son's birthday party," as he headed for the door. But he was smiling. This sounded like a good one, a chance to match wits with some real bad guys. It was a welcome break from doing background investigations on appointees to the Atomic Energy Commission.

"Give my wife a call, will ya? Tell her to go ahead without me."

"Okay, Ben. We'll handle it."

Barron turned to Landry. "Tim, how about bringing your car around front while I finish packing my bag. I'll have you drop me in the area and then come back here to cover the phone."

"Okay, Buddy. I was going to work late, anyway. Wife's out of town."

That was typical of Landry. Always ready to help. Most agents were team players, but Landry took it a step farther. He could make you feel like you were doing him a favor by calling on him.

"Thanks, Tim. I'll be ready as soon as I get my 'moving-in bag' loaded and make a call to the residence."

Barron pulled a canvas gym bag from his equipment locker. It already contained two changes of socks and underwear, a pair of jeans, knit shirts, shorts, an old pair of running shoes, and toilet articles. From the equipment room, he added a tape recorder with a telephone attachment, a supply of tape cassettes, binoculars, a hand-held radio, evidence tags and envelopes. Barron packed the bag while following a checklist he had prepared after attending a training session on personal crimes at the Academy a year and a half ago.

Lance recalled cases in which the subjects warned the victims not to contact any law enforcement agency. Some claimed to have the house under surveillance. Although this was rarely, if ever, true, the FBI practice was to make their entry into a case as unobtrusive as possible. No need to take a chance on upsetting the kidnappers. Also, an undue amount of coming and going might start the neighbors speculating.

In this case the kidnappers apparently made no demand of secrecy since Kogan called the police and Vickers's marked cruiser was probably sitting in the driveway right now. Nevertheless, Barron was going to take his moving-in bag and walk in. The bag would save him a lot of coming and going in the next few days if this turned out to be the real thing.

Lance dialed the Kogan residence and tried to call up a mental picture of Corporal Don Vickers, whose name sounded familiar. He had made it a practice to get to know as many local law enforcement people as possible, but he couldn't recall Vickers. He was still working on it when the phone was answered with a gruff, "Yeah?"

"Excuse me, sir. Is Officer Vickers of the Springfield Police Department still there?"

"Who the hell wants to know?"

"I'm sorry sir. This is Lance Barron with the FBI. May I speak with Officer Don Vickers?"

"Here, it's for you. Some guy who says he's with the FBI."

"This is Corporal Vickers."

"Corporal Vickers. This is Lance Barron, FBI. Your dispatcher gave me a brief report of the situation there. Has there been any change since you put out the APB?"

"No. The situation is still the same. No reported sighting.

They've probably ditched the car by now, but we haven't had a report of it."

"How long will you be able to stay there? Are you required to return to your regular patrol?"

"No, sir. My supervisor has authorized me to stay here until I am relieved. I imagine he will send a detective over to take charge of the investigation…unless you guys take the case."

"As I understand it, there was an armed abduction. Is that correct?"

"Yes, sir. That's what happened according to Mr. Kogan."

"Were there any other witnesses to the abduction?"

"No, not that I know of. I've talked briefly with Mr. Kogan. He thinks the kidnappers were black men, although he admits they were pretty well covered up."

"What did they say? Did they mention money?"

"Only one of them spoke. As they left, one said, 'You'll hear from us.'"

"Okay, Corporal, it sounds like a case we will want to get into. I'll see you there within the hour."

Lance Barron was forty-one years old. He had been in the FBI almost eleven years. He had been transferred six months ago to the Springfield, Missouri RA, Kansas City Division, after spending a year in Cincinnati, nine years in the Washington Field Office, and a year at FBI Headquarters.

Lance had worked several kidnappings in the Washington, D.C. area but only a couple were classic ransom kidnappings. Several were drug deals gone bad. One was a grab-and-rape case.

One of the classic cases involved the seventeen-year-old son of a wealthy pharmaceutical wholesaler. The father paid a ransom of $200,000. His son was released unharmed, but when Lance was transferred two years later, the case was still unsolved. There were still occasional leads, and there was always the hope that some of the ransom bills would turn up. The serial numbers were still in the National Crime Information Center computer.

In addition to those cases, Lance had covered numerous leads on kidnapping cases being worked in other divisions, and he had studied the case files of every kidnapping on record in the Washington Field Office and the Kansas City Division.

A kidnapping is different from most other crimes in that law enforcement enters the case while it is still in progress. The investigator has a chance to deal, sometimes directly, with the criminal. The kidnapper must expose himself to some degree in order to communicate his ransom demands and set up a way to collect it. The challenge to the investigator is to learn all he can from these exposures without further endangering the victim. Lance Barron had prepared himself for this moment.

Tim Landry retrieved his Crown Victoria from the lot while Lance finished packing. Lance checked the hand-held radio with a call to Landry. "KC-21 to KC-19. How do you read?"

"Loud and clear, 21. I'm at the appointed place."

"Okay KC-19, I'm on the way." Lance secured the office and set the intrusion alarm. He lugged his briefcase and equipment bag down the back stairs to Landry's car. "You know the area don't you, Tim, Brentwood South?"

"Yeah, it's only a few minutes away."

As they headed south on Glenstone Avenue past all the fast food places Landry said, "It's nearly six o'clock, Lance. Don't you want to get something to eat before you go into seclusion? You might be confined there for a while."

Lance knew Landry was ribbing him about "moving in" but he didn't mind.

"No thanks. I'll sponge off Mr. Kogan if I have to. Feel free to pick up something for yourself after you drop me off. Get back to the office as soon as you can, though, in case Ben needs to contact us."

Food, Lance thought. *I guess I'll always associate food with getting this job…and almost not getting it.* He smiled at the memory.

★ ★ ★

Lance Barron was a disillusioned high school football coach in Beaumont, Texas, when he became interested in the FBI. He had just finished a disastrous season and had vowed to look for employment in a more stable atmosphere, when he had a chance encounter with an FBI Agent who was recruiting graduating seniors to fill clerical positions in Washington, D.C. The agent mentioned that the Bureau also had occasional openings for Special Agents but the competition for the limited slots was intense. Lance learned that his master's degree, his six years as an Air Force pilot and four years of teaching/coaching experience qualified him to make application. Lance had enjoyed the tight organization and discipline of the military. He pictured the FBI as being similar. He conferred with his wife and decided to apply.

Lance's application started a series of tests, personal interviews, and physical examinations that sometimes seemed to be designed to drive him away. The process took the better part of a year and would require no little sacrifice on Lance's part.

When he made application, Lance, who had played four years of college football, was carrying 238 pounds on his six foot, one and one-half inch frame. He was well into the qualifying process before anyone mentioned the Bureau's weight program. He had noticed, however, that the few agents he had met were all trim.

One day the agent who was handling his application casually mentioned the weight program and asked Lance what he weighed. Lance gave him the 238 pound figure. The agent winced and checked his chart. "Uh, Oh. Mr. Hoover won't like this. Based on your height and age, the most you can weigh on your entrance physical is 190 pounds!"

Lance was shocked. The physical was three months away. Could he possibly lose forty-eight pounds in ninety days? He was doubtful when he gave his wife, Patsy, the news that night. "It will be tough, Lance, but if you want to try it I will do all I can to help you." She was as good as her word as she planned menus and kept the children's goodies out of his sight.

Three months later on the day of the physical, Lance knew he was close to the mark, but to make sure, he took a steam bath in Beaumont before he and Patsy began the ninety mile trip to Houston. They arrived early. Still concerned, Lance visited a gym where he took a sauna. When he stood up after dressing he was so weak he almost blacked out. Patsy had to drive him to the site of the physical. At her suggestion, he bought and ate a small jar of honey which he hoped would give him enough quick energy to get through the exam.

Lance, with several pounds of liquid left in the steam bath and sauna, made the weight at 188 pounds, but he was unable to give a urine sample! The examining physician said, "You'll have to come back next week and finish the physical." Lance was afraid to ask if completing the physical only meant giving a urine sample or if it would involve another weigh-in. He continued dieting during the week, just in case, but on the re-test they only took the urine sample. He passed with flying colors. He celebrated by eating a two-piece meal from Kentucky Fried Chicken, bones and all.

Lance smiled as he recalled that long ago weight battle. When he was preparing to leave for New Agent training, one of his former football players told him that rumors had circulated around campus that he had cancer.

Lance's experience with the Bureau's weight program was not unique. There were stories in every office of the drastic efforts agents made to reach the weight limit, not only on their entrance physical but on ensuing annual physicals or during surprise inspections. He knew one agent who bought a special suit to wear while the inspectors were around. It was two sizes too large and gave him such an emaciated appearance, no inspector ever picked him out for a surprise weight check. He knew several others who decided to take annual leave for the week the inspectors were in the office, rather than face the possibility of an unscheduled weigh-in.

In light of such stories, Lance stayed with his diet and exercise program and made the weight loss permanent, but he still tried not to think too much about food.

★ ★ ★

Tim Landry turned east on Battlefield Road, a wide four-lane boulevard with bluegrass and young trees in the esplanade. "The house is about a mile from here, Lance."

"Okay, let's drive by once and have a look at it and then I'll walk back to it."

Brentwood South was one of the earlier fine residential developments in southeast Springfield. Most of the houses were now around twenty years old, brick, three or four bedrooms. It was an area of manicured lawns, trees and flowers. Most of the residents were older couples. There were few children.

As Tim Landry turned north on Martin Avenue and started checking house numbers, Lance said, "The PD cruiser is in the driveway ahead on the right."

They saw no outdoor activity as they eased by the house and continued down the block. There were no cars parked on the street. All were in driveways or garages. Lance observed, "It would have been tough for the kidnappers to stake out the house and wait for the girl in this neighborhood without being noticed. Maybe we can dig up something with a canvass of the neighbors."

"You sound like we are already in it," said Landry.

"Yeah, I have a feeling this is the real thing."

Lance had Tim turn left at the next corner. They traveled two blocks west and then south for a block. As they approached Battlefield Road again Lance said, "I'll get out here. Get yourself something to eat, Tim. I'll be in touch when you get back to the office."

"Okay, Lance. Good luck. Let me know if you need anything."

Lance felt a little foolish as he headed down the sidewalk with his briefcase and equipment bag. He overcame that, however, as he looked down the street and tried to visualize what had happened here.

The kidnappers were right here on this street less than two hours ago! Were they following the girl's car or had they known in advance she would be home? Had they followed her before to find out where she lived and what her daily routine was? Did any of the people in these houses see her being dragged to her car? Did anyone notice a strange car driving through the neighborhood? What kind of car? How many people in it? Were they black men? Her dad thinks they were. If I had all the knowledge these people have would I know who the kidnappers are?

There's her house. There's the driveway where she parked her car and where they later forced her back into it. A red Mustang. Did any of you neighbors see that? If the kidnappers left here in her car, how did they get here? Someone had to drop them off. Who did? Didn't some of you see them in their dark coveralls and ski masks? Why didn't you call the police?

It gives me an eerie feeling to be right here where it happened. Surely there is some essence of the crime still here. Something I can touch, see, smell.

It was 6:05 when Lance rang the doorbell at the Kogan residence. The door was jerked open by a small man wearing a double-breasted gray business suit. There was a uniformed police officer standing behind the man. He had his right hand on his holster. Neither was in a cordial mood.

Lance pulled his credentials from his shirt pocket and flipped them open toward the man he took to be Kogan.

"Good evening, sir. I'm Lance Barron with the FBI." Turning toward the policeman he said, "You must be Officer Vickers. I believe we've met."

Vickers said, "Oh, yeah. How are you, Mr. Barron?" He extended his hand and said, "I remember you. You taught a segment on the FBI at a class I was taking up at Drury."

The small man exploded. "Goddammit! Is this old home week

or something? I don't want to stand out here and listen to you guys jaw. Are you coming in or is this clown leaving? It don't matter to me. Just make up your frigging minds."

"I'm sorry, sir. May I come in? I'm here to talk with you about your daughter. Have you heard anything more?"

"Not a damn word. How can the police miss a red Mustang this long. Hell, they could be halfway to St. Louis."

"They've surely dumped the car by now," said Vickers.

Kogan was ready, "Yeah, you've been saying that for an hour. Hell, if they dumped it, it would be even easier to find."

"Well, that would depend on where..."

Lance interrupted, "Let me suggest that we go to where we can all sit down. I need to get some basic information to establish if the FBI has jurisdiction."

Kogan led the way down a short hallway. As they turned into his office, he said, "This is where the son-of-a-bitch stuck the gun in my chest and pushed me over on my desk. They weren't in here a total of a minute. Maybe less. Took her out through the garage there. Same way they came in, I guess. I heard her open the garage door with her opener. I had left my car in the drive. I was going back to the airport after supper. I guess they just followed her in here. And, well, I've already told this guy all about it. What else do you want to know?"

Before Barron could answer, Kogan's phone rang.

"Yeah?...Yeah, there's an officer here. I guess it's him."

"It's for you, officer," said Kogan as he thrust the phone toward Vickers.

Barron turned back to Kogan, "What did the kidnappers tell you to do?"

"Not a damn thing. As they drug Jenny out, one of them said I'd hear from them. I chased after them but I couldn't do anything. I saw them push Jenny into her car, and they burned rubber getting out of here."

Vickers hung up the phone and said, "The Missouri Highway Patrol found your daughter's car on 65 Highway a mile north of I-44 just inside the city limits. It was unlocked and the keys were in the ignition. No one in or around it. We have dispatched a tow truck up there. They will take it to our garage for processing."

"What time?" asked Lance.

"Let's see, Sergeant Sheffield, MHP, called the dispatcher at 5:35 P.M. to verify the tag. He had heard the APB."

"If they drove directly from here to where the car was found, about how long would that have taken?"

Vickers said, "At this time of day, with the traffic and the lights, I would say twenty, maybe twenty-five minutes."

"So the car could have been there fifteen or twenty minutes."

"Right," said Vickers.

"Now Mr. Kogan, I was questioning you about what happened here with the kidnappers."

Kogan paused and then said, "I've been over all of that with the officer here. Why don't you just ask him your questions?"

Lance said, "That will be fine for the present. Are there any other family members here?"

"No, uh, well, yes, her mother is here...but she didn't see anything, uh...she's emotional. She's taking this hard...She's not well."

It was obvious Kogan was uncomfortable on this subject. Lance decided not to pursue it. He turned to Vickers. "Corporal, if you have written up your report, let me take a look at it."

"Sure, I just hit the high spots, though."

"Good. Let me look at that."

The first paragraph of Vickers's report contained the line, "Occupation: Owner of Kogan Aviation." Lance immediately connected Kogan's face and name with the numerous newspaper articles he had seen recently about Kogan's battle with another aviation company over a contract. He had also seen him on the TV news several times. *That dispute could be behind this. I wonder if that has occurred to him.*

After reviewing Vickers's report, Lance again went over the description of the kidnappers with Kogan. Kogan was vague. "One was big, the other small. The small one had a squeaky voice, high-pitched." Kogan seemed irritated at having to repeat the descriptions. Lance noticed that Kogan didn't mention the men's race even though Vickers's report indicated that Kogan said the men were black. Lance decided not to bring it up directly but asked, "Mr. Kogan, could you identify these men if you saw them again?" Kogan's face reddened and his jaw tightened. "I could, by god, if they were dressed like they were today." Kogan must have realized how ridiculous that was. He followed with, "But I'll bet you Kline and his crowd at South County are behind it."

Lance took note but moved on to the action of the men while they were in the house. Kogan went, step by step, through the movement of the two men during the abduction. His account was close in all details to Vickers's report. "Do you think your neighbor saw them leave?"

"I don't know. I didn't see anyone out there, but he spends most of the day, every day, out there working on his flowers and vegetable garden. Doesn't have a damn thing else to do I guess."

"What's his name?"

"Hell, I don't know. I'm trying to make a living in a very competitive business. I don't have time for gardening...or neighbors."

Lance said, "If you will excuse me, Mr. Kogan, I have a couple of local calls to make and one long distance. I'll bill the long distance call to my calling card."

Kogan made no comment, nor did he volunteer to move away from the desk to give Lance privacy.

Lance called the FBI Field Office in Kansas City. He asked for the Special Agent in Charge, or SAC, expecting a transfer to Mr. Palmer's unlisted home phone. But the operator said, "He's still in the office, I'll ring him."

"This is Paul Palmer."

Barron briefed Palmer on the incident, then added, "We will need some extra manpower and equipment, of course."

Palmer asked, "There was definitely an abduction then? It's not going to turn into a runaway teenager, a disgruntled boyfriend, a fight over custody or something like that?"

"No, sir. I'm at the residence now, and according to the father, the two guys came right into the house and grabbed her. One showed a weapon."

"What do you recommend, Lance? A preliminary inquiry or a full scale investigation?"

"I think it's a real one, sir. I recommend we get into it now under the presumptive clause."

After a slight pause, Palmer said, "You're right, Lance. An armed intrusion into a residence. There's no doubt that qualifies as an abduction. What kind of manpower are you thinking about?"

"I figure with our five guys here all working it, we can get by with the surveillance team from up there and a couple of air surveillance units to cover the ransom drop."

"You think that's enough? I'll send a couple of the Joplin guys over as well. I don't want to be caught short if we have a bank robbery or something else on top of this. I'll come down and run the command post out of the RA as long as you are tied up there. You do plan to stay there at the residence?"

"Yes, sir, I'm here for the duration."

"I'll put the people from here on standby tonight and we'll wait and see what develops…Oh, Lance, one administrative matter. You know we have to notify FBI Headquarters and surrounding offices by teletype when we open a kidnapping case. Let me get the night clerk, and we will get a file number."

"Okay, sir, I'll hold, but we don't want to tie up this number too long."

"It won't take long."

While waiting, Lance became fully conscious of something that had irritated his subconscious since he sat down. Kogan was sitting right at his elbow and taking in every word that was said. While the conversation was not confidential, Lance disliked Kogan's blatant eavesdropping. In addition, Kogan was constantly drumming the desk top with his fingers. Lance, for the first time, noticed how small Kogan's hands were. His fingers were so pointed it appeared they might puncture the desk top as he drummed away.

SAC Palmer came back on line. "What's the title of the case, Lance?"

Lance wrote it out in Bureau form as he gave it to Palmer:

UNSUBS (3);
Jennifer Marie Kogan - Victim;
Kidnapping;
OO:Kansas City
ARMED AND DANGEROUS

"Okay, Lance, your file number is KC 7-2552."

"Got it. KC 7-2552. Tim Landry is manning the phones at the RA tonight. I'll be in touch with him. We can communicate through him until we get our extra line in here."

"Okay, Lance. Sounds like you have things well in hand there. Let me know of any new developments until I can get down there."

"Thank you, sir."

As Lance hung up, he sensed that Kogan was about to speak, but he wanted to reach Castle before he left the phone company. "It's a go, Ben. We'll need the trap-and-trace. Can they get it on tonight?"

"Yeah, they went ahead and made most of the connections. We were waiting for the final word."

"That's great, Ben. What about the AUSA? Did you get in touch with Paul?"

"Oh, yeah, and you know him. He said it was no sweat; go

ahead and do it. He will get us a memo for our file tomorrow."

"Good work, Ben. What about the extra line? Did you get around to that?"

"Oh, yeah. We have a little problem there. They can get it in tomorrow morning, but they have to have a signature for billing purposes. I told them the FBI would stand good for the bill, but they said they had to have a real person. I signed for it…I used your name. Hope that was okay." Castle could hardly suppress the laughter.

"You joker. I'll get you for that."

"I had to get even. You caused me to miss my son's birthday party."

"Go on home from there, Ben. Tim is still in the office. I'll call him now and have him get everybody in early tomorrow. Good work, partner."

"Okay. I'll be in early. You're staying over there?"

"Yeah, I'll be here for a while. We have a lot of ground to cover. So long."

Kogan was still in place, drumming away and looking more irritated by the minute. Lance still had to get Landry updated, and as a precaution, he wanted to get the recording device hooked up to the phone.

He dialed the RA. Landry answered immediately.

"Tim, I talked with the boss in Kansas City. We are in it full scale under the presumptive clause." Lance went over the manpower plans with Landry and gave him the case title and file number. "Call our other guys—Ben already knows—and have them come in early tomorrow. They are to drop everything unless it has a short Bureau deadline. We're giving this one the full court press."

While talking with Landry, Lance retrieved the tape recorder from his bag and attached the suction-cup-held microphone to the telephone receiver, placed a used cassette in the recorder, and watched the tape move through the recorder as he talked. "One more thing,

Tim. First thing tomorrow do a discreet neighborhood investigation. Restrict it to two houses on either side of the Kogan residence. See if anyone saw anything suspicious. Play it low key. No mention of the kidnapping or the Kogans. Use your personal car and wear casual clothes. The neighbor on the south is a good bet. Someone had to drop the kidnappers off. Maybe he saw something."

"I got ya, Lance. I'll take care of that and the teletype. Anything else?"

"No, that's it for now. Thanks, Tim. I'd better get off this phone. I'll give you our new number early tomorrow. So long."

Kogan was ready, "What the hell about my calls? I can't tell people not to call."

"No, sir. You should not change your normal calling pattern nor ask anyone to change theirs. Except for being here rather than at the airport, don't change anything. We will have the trap on this line so we hope they will use it. I must point out, however, that there's no guarantee they will call. They might mail the ransom demand, or drop it at your office, or leave it on the windshield of your wife's car, or any one of a dozen other possibilities. We will be prepared for the most obvious, the most convenient, the least risky for them: the phone. If they choose something else, we will adapt."

Lance had rewound his test tape as he talked. He was about to replay it when Kogan, right in his left ear, said, "Tell me Barron, is the FBI worth a shit?"

Vickers, who had been sitting quietly across the desk, bristled and started to get up. Lance held up his hand and Vickers sat down but still gripped the edge of the desk with both hands.

Lance turned toward the diminutive Kogan, "I beg your pardon, sir?"

"Well, you seem to have taken charge here. You and these other guys you're talking to. I think all of you ought to be out there looking for the bastards that did this and trying to get my daughter back. If you and the big FBI are gonna be in charge of getting her back, I just wondered if you're worth a shit."

"Look, Mr. Kogan, I'm not going to spend valuable time defending the FBI. I can tell you this, though. No one can guarantee the safe return of your daughter. No one!"

Kogan's jaw tightened and his eyes narrowed, and Barron wondered if Kogan might be foolish enough to take a swing at him. He continued, "You must convince yourself of this fact, Mr. Kogan. You are not in charge of this situation...I am not in charge...The FBI is not in charge...*The kidnappers are in charge!* They are going to be calling the shots and we are going to be making the best responses we can. Jenny's safety is our first priority. That will be true throughout this investigation.

"We will consult you on every issue we can. You will make some of the decisions. If they demand a ransom, and I expect they will, you will decide if you will pay it. I won't make that decision. The FBI won't, the police won't. You will.

"In some cases the victim's family has decided not to pay. In others they have decided to go through the ransom drop using a dummy package rather than real money. Regardless of your decision, we will support you. If you choose a dummy package, for instance, we will make up a package of the proper dimensions and then carry out the drop just as we would otherwise...But it will be your decision.

"There are other areas where we will make decisions based upon our experience in working these cases. But your daughter's safety will always be the first priority.

"I have a daughter a little younger than Jenny. I think of her often when I study these cases and see how distraught the parents are. I wonder how I would respond if I were in their position. The only conclusion I have reached is this: if it should happen to me, and God forbid that it should, I hope and pray that it would be handled by the FBI. That's the best assurance I can give you, Mr. Kogan...Now, lets get to work."

Kogan replied, "You better hope we get her back safely, Barron, or I'll sue your ass and the FBI's for all you're worth and then some."

Lance refused to respond to that asinine threat, but he seriously questioned the character of the man who made it.

"Let's get back to that list of persons, such as disgruntled former employees, who might have reason to seek vengeance against you." *There must be quite a list,* Barron thought.

"I've already told you who I think is behind it, that bastard Jim Kline over at South County Charter. He's tried to get me in a jam with the FAA, and he's hired some of my best pilots after I've trained them. He would do anything to get even with me now that I have the Global Business Machines contract sewed up. He was in the running to the last day, and I know he spent a ton of money trying to beat me. It's got to be him. He has blacks working for him, too. Why don't you ask him about it?"

"We'll get around to Mr. Kline. Let's stay with the disgruntled employees? Someone who might have left with hard feelings."

Kogan admitted firing two pilots and two mechanics in the past year. He identified them by describing in detail the incidents that led to their firing, but when Lance asked for their names, Kogan said he couldn't remember. "You can get their names from bookkeeping," he said.

Lance wanted to move on, but Kogan was enjoying himself. He told how one of the pilots he fired had flown a one-way, one-person charter to Shreveport, Louisiana in a Cherokee Six. "When the clown arrived back in here, I saw him unload a brake assembly and leave it at the operations desk. I checked and saw it was to be picked up by South County Charter. I confronted the pilot and asked him why he didn't turn in the freight charge. He denied that any money was involved. He said the Fixed Base Operator in Shreveport asked him to bring the assembly back to Springfield where South County would pick it up. He claimed he just did it as a favor for a fellow pilot. He wanted me to call the Fixed Base Operator in Shreveport to verify his story. To hell with that! Even if he didn't take money, he was being disloyal to me by doing a favor for South County. The dumbshit should have know better. When you're in a competitive business, you don't go around doing favors for your competitors. Would you believe that after I fired him, he had his wife call me up and beg me to take him back?"

"What is he doing now?"

"How should I know? I don't keep up with them. He's still around, though. I hear him on the radio. He's probably working for Kline."

The other firings were similar. Not a one involved a crime or even a breach of discipline. All involved employees who seemed to Lance to be trying to do their job. At most they made a mistake in judgment which Kogan perceived to be stupid or, even worse, disloyal. Lance found it interesting that Kogan remembered every incident clearly but could not remember the names.

Kogan watched as Lance tested the trial tape he had made during his conversation with Landry. Both sides of the conversation were clear and crisp. He inserted a new cassette and set the instrument on RECORD.

Making sure he included Vickers in the conversation, although he did not anticipate his staying much longer, Lance said, "We are assuming the kidnappers will call on this number with some sort of instructions about the ransom. By the way, Mr. Kogan, how many extensions do you have on this line?"

"Well, we have one in the bedroom and one in the kitchen. Then my daughter has her own phone in her bedroom, but it is a different number."

"I request that the extensions in the kitchen and the bedroom not be answered at those locations. We want to answer it here, where we have the recorder hooked up. Will that be a problem?"

"I'll see that it isn't. We have a rule here that if I am in the house,

I will answer the phone. Most of the time it is for me. My wife doesn't get nor make many calls."

"Fine, I have the tape recorder set on FORWARD and RECORD with the PAUSE button depressed. When any one of us answers the phone, we want to release the PAUSE button to start the recorder in the event it is the kidnappers. If we determine it is not the kidnappers, we press the PAUSE button again to stop the recording. We have no idea, of course, when a call might come in. We might be asleep but we only have to remember one thing…release that PAUSE button.

"Recording the call is doubly important. For one thing, it is great evidence when the kidnappers are identified. Voice prints have been used to match the voice of the caller with the voice of the defendant to the exclusion of all others. In a few cases, background noises picked up on the recording were used to locate the place from which the call was made.

"The tape also gives us a record of the instructions. Sometimes the instructions for preparing and/or dropping the ransom are complex. In the excitement of the moment, we might not get it right. I will make a work copy of the original as soon as we can rewind the cassette. I ask that you allow me to insert and extract all original tapes and make all copies. We must maintain a chain of custody on the original tapes for trial purposes. It is much simpler if only one person has custody. We will preserve the original for evidence. We can play the copy as many times as we need, to get the instructions right.

"Any questions on that, Mr. Kogan?"

Kogan grunted and looked uninterested. Lance quickly went through the routine again and then said, "One last item. If the call is from the kidnappers, we do not want to hang up the phone at the end of the conversation. We can enhance the technicians' chances of tracing the call if we leave the line open after the call is completed."

Kogan asked, "I'm supposed to handle all that after you leave?"

"I'm glad you brought that up, Mr. Kogan, and I apologize for not mentioning it sooner. With your indulgence, sir, I intend to stay here, in your office, until this situation is resolved. I brought some clothes and personal items. If I decide to sleep, that couch over there will be fine. I don't know how long this will take, but I'm good for several days."

Kogan seemed to be relieved that he would not have the responsibility of handling the expected call and in a show of warmth that was inconceivable an hour before, he said, "Well you'll need something to eat. I'll see what I can rustle up."

"That's thoughtful, sir. Anything will be fine. The lighter, the better."

"How about you, Biggers?" Kogan growled. "I don't think we have any donuts." Only Kogan thought it was funny.

"No thanks," Vickers said, then under his breath, "you damn midget."

Kogan left for the kitchen, and Vickers started preparing to leave. Barron said, "I appreciate your holding things down 'til we could get over here and decide what we were going to do. We are going to need a lot of assistance from the police department. You know—running tags, getting criminal records checks, things you folks can do a lot faster than we can. We are going to have our command post set up in the FBI office. If you are agreeable, I'd like to call your chief in the morning, or better yet, have my boss from Kansas City call him and request that you be assigned to this case. You would be working out of the command post. It would be a tremendous help to us and, who knows, the case might wind up in state court anyway if the girl hasn't been taken out of state. What do you think?"

"It sounds great to me, Mr. Barron. It sure beats traffic accidents and barking dogs."

"Hey, Don, call me Lance."

As he closed the door behind Don Vickers, Lance checked his

watch. It was 9:15 P.M. He hoped his children were in bed. And then it hit him like a two-by-four. Today was his son's first baseball game. He promised he would be there at six! He hadn't even called! He knew Patsy had defended him and smoothed it over to make him look as good as possible under the circumstances. But he felt terrible about it.

The appetite he had was now gone, but he forced down a few bites of the sandwich Kogan had brought. When he called home, all he could say was, "I'm sorry, darling. I'm on a big one and I might not be home for a few days. How did Barry take my not showing?"

"Oh, he kept looking for you during the game, but you know how kids are. He got a couple of hits and made a great catch for the final out. He was the center of attention for a while and that helped. I told him I knew you would've been there if you possibly could have. He went to bed happy. His little sister told him she was proud of him for being the star player. That helped."

"God bless you, Patsy. Hug them for me. Tell them I love them. I hope they will believe it."

Lance Barron had been an FBI Agent for over ten years. He loved his work. He could not think of anything he would rather be doing, even if he did occasionally get a call at 5:31 in the afternoon after a full day's work, a call that caused a complete change of plans. Yes, he loved his work, but he didn't like having to break a promise to his children. He had to work on that.

CONTACT

(a) Whoever transmits in interstate commerce any communication containing any demand or request for a ransom or reward for the release of any kidnapped person, shall be fined not more than $5000 or imprisoned not more than twenty years, or both.

—18 U.S. Code, Section 875 (a)

Lance Barron continued his interview of Charles Kogan, using Corporal Vickers's notes to avoid the duplicate questions that seemed to annoy Kogan.

"How much formal education do you have?"

"What does that have to do with my missing daughter? Not a damn thing, that's what. I'll tell you one thing though. I'm not one of you college boys." Kogan grinned with apparent satisfaction at this revelation.

Lance skipped several questions to avoid Kogan's anger, but he couldn't skip them all. "Have you ever been arrested?"

"Hell, no, but what if I had? Would you still work the case?"

"I'm sorry, Mr. Kogan, that you object to some of the questions. We get as much background data as we can. It often proves useful. You can refuse to answer."

"And you'll write down that I refused to answer. That makes me look bad. It's better if you don't ask. Let's get on to something that pertains to my daughter."

"All right, there are several items I need to discuss with you and your wife, and I have some forms for you to sign."

"My wife won't be much help to you. I'll be making most, if not all, of the decisions."

Lance was relieved when the phone rang. Kogan started to reach for it, but Lance held up his hand, released the PAUSE button, let it ring a third time, made sure the recorder was running and then motioned for Kogan to answer.

"Chuck Kogan…Yeah. He's here…Who?…Okay."

Kogan pushed the phone toward Lance. "Some guy from the highway patrol."

Lance reset the PAUSE button and answered, "Lance Barron." He wrote 9:34 P.M. in the log.

"Yeah, Lance, Harold Sheffield, here. How are you?"

"Hey, Sergeant. Haven't seen you in a while. How are things in the Patrol? They still have you working cattle thefts?"

"Yeah, we're still hoping to get you folks involved, but that's not the reason I called. I'm the one that spotted the red Mustang out on 65 North this afternoon."

"Hey, good work, Harold. We were glad to get the report."

"Yeah, well there was something else I noticed that I want to pass on. Tim Landry gave me your number there; said I ought to give it directly to you.

"This might not amount to anything but it seemed so unusual I decided to call. That Mustang was on the left shoulder. That's what caught my attention. I had heard the APB while I was on my way south a little before 5:30. I was hurrying to Troop G. I had some papers a trooper needed for a court appearance. I didn't even go in. I just gave him the papers and started back north. It was about 5:30 when I left the Troop. I had forgotten about the APB. If the Mustang had been off on the right side—that's where most of your breakdowns limp to—I probably wouldn't have noticed it, but it was on the left. I remembered the APB and called it in. I stayed out there until the locals arrived and then shuffled on back to Buffalo. But something about that car being off on the left kept gnawing on me until I finally figured it out. That was the second car I had seen off on the left in a matter of fifteen or twenty minutes! On my way south before I heard the APB, I saw a car off on the left. The strange thing about it though, and this is what kept gnawing at me, was that those cars were no more than two or three hundred yards apart through the woods.

"It might not mean a thing but it was unusual enough I had to call."

"That's interesting, Harold. What time was it when you saw the southbound car?"

"I heard the APB before I got to Troop G but after I saw the first car, so it would have been 5:10 to 5:15."

"Anybody in it?"

"No. Nor around it. I would have stopped but I was hurrying to meet the guy. The car was well off the pavement and parked straight. It wasn't creating a hazard, and it didn't look like it was broken down."

Lance could feel his pulse rising but before he could ask the key question, Harold continued, "I sure don't want to mislead you, and there might not be any connection. It just seemed odd; two in the same day off on the left, close together and at about the same time."

Lance thought, *Some people are so conscientious it almost cripples them. This guy is a jewel.*

"What do you think it was, Harold?"

"I know it was a big car; blue, dark blue, and...I...I think it was a Cadillac." Sheffield sighed, "I couldn't rest 'til I got that to you."

"That could be very helpful, Harold. The proximity to the Mustang and the time frame would suggest a connection. We know they left here in the Mustang. The PD said there are no houses in the recovery area. They had to change cars. That could be the car."

"Well, I thought I'd better give it to you. The police out there didn't know anything about the case except what was on the APB. What do you have going?"

"It's a sensitive situation, Harold. We must keep the lid on for a while. I know you understand. We will have information to release soon. We will probably be begging you guys and Springfield PD for help before it's over, but right now there's a life at stake, and we must march to someone else's drum."

"Sure, I understand. No problem."

"Thanks, Harold."

"Good luck, Lance."

Kogan had heard Lance's side. Lance filled in the gaps for him while trying not to show how elated he was.

"Why don't you find out what kind of car Kline drives?"

"We will get to that soon, Mr. Kogan. You can bet on it. That will be Corporal Vickers's first lead tomorrow."

"By the way," said Kogan, "my wife took a couple of calls earlier this evening on Jenny's phone. Jenny's girlfriends calling. She didn't know what to say. She asked if Jenny could call them back. Kind of stupid, I thought. Jenny won't be calling anyone back for a while."

"This is a good time for us to go over situations like that. I want to meet your wife anyway. It looks like I'll be a house guest for a few days. Why don't you ask her to join us so we can cover those items I mentioned."

"I'm going to handle all the decisions. I'm not sure she's up to talking about this."

"If she is going to be handling phone calls on Jenny's phone, we need to talk about what she should say. I have some suggestions I want to share with both of you. You heard what I told Sergeant Sheffield. He is a friend and a trustworthy law enforcement officer. He can guess what is up from the APB and our conversation. But I'm not going to be the one to give him any details when your daughter's life is at stake. He knows how dangerous it would be to have people speculating about it. He understands, but I'm not sure your daughter's friends would. If they knew the situation and started talking about it, and they *would* talk, it could jeopardize Jenny's safety. We must keep this situation from the public for as long as we can and hope we can get to a successful resolution before it leaks.

"If the kidnappers have not called by tomorrow morning, I suggest that you go to your office as usual. We don't want speculation to start out there. Since I will be staying here covering this phone and directing our investigation, it would be nice if I could meet your wife."

Kogan growled something about the overbearing FBI and stomped off to get his wife.

Jenny was in a fitful sleep when she heard the phone ring in the distance. She started to sit up but bumped her head on the lid and remembered where she was. *How long have I been asleep?* She was trying to piece together all that had happened when she heard someone on the steps and then the squeaking of the lid.

"You need to get up, honey. Do you need to go to the bathroom? I should have thought of that sooner." It was the lady. "Here let me help you up. They called. They're on their way out here. They have something they want you to do."

Jenny had not had a chance to answer, but she wasn't going to interrupt someone who was getting her out of that coffin.

The lady helped her stand and step over the side. It felt wonderful to be up and moving about. The lady gently held her arm and guided her up the two steps she remembered coming down. *This should be the room with the tile or linoleum floor.* Jenny thought she heard the sound of a refrigerator off to her right, and she recognized the faint smell of a garbage disposal on her left. She moved straight ahead onto a carpeted floor. Jenny's shoulder brushed the wall on her right just as the lady pulled her to a stop.

"This is the bathroom. I'll open the door for you. I'll wait right here. You'll have to leave the blindfold on. They might arrive before we could get it back on."

As Jenny moved into the bathroom, she heard the door close behind her. She cautiously moved ahead but bumped into what felt like a clothes hamper and lost her balance. She reached out and caught a plastic curtain as she almost fell into the bathtub. She angrily pulled the blindfold away from one cheek. She tilted her head all the way back and saw enough to get her bearings. The tub covered one entire end of the small bathroom. There was a tiny window above the tub. A flimsy curtain covered the closed window, but she could see the darkness outside. *Darkness and freedom right out there. I'm so close.* She had a momentary urge to dive through the window.

A light rapping on the door startled her. "Are you all right in there? You need to hurry."

"Okay, I'm having a little trouble finding my way around. I'll be right out." Jenny quickly used the bathroom and washed her hands in the small lavatory. She pulled the blindfold away from her cheek again. She saw a white medicine cabinet with a mirrored front over the lavatory. She caught a glimpse of herself in the mirror, head tilted far back. She saw the birthmark under her chin that she thought ruined her appearance but which no one else, not even Jason, ever noticed. *My hair is a mess.*

There was a louder knock and the lady opened the door. "I'm sorry, honey, but J.D. told me to have you up and ready."

"I'm sorry, but it's a little tough finding my way around in here."

Jenny thought, *Mom is always saying that civility is contagious. I guess this is what she means. Here I am, being held hostage but exchanging "pleases," "sorrys," and "honeys" with my keeper.*

Lance was bringing his log up to date when the phone rang. He started the tape recorder and after the third ring, picked up the receiver. Kogan was on the line, barking out something about not calling him at home. The other party, a female said, "I'm sorry, Mr. Kogan, but you left specific instructions that if the Fort Wood Charter was…"

Lance hung up and turned the tape recorder off. *She will probably be Kogan's next ex-employee,* he thought. He added another item to the list of things to discuss with Kogan. Lance thought they had agreed on the procedure for answering the phone. Kogan apparently had other ideas.

Kogan entered walking in front of a lady who was at least six inches taller than he. She was wearing a floor length pink dressing gown. Her dark hair, worn in a bun, had a few gray streaks. Her eyes were downcast. As they single-filed across the floor, she towered over her husband.

When Kogan stopped in front of Lance, the lady stopped, still behind Kogan and maintaining her distance.

Kogan stated with no emotion, "This is my wife."

Lance had to step to the side to address her without going through Kogan. "Mrs. Kogan, I'm Lance Barron. I'm pleased to meet you. I'm sorry it has to be under such trying circumstances."

This tall striking lady's chin was still almost on her chest, but she raised her eyes far enough for him to see the sadness. She quickly lowered them and searched for a reply. She finally said, almost in a whisper, "Welcome to our home."

In sharp contrast Kogan barked, "Now let's get on with it." He turned and headed for a chair. His wife waited until he passed, then followed him across the office. When Kogan mounted the "throne" behind his desk, his wife took a small chair behind him and slightly to his left.

As Lance watched this ceremony he wondered, *Was it the American Indians or maybe the Japanese whose custom required their women to stay always a walking pace behind their men? I didn't know we practiced it here.*

Kogan said, "I want to say right up front, and my wife agrees with me on this, that I will make any decisions that are left up to me, that is to…us, uh…to this family."

Mrs. Kogan had found a spot on the carpet to study. She voiced no dissent.

"Now, Barron, what did you want to talk about?"

Lance moved his chair so as to include Mrs. Kogan. "First, I have some forms for you to look over and sign. One is a release for the phone company to install a device on your line which will trap-and-trace all incoming telephone calls. This is standard procedure in cases of this type."

Kogan grunted.

"The second form is similar but authorizes us to record both sides of conversations coming into and out of this phone. It is our intent to only record calls from the kidnappers. Will both of you sign these forms, please."

Kogan read the forms carefully, then signed. He then held them over the back of his chair with no comment. When Lance noticed, he handed them to Mrs. Kogan along with a pen and his note-book. She whispered, "Thank you," and signed without reading.

"The last form is your consent for the postal service to put a mail cover on your address. All mail for you will be inspected, but not opened, at the post office. If the inspectors see anything suspicious, they will hold it for us. By having mail checked at the post office, we would get a mailed ransom demand at least one day earlier. The interception would also reduce the number of persons handling the communication, enhancing our chances of raising fingerprints from it."

Kogan read and signed the form without comment and then sent it by the same route to his wife, never looking back, never consulting her.

Lance addressed the next item to Mrs. Kogan. "I need the latest, most accurate photograph of Jenny you have. We can make a copy of it and get the original back to you if you wish."

Mrs. Kogan looked all the way up to Lance's eyes at the mention of Jenny's name and smiled briefly. "I can do that. Her school pictures are good and we have extras." She suddenly stopped and lowered her voice, "Is that all right, Charles?"

"Yes. Get it."

There was silence as Lance watched Mrs. Kogan plod out with head lowered. Kogan seemed to feel obligated to fill the void. "This has been hard on her."

Lance said, "I can imagine." He thought, *I'll bet Mrs. Kogan's misery started long before this kidnapping.*

"Now, Mr. Kogan, we agreed earlier that we would answer calls to your published number only here on your office extension. Isn't that correct?"

Kogan paused long enough to turn and glare at Lance before saying, "That's what you suggested, yeah."

"If the call you took a little while ago had been the kidnappers, we would have missed recording the first part of it. You answered it before I could get the tape recorder going."

Kogan fumed as Lance repeated the phone-answering procedure and patiently explained why there was no need to hurry the process. "Think about it. The kidnappers know you aren't going to ignore them. They have to contact you before they can get what they want. So, we don't have to hurry!"

Mrs. Kogan had quietly returned and had taken her seat behind her husband.

When Lance turned toward her and smiled she said, "Here are several of this year's school pictures."

Lance took them and for the first time Jennifer Marie Kogan became a real person.

"She's beautiful. I know you are proud of her."

Tears appeared in Mrs. Kogan's eyes. She started to answer but then turned toward her husband as if to ask, *What is the official family position on being proud of our daughter?*

Kogan was losing patience. "We ought to be doing something about getting her back here."

Lance forged on. "Mrs. Kogan, would you take this five-by-seven and write on the back your daughter's full name, date and place of birth, color of eyes, color of hair, height, weight, any identifying scars or marks and a description of the clothes she was wearing. Here is a card listing the information we need."

Lance turned back to Mr. Kogan, "I see from Corporal Vickers's notes that you have a son and daughter in addition to Jenny. Have you told them about the situation with Jenny?"

Kogan, with dripping sarcasm said, "No, I haven't, but I imagine my wife has."

Mrs. Kogan looked up from her work on the picture. She looked cornered and afraid. "I thought they should know, Charles; after all…"

Lance put up his hands to interrupt, "That's fine. There is no problem with telling them. Do they plan to come home?"

"We didn't discuss that. They were both concerned and asked if there was anything they could do. Our son is in a new job. He lives in Des Moines. Kerry, our other daughter, is in college at Warrensburg."

"There is no problem with notifying them. It is up to you and them if they come here. We just need to keep things looking as normal as possible. If both came home at the same time, it might cause the neighbors to wonder why and start asking questions. You need to be prepared for that. As I said earlier, we must keep this situation quiet as long as we can.

"Mrs. Kogan, I understand you have already had calls from Jenny's girlfriends."

Kogan interrupted, "Yeah and I'm surprised that Yeager boy hasn't called. He's usually on the phone half the time."

Lance continued, "As for what to tell her friends, I can't give you an answer that will fit all situations. Both of you need to be thinking about what you will say to people who inquire. I suggest you call the school tomorrow and report Jenny ill. That will hold for a day or two, but her friends will still inquire. You must have a story for them. I will not attempt to tell you what to say, but we must keep this situation from becoming general knowledge. If it does, believe me, it will be a circus: crank calls, people claiming to be the kidnappers trying to collect the ransom, reporters, and good, well-meaning people driving by, gawking, taking pictures, following you. It would become impossible to set up an exchange the kidnappers would accept.

"There may be a few, a very few, persons you can trust with the truth, but you must impress upon them the danger to Jenny if they violate your trust. It is imperative that we keep it out of the media and away from the general public. Jennifer's safety depends on it."

"What if the newspaper calls me here or at the airport?"

"That could happen. Some reporters have sources with their ears to the ground for information such as this. If you are contacted by the news media and they seem to know something, refer them to me. I have a good relationship with the local editor. He is a responsible person and has worked with us in the past by holding up on a story when a life was in danger or the outcome of an investigation was at stake. But he also has an obligation to his readers and we can't expect him to sit on a story for long.

"Our relationship with the local TV stations has been all right, but I'm not confident we could get all three to go along with holding up on a story. Their competition with each other is fierce. Fortunately they don't have time to dig quite as hard as the newspaper. If you are contacted by a TV station, refer them to me, also. I believe they will cooperate up to a point.

"I haven't given you any concrete answers. There are none. People are going to ask questions. Just do some thinking in advance and give them as little information as you can.

"You also need to be thinking about whether or not you will comply with the ransom demand. Mrs. Kogan, I went over several of the options with Mr. Kogan earlier. Pay or not pay. Use real money or a dummy package. Another consideration is, can they give you assurance that Jenny is still...safe," Lance found it impossible to use the word *alive*, "before you pay the ransom. That is also a good question to use to keep the kidnapper on the phone."

Mr. Kogan had been quiet for as long as he could manage. "Is there any chance the FBI, the federal government, will put up the money? It's a federal crime, isn't it?"

"No, sir. That is, yes, it is a federal crime; but there is no chance the government would put up the ransom money. We will help you get the money in the proper form, but it will be your money. We'll talk about that at the proper time."

"How much do you think they will ask for?"

"I'm not going to speculate on that. I don't know, nor do I need to know, your financial status. The kidnappers may know. They will ask for all they think they can get."

"Have there been any cases where they took less than they asked for?"

"I don't think we ought to pursue that, Mr. Kogan. It would be speculation. I don't want to mislead you or influence your thinking by talking too much about what has happened in other cases. Every case, *every case*, is different. I know it is a terrible burden to make these decisions but you two will have to live with them."

Mrs. Kogan, who had not spoken since she admitted calling the older children, suddenly pled, "Oh, Charles, let's give them what they want."

Her hand went to her mouth, and she burst into tears.

Lance looked to Kogan. *Why, for heaven's sake, don't you hold and comfort this poor woman?*

Kogan didn't seem to notice the tears. "That would be the easy way out. I'll do what I think is best when the time comes."

As Mrs. Kogan sat sobbing in her chair, Lance said, "Yes, why don't we wait and see what they ask for. You don't have to make any choices yet, but you do need to think about your options."

Lance went through the phone procedure again, this time

including Mrs. Kogan. When finished, he looked directly at Kogan and asked, "Is that agreeable to you?"

"It looks like you're calling the shots."

"I realize the procedure I have outlined might result in my answering some of your business and personal calls. If a caller asks who I am, I will say I am a family friend. If they ask you who answered the phone, you should give the same answer."

"I don't want my wife answering any calls from the kidnappers."

"I understand that, Mr. Kogan, but she normally answers the phone when you are not here. We want to make things as normal as possible. Since we don't know when they will call, it will be better if we allow her to answer all the calls she can reach in a reasonable number of rings. The only change is she would be answering on this extension. And, I will be here to assist her."

"You've got all the answers, don't you, Barron?"

Lance ignored the remark, "I have started a log here to record all telephone calls, in and out. This will be important later when we are reviewing the telephone company trap records and preparing for trial. We don't need to log business or personal calls, but only those calls that relate to the case. If either of you should take a call from the kidnappers, please log the time it began and ended. That information could be critical if we get a good trace."

Kogan seemed to be bored. He finally said, "I get the picture. We've just about talked this thing to death. I think I'll go on to bed. I don't think you're gonna solve this thing by sitting around here talking about lists and logs. You need to be out there talking to Kline and his crowd and finding out where they were when this thing happened."

"We will do that, Mr. Kogan, but we must be ready here first. Remember what the kidnapper said? 'You'll hear from us.' That first contact, whether by phone or some other means, is a great chance to learn more about the kidnappers. We must take advantage of it."

Kogan was already nearing the door, followed, at a respectful distance, by his wife.

"It was nice to meet you, Mrs. Kogan."

Mrs. Kogan stopped, turned and for the first time, looked directly into Lance's eyes. She silently formed the words, "I'm sorry," and continued on.

"We'll do all we can to get her back safely, ma'am."

After the bathroom break, Lady led Jenny through the room that smelled like a kitchen and down the two steps. But they didn't turn right, toward the box. Lady led her to the left and said, "Just sit here, I'm sure they will be here soon."

The metal chair reminded Jenny of the ones her mother used to set up for bridge parties. She rested her arms on a small table. She could hear Lady breathing directly across from her, but she said nothing.

Jenny thought of Jason. *I wonder what he's doing. Does he know about me? I guess it is still Thursday. If it's Friday he has gone to Columbia with the track team. He was supposed to call me when he got back. I guess Mom will tell him what happened.*

The barking dogs and then tires crunching on gravel brought Jenny back to reality. She heard Lady's chair slide on the concrete floor. "They're here."

Jenny heard heavy footsteps across the kitchen and then Boss's voice. "Do you know how to use this?"

"Yes," Lady answered.

"Okay, here's the message. Make sure she reads it word for word."

Jenny heard whispering behind her, and then Boss spoke out, "Listen, girl, I'm going to let her remove your blindfold. You better not turn around or look around. Just read the message exactly the way it's written. If you mess up, we'll just start over 'til you get it right. You understand that?"

"Yes, sir."

"I'm going to be right outside so don't try anything. The sooner we get the message to your little ole dad, the sooner we learn how much he *luves* you." Boss chuckled as he went up the steps and closed the door.

From behind her, Lady said, "I'm going to put a little vaseline on your hair to help me get the tape off. I'll be as gentle as I can."

When the blindfold slipped off, Jenny was blinded. She rubbed her eyes and saw that the room was dark except for a blinding ring of light on the table in front of her. A goose neck lamp was the source.

Jenny continued to rub her eyes as Lady placed a small microphone on the table. The cord stretched into the darkness. "When I start the recorder, read the paper word for word."

Jenny felt Lady lean around her shoulder on the left. She saw a tanned arm wearing a watch with a jewelled band enter the lighted circle. There was a silver friendship ring on her pinky.

"Are you ready? Pick up the paper."

Jenny rubbed her eyes again and picked up the single sheet of printer paper. She had trouble focusing even though the print was clear and large.

"Here we go. Read!"

"Daddy, this is Jenny. I'm okay, but you must follow these instructions and do exactly as you are told or you will never see me again." Jenny sniffled, then continued, "Get together $300,000 in unmarked twenty-dollar bills. We want it in a briefcase. When you have it ready, put an ad in the Springfield newspaper under PERSONAL. Mention Jenny. Hurry, Daddy. No cops. You will hear from us."

Jenny turned to hand the paper back.

"No, Jenny, don't! Put it on the table."

"Okay, I'm sorry, I forgot."

It lifted Jenny's spirits to have someone, even a kidnapper, call her by name.

Lady reapplied the blindfold but she used several layers of gauze before applying the tape. Lady said the gauze would keep the tape from sticking to her hair. Jenny thought, *But it will make the blindfold a lot harder to lift. Oh, well, about all I can see from the box is whether it is daylight or dark anyway.*

"Are you through out there? Is her blindfold back on?"

"Yes, she's all tucked in."

Boss's heavy feet announced his approach. "Let me have the cassette. Did you check it?"

"No."

"Dammit. You should have checked it. I told you to."

"Look, J.D., I use a tape recorder every day, five and a half days a week. I know how to use it."

"Okay, don't get smart. I'm gone."

"Tell Ronnie to bring us some food when he comes back. I know the girl is hungry."

Jenny heard the car start and the crunching sound of gravel gradually subsided. She repeated to herself, *I'm going to remember this. Boss is called J.D., Ronnie is around here somewhere, and Lady uses a tape recorder five and a half days a week. Boss is called J.D., Ronnie is around here somewhere, and Lady uses a tape recorder five and a half days a week. I'm going to remember that much, no matter how long they hold me.*

I know Daddy will hurry. They want $300,000. Isn't that an awful lot of money? I'll bet he has it, though. Like Mother says, "He's a good provider."

As Jenny turned over in her mind all she had learned during the break, she realized Lady was right about her being hungry. The nausea she had felt earlier was gone, and her appetite had returned. *When did I eat last? In the school cafeteria at noon. Jason and I. I shared my fries with him.* She smiled at the thought. *Was that today? No yesterday. I'm losing track of time.*

The dogs announced the arrival of a car. Jenny listened carefully and was able to hear laughter from the kitchen. Then there were footsteps on the concrete, the lid was opened and the aroma of hamburgers was unmistakable.

"He brought us some food, Jenny. I hope you like Hardee's."

She heard Lady drag a chair to the side of the box. "Sit up if you like. I'll stay here with you." She touched Jenny's shoulder and Jenny reached up and took the hamburger. "Here, let me unwrap it for you. There's a milkshake too. I'll hold it until you're ready."

Jenny was pleased to find the hamburger warm and delicious. She quickly ate a couple of bites and then put it on her lap and held out her hands for the milkshake. Lady handed her the large, cold cup. She sipped a few swallows and handed it back. She reached again for the hamburger. Gradually the silence and this absurd ritual started to bother her. Here she was blindfolded, sitting in a box, eating, with a stranger sitting a few feet away, holding her food and, she supposed, watching every bite she took, every move she made. To break the silence, Jenny asked, "How did you get involved in this?"

"Here, have some more milkshake."

Jenny repeated the question.

"I'm not going to talk about it." Lady's tone was not angry, but determined.

Jenny tried again, "You seem so nice. I can't believe you are a part of this."

The reply was firm, "Listen, I told you I am not going to talk about it. You would never, ever understand."

Suddenly the door opened. A high-pitched voice squeaked, "Hey, what's going on? Get her back in there and close it."

"Okay, we were just finishing up." Then to Jenny, "Here's your shake and some straws. Maybe you can finish it."

"No, I don't want any more, thank you." Jenny had lowered her voice to a whisper, "Am I going to get out of this without getting hurt?"

"If I have anything to do with it, honey, you will. There is no plan to hurt you, or I wouldn't be involved. I can control one of the guys, but the other one, I don't know. Now let me get this closed. Try and get some sleep."

"What day is it?"

"It's Thursday, honey."

Jenny tried to hold the lid up. She begged, "Come back as soon as you can. I don't think I can stand it in here. There's nothing to do. Please, please, don't leave me in here so long."

Then she was alone.

★ ★ ★

Lance was in the deep early part of sleep from which it is so difficult to awaken when he heard the phone ring. He had left all the lights on. The desk and the phone were only six feet away, but it felt like he was knee deep in fresh concrete as he made his way, reaching to release the PAUSE button. The digital clock on Kogan's desk read 1:50 A.M. *Was that the third ring?* The tape recorder was running. Lance was fully alert by the next ring but decided to let it ring one more time to see if Kogan was on the way. Finally he answered, "Kogan residence."

There were several clicks on the line. Lance thought the caller was hanging up. Then a female voice, "Daddy, I want you to listen..."

Chuck Kogan yelled, "Jenny, are you all right?"

Lance was frozen for a moment as he heard the female voice still speaking, "...follow these instructions and do exactly..."

"Jenny, tell me where you are." It was Kogan again.

"...see me again."

Suddenly, it made sense! Lance covered the telephone with his hands and yelled at the top of his voice toward Kogan's bedroom, "Mr. Kogan, get off the phone. It's a recording, it's a recording! Get off! Get off! She can't hear you."

The voice continued "...$300,000 in unmarked twenty-dollar

bills. We want it in a briefcase. Put an ad in the Springfield paper under PERSONALS when ready. Mention Jenny. No cops. Hurry, Daddy. You will hear from us."

There was a click and the phone went dead. Lance was perspiring and his throat throbbed. He turned off the recorder and laid the telephone, uncradled, on the desk.

Kogan entered. He was in his pajamas. He looked like a child and, like a defiant child, he attacked. "Why the hell didn't you answer it? I thought you were going to let them hang up."

"And I thought we were in agreement about where we would answer and that we didn't have to hurry. I hope you didn't blow it."

Lance caught himself. "I think we got most of the instructions. I'm sure our voices overrode part of it."

Lance pulled the original and started the copying process. While waiting he read his notes to Kogan, "300,000, unmk, 20s, briefcase, Spg. paper, Jenny, hurry, no cops. Did you get anything else?"

Kogan, still in a pout over Barron's reprimand, said, "No, but I heard enough. I ain't paying any crooks $300,000."

Lance removed the original and labeled it, "KC 7-2552 #1." He added his initials and the date and then secured it in his briefcase. The copy was clear and crisp. Jenny's voice was unfazed by her father's interruptions. She seemed to be reading. Her voice was a monotone. Even when she said, "Hurry" there was no emotion. Her use of the word "cops" seemed unnatural and she referred to herself in the third person. In spite of Kogan's shouting and Lance's muffled "Get off! Get off!," Jenny's instructions seemed to be complete. The closing, "You will hear from us," sounded familiar.

Kogan paced and fumed as he heard himself shouting at a tape recording. "Let me ask you something, Mr. Smartass FBI. You've been saying how much we'd learn when they contacted us. What did we learn? We learned the bastards can make Jenny use a tape recorder. Big deal. What else did we learn?"

Lance took a deep breath. He fought to control the inclination to tell Mr. Kogan how close he had come to fouling up what could be the only instructions they would get. He calmly said, "We learned they want $300,000. You'd better start thinking about that. The sooner we run that ad, the better it will be for Jenny."

THE PACKAGE

If two or more persons conspire to violate this section and one or more of such persons do any overt act to effect the object of the conspiracy, each shall be punished by imprisonment for any term of years, or for life.
—Title 18, U.S. code, Section 1201 (c)

It was a short night for Lance but he was up at 5:00 A.M. He shaved, put on his jogging gear, and took a run around the neighborhood to "shake the wrinkles out" as he once heard Willie Nelson say. After the ransom call and the aborted discussion with Kogan, he had a lot of wrinkles. Kogan's opinion of the investigation had apparently reached a new low. He had continued his pout over almost fouling up the ransom call. Then there was the disappointment over the trap-and-trace. Lance had used Jenny's phone to call the phone company. They said they were short-handed in engineering on the midnight-to-eight shift. They were not able to trace the call to its origin before the automatic hang-up occurred. They had determined that the call was from outside the Springfield service area. It came from a trunk to the south. The report had brought about another tirade from Kogan, "Dammit, Barron, I wish one time you could produce some results. So far you haven't been right on anything."

Lance had ducked and tried to steer Kogan's thoughts toward the ransom payment, but Kogan refused to discuss it and went back to bed. Lance, too, had hoped for better results from the phone company, but he knew the trap-and-trace was a delicate process. It was not a total failure, anyway. If the next call was placed from the same phone, or a phone in the same area, the phone company could start from the trunk where they lost this call and be that far ahead in the trace.

Lance had stretched out on the couch in Kogan's office for the second time. His last thoughts before sleep were of Jenny Kogan's face from her school picture and two words from the tape: "Hurry, Daddy."

A couple of hours' sleep and the short run had refreshed Lance. He had showered in the guest bathroom and was back at Kogan's desk at 5:45 when Mrs. Kogan came in with breakfast. She glanced over her shoulder then whispered, "I'm so afraid Charles is going to refuse to cooperate with the kidnappers. I hope you will reason with him. He won't listen to me. I can't stand it if anything happens to Jenny."

"I understand, ma'am, and I'm sorry. I will go over the options with him, but I know you understand that you two must make the decision."

They heard Kogan approaching. Mrs. Kogan said, "I'll get more coffee."

"Thank you, Mrs. Kogan, I hope you will join us. We have some decisions to make." She nodded to her husband and left.

"Good morning, Mr. Kogan. Your wife served me a fine breakfast. I hope you had a restful, albeit short, night."

"What's your next bright idea? I don't understand the failure of the phone company. Why didn't they bring in extra people?"

"Running a trap-and-trace is not a part of their normal business. They cooperate with law enforcement when they can. They have been very helpful in the past and I'm sure they will be in this case. We did get some information. We know they didn't call locally."

"I don't know, Barron, how you ever get anything done. If I was running this show I'd be out there rattling some doors and telling some people off. I wouldn't be sitting around here waiting for some lazyass telephone people to do my work for me."

"We have plenty to do, Mr. Kogan. The contents of the call, the instructions, are more important to us right now than knowing where the call came from. The ball is in our court. We must start making some of those decisions we discussed. I don't expect any further contact from them until we put that ad in the paper.

"I did a little work on the package before I went to sleep. I don't believe they realize how large $300,000 in twenty-dollar bills is. I have a formula for figuring the size. According to my figures, we can't get $300,000 in twenty-dollar bills into a briefcase. The average briefcase, like mine here, is 18 inches by 12 inches by 3.5 inches, inside dimensions. That gives it a volume of 756 cubic inches."

Lance showed the figures to Kogan as he went but Kogan showed marginal interest. Lance was determined that Kogan understand why they could not comply exactly with the kidnappers' instructions. Failure to use a briefcase might be considered a serious deviation by the kidnappers. Lance had an alternative to suggest, but he wanted Kogan to know, up front, why they would not be using a briefcase. He continued, "Banks store paper money, regardless of denomination, in stacks, called straps, of one hundred bills. A strap of twenty-dollar bills would total $2000. Your package will take 150 straps. A strap of used bills is .43 inches thick, and all bills are 6.14 inches long by 2.615 inches wide. This ransom package will have a volume of 1035 cubic inches. It cannot be put into a briefcase."

"I'll bet the bastards will take it any way we want to give it to them. Right?"

"They might, but they might become suspicious and scrub the plan. We want to *appear* to comply in every way we can. I suggest that we use a mapcase, like the ones your pilots use. An average mapcase, or catalogue case, is 16 inches by 11.5 inches by 7 inches. It, then, has a volume of 1288 cubic inches which gives us plenty of room for the ransom. It is close to being a briefcase and it would be a natural for you, a man in the aviation business."

"I'd like to give it to them in a case of dynamite."

Lance went on, "Our Technical Services Division at the lab keeps several kinds and sizes of briefcases and suitcases on hand. They will send us one air express once we decide exactly what we need."

"Hold on just a damn minute. I haven't said I was going to pay it. I've got a lot of questions before I agree to anything."

"That's fine, sir. Let's talk about it."

"There was something they said, or had Jenny say, that I didn't understand. What do they mean 'unmarked bills'?"

"Criminals often use that term, and I'm not sure they know what they mean.

"We have several ways of marking bills. We could, for instance, use ultraviolet powder or paste which can only be seen with a special light. Or we could sprinkle the money with shark liver oil which makes it easy to locate with 'sniffer dogs.' What they probably mean, however, is they want money with unrecorded serial numbers. Ironically, there is no way they can know whether we recorded the serial numbers or not. We *will*, as a matter of fact, record the serial number of every bill in the package, along with all the other variables that make each bill unique. We will have all that data on record for each bill in order to prove in court beyond all doubt that a particular bill was a part of the ransom you paid. That's one of the decisions the FBI makes. Recording those numbers poses no threat to Jenny because the kidnappers have no way of knowing that we did it, until they are charged and tried, of course."

"If I decide to put up the money, are we just going to pay them off and let it go at that? What are you going to do to protect my investment?"

Lance noticed that Mrs. Kogan had quietly returned and had taken her spot behind her husband.

"I will summarize what I have told you earlier. Then I will try and answer your question.

"Our number one priority is the safe return of your daughter. We cannot win if we don't accomplish that. And we can't lose if we do. With that in mind, we must *appear* to comply with the kidnappers' demands.

"Our second priority is the coverage of the ransom drop *undetected by the kidnappers* in order to bring about their apprehension *after* Jenny's release. We fully intend to cover the drop. We will talk later about the type of surveillance we will use.

"Our third priority is the recovery of the money and the conviction of the kidnappers."

"Those are mighty highflown words, but they don't tell me what I want to know. In everyday working man's words, what are you going to do to get my money back? I need that information before I can make a sound decision."

"There is no way I can cover everything we will do, Mr. Kogan, because we are in a reactive mode. Many of our actions will be based on what the kidnappers tell us to do. So far their demands have been fairly reasonable."

"The hell you say! You think $300,000 is reasonable? It might be for the federal government, but for a small businessman..."

"I know it's a lot of money. As I said before, I don't know what your financial status is. What I do know is that they did not put us under an unreasonably short deadline. They allowed you to let them know when you have it."

"Big deal. But let's get back to what you are going to do to protect my money."

"We will send an accountant, an FBI agent who is an accountant, with you to the bank. What bank do you use?"

"Commerce, the Commerce Bank down on Boonville."

"Our agent will work closely with whatever Commerce Bank official you decide to use to fund the ransom payment. We will have the bank official handle the microfilming or photocopying of the money. That is so we will have a clean chain of custody. He can later testify that a particular bill, to the exclusion of all others, was a part of the ransom package he prepared and photocopied for

Mr. Charles Kogan on a particular date at the Commerce Bank, Springfield, Missouri. And you can testify that you took the package from that bank official and had it in your possession until you delivered it to a particular location on a particular date as directed by the kidnappers in exchange for the release of your daughter."

"I thought it was illegal to photograph money."

"Normally it is; however, there is a section of the United States Code that allows copying, in black and white only, for certain purposes, one of which is law enforcement. We'll take care of that through the local Secret Service Office."

"Okay, Okay, what else are you going to do?"

"The entire list of currency, in this case 15,000 twenty-dollar bills, will be scanned into the NCIC computer in Washington."

Kogan was becoming impatient. He wanted to hear about kicking doors down and dragging suspects in for a session under the flood lights.

"What will you do if I say I won't pay?"

"Do you mean, go through with the drop but without real money in the package?"

"No. I mean don't do a goddamned thing. Just don't do it. Wait 'em out."

Lance tried hard not to show his emotions. Before he could calm himself enough to answer, Mrs. Kogan rose from her seat and said, "Oh, Charles, please! They have our daughter."

"You think I don't know that? You just stay out of this. I'm trying to make a sound decision."

Mrs. Kogan looked to Lance with her sad eyes and sagged back into her chair.

"Tell me, Barron, do you have any figures on what the odds are if we do pay the ransom and what they are if we don't? Does it improve our chances if we pay?"

Lance had hoped Kogan would not ask that question. He hesitated as long as he could, not wanting to say what he knew he had to. "No, sir, Mr. Kogan, I'm sorry to say there is not a strong correlation between paying the ransom and achieving the safe return of the victim."

Kogan smiled. "So some people pay and don't get their kids back. Is that right?"

"Yes, sir."

Kogan continued a little louder, "And some people don't pay and do get their kids back." Kogan turned toward his wife to make sure she was listening. "Is that right, Barron?"

The answer was obvious. Lance was tempted to balk but finally said, "Yes, sir."

Kogan was on a roll. "And there is no connection between the two. Is that right?"

"Well, no, sir. Not of any statistical significance." Lance wanted so badly to add, "But how are you going to feel for the rest of your life if you don't do everything you possibly can to save your daughter?"

Mrs. Kogan was suddenly on her feet, "Charles Kogan, what are you thinking? This is our daughter, not some race horse you are betting on! Who cares what the odds are? We don't need that money. We have to think of Jenny. How can you think of anything else? She's waiting somewhere, barely keeping her hopes alive probably. And do you know what she is clinging to? Her belief that we are doing all we can to save her. And here you are talking about odds! The devil with the odds. How could we go on living if we didn't help her? Oh, Charles, please, please."

Kogan had gotten up when his wife started her plea, but he made no effort to stop her, or reassure her, or comfort her. He didn't even face her. He just stood and looked at the ceiling until she finished. "I'm trying to get information here. Will you please control yourself."

Lance was embarrassed to be a part of this sad scene. He said nothing.

Mrs. Kogan, now sobbing, finally sat down. Her husband followed suit and then said, as if nothing had happened, "You said something earlier about a dummy package."

"Yes, sir, that's one of your options."

"Would you use counterfeit money?"

"No sir, not a chance. That would definitely be against the law. But, if you should choose that option, we would fix up a mapcase in the same way we would with real money. We would fill it with straps of paper of the same size and weight as real money. We would set up the drop and conduct the surveillance in exactly the same manner as with real money. We would put the same electronic tracking device in the mapcase as we would with real money.

"Of course, as soon as they opened it up they would know we had not complied…"

Kogan interrupted, "What do you mean, electronic tracking device?"

"I didn't get to that before, and I am not going into a lot of detail now. I'll just say that our lab will place a very small transmitter behind a false wall in the mapcase. The transmitter will emit a signal which we can follow with a special receiver mounted in one of our vehicles."

Kogan became more animated than he had been since before the ransom demand call. "Now that sounds like something that will do some good."

Jenny awakened with a start. Someone was opening her coffin. She almost turned over the remains of the milkshake Lady had given her. How long had she been asleep? It must have been hours. The milkshake was thin and warm.

"You need to go to the bathroom before I go, honey. I'll be gone for a while and I don't want you to get in a bind."

Lady helped her over the side and led her up the steps through what she now felt sure was the kitchen. She entered the bathroom without incident this time and found things situated as she remembered them. She called out through the door, "Any chance I could take a shower? I'm really starting to feel grungy."

"No, I'm afraid not, honey. We don't have time. The shower doesn't work. Maybe we can arrange for you to take a bath tomorrow if I have time. I'll ask them about it. Okay?"

While Lady was talking, Jenny pulled her blindfold away from her right cheek and tilted her head back. Sunlight was streaming through the small window over the bathtub. She had the same impulse she had before to dive through, but in the sunlight she saw how far it was to the ground. Still, that window kept telling her it represented freedom. "I'll work on that," she told herself, "I have a lot of time."

Jenny washed her hands and left the water running to cover the sound as she quickly made inventory of the items in the medicine chest, hoping to find something with a name or address. They apparently had removed all the prescription drugs. In fact there were no drugs, not even aspirin. But there was toothpaste, mouthwash, dental floss, two toothbrushes, eye shadow, perfume and lipstick.

"Time to go, honey. Are you about done in there?"

"Okay, I'm on the way."

Jenny quietly closed the medicine chest, turned the water off, and opened the door. "Any chance you could get me toothpaste and a toothbrush?"

"I'm going into town now. If I get a chance, I'll do that. Oh, yeah, I have some food for you. The guys brought some raisin biscuits. I left them down by your box. They're probably cold but still fresh. They were nice and warm, but I didn't want to wake you. I let you sleep as long as I could."

As they started back through the kitchen, Lady, in a sterner voice said, "Listen, I know it must have occurred to you that you could remove the blindfold while you are in the box. J...uh...the guy, has asked me three times if there was any sign you had messed with the blindfold. He said if you messed with it, he would tie your hands together again. And, honey, he's mean. If he thought you saw him and could identify him, I hate to think what he would do to you. And to me, too. So please, for your sake and mine, don't fool with the blindfold. Okay?"

"Okay, but you can't imagine how hard it is, being locked up in there. Sometimes I almost panic. It's so dark and so quiet and there is nothing to do. I wish I could sleep 'til this is over, but I can't. How much longer do you think I'll have to be in there?"

"I don't know, honey. I think it's up to your father, now."

"Can't you leave the lid open? I promise I won't get out. Just don't lock me in there, please, please, Lady."

"I have to go in to work, honey. I was supposed to be off all week but they called me to come in. I told the guys one of them needed to be out here while I'm at work. One is out of town but the other one was supposed to be here."

"No! You mean no one will be here? Please don't do that. What if something happened like the house catching fire? Leave the lid open or at least unlocked. I won't go anywhere."

"I'm really sorry, honey, but if I left it open or unlocked and the one guy found it that way, I don't know what he would do to me. I'm afraid of him, and he gave me strict orders to keep you in the box with the lid closed and locked. I have to do that. Believe me, honey, I don't like it. Just try to relax and sleep as much as you can. Here, take your biscuits with you."

Jenny took the sack and threw it violently in the direction of Lady's voice and said, "Keep your biscuits! You're as bad as they are! Worse! You could help me but you won't." Jenny broke into pitiful sobs as Lady helped her over the side of the box.

"I'm sorry, Jenny. I know you don't understand, and I doubt you ever will. I don't like what I'm doing, but it is my only way out of the situation I'm in. I've got to go now. I'll bring you that tooth-brush if I can. And, here, you better take your food. You ought to eat something."

Jenny heard the lid close and Lady's departing steps. She heard the front door close and the automobile sounds and tires on the gravel. Then she suddenly saw the whole picture. *Lady doesn't like what they are doing to me. Lady is going to let me escape! Of course! That's it! Lady told me I would be here all alone. She didn't have to tell me that. She could have told me one of the guys was here. How would I know? I'll bet she only closed the lid! She didn't lock it. I can get out of here. I can go through that bathroom window if I have to!*

Jenny sprang forward. Her forehead banged on the lid and she fell back. She pushed upward with the heels of her hands. It was no use. The lid was locked.

What a fool I am. She's not going to help me. Maybe no one is. Jenny chastised herself for being such a dope as to think getting away would be that easy. She finally calmed down. She even ate a couple of the beat-up raisin biscuits.

To pass the time Jenny tried to imagine what her mother and father were doing. She knew her father could handle this situation. He would handle it like a business deal. It was like another contract, a bid on another airplane. He would work out the details and eventually get his way, but her mother would be grieving. She always seemed sad, anyway. *I'm sorry, Mom, to cause you to worry. I'm going to make it up to you when I get out of here. I'm going to see if I can make you laugh at least once every day. I'll bet I can. That will be my goal. My gift to you. I'll probably get myself a joke book or some-thing, but I am going to do something, sing something, say something that will make you laugh. You deserve that, Mom. We used to be that way. I made you laugh without even trying. I don't know what happened to you. Maybe nothing. Maybe something happened to me. But we must get back to that, Mom. Okay?*

Jenny's thoughts rambled on as she gradually recovered from

the silly idea that Lady would let her escape. She thought of her big, black Labrador retriever, Peaches. What a stupid name for a dog! She actually laughed a little as she thought of Peaches pushing his bowl across the floor at feeding time, just to remind her. Peaches cried for her when she was gone. Her mother told her that when she went to cheerleader school last summer, Peaches cried and went around the house looking for her every day at feeding time. *Don't cry, Peaches. I'm coming home as soon as I can.*

Jenny found it a little surprising that she thought of Peaches before she thought of Jason. She smiled. *Oh, well, I've known Peaches a lot longer.*

She wondered how Jason would react to what had happened to her. She was pretty sure he wouldn't cry. She had never seen him cry. Even at that sad movie where she saw several grown men tearing up, Jason didn't. She didn't think anything of it at the time. Now, thinking about it for the first time since, it bothered her. She couldn't figure out why. She had never seen her father cry either.

Jenny didn't know how long she had been asleep when she heard the heavy footsteps in the distance. She cringed as they came across the kitchen and down the steps to her level. She knew it wasn't Lady. The lid opened. As soon as he spoke, she knew it was Boss, "I see you are still with us. Are you being a good girl?"

Jenny didn't answer.

"I never did get much of a chance to see you close up. Let's see if that blindfold has been messed with." Jenny cringed as he ran his finger between the tape and the side of her head. "I wouldn't want you to be trying to get a look at me. You wouldn't do that would you?"

Jenny felt his breath, smelled the beer. His head was inches away.

"I'll bet your daddy liked that nice recording you made for him. Do you think so?…What's the matter? Don't you want to talk?

Aren't you lonely down here?…Do you like the little box we made for you? You seem to have plenty of room in there. Do you think there's enough room in there for two of us?" He chuckled and then said, "We might have to lay on top of one another…Hey, that wouldn't be so bad, would it? Huh?…Why don't you answer me? Are you a shy girl? You don't look like you'd be shy. You look like one of those Dallas Cowboy Cheerleaders…I'll bet you're not shy with that big old boy we saw you with."

He chuckled deep in his throat. "Huh, huh, huh."

Jenny had not moved. She was terrified. She knew if she said a word she would cry. She prayed.

"Let's see what you've got there under that sweater. What does that say on there, Dallas Cowboys?…No, GHS. What's under your GHS sweater, Miss Dallas Cowboy Cheerleader? What do you have under there? Let's see. Some nice, firm titties, I'll bet. Huh, huh, huh."

He pulled Jenny's sweater up toward her head. Without thinking, Jenny suddenly raised both her arms upward from her sides, grabbed Boss's arm, and brought it straight to her mouth. She bit the muscular part of his forearm just below the elbow with all the force she could muster. He bellowed. She held on as he jerked backward. His reaction was so violent it pulled her into a sitting position before she could turn loose. He roared, "You little bitch! You'll be sorry for that!"

Jenny slipped back down into the box and held both her arms up to protect her head from the expected blow. Boss reached in and caught her by the hair. She screamed as he jerked her head toward him. She heard the kitchen door bang open. Someone tumbled down the steps. She heard a chair scraping on the concrete floor just as Lady screamed, "No, J.D., no!"

Jenny heard Lady grunt with exertion, then a thud and a metallic crash. The man groaned and released his grip on Jenny's hair as Lady shouted, "Knock that off, J.D.! Do you hear me?"

Jenny slipped farther into her sanctuary, assumed the fetal position and sobbed into the darkness behind her blindfold.

Lady, panting from her effort, but resolute in her delivery said, "You listen to me, you lousy bastard. I agreed to this deal on condition that this girl would not he hurt in any way. I meant it. You apparently didn't, you slimy pervert, but that's the way it is going to be. Do you understand me?"

J.D. moaned. Lady paused, breathing heavily, then repeated even louder, "Do you understand me?"

J.D. mumbled, "I wasn't going to hurt her."

"Bull shit! If I hadn't come home when I did…and by the way, just in case you have some bright idea about cutting me out of the deal or cutting my throat, you better listen to this.

"There is a safe deposit box somewhere in this area rented in my name. Inside is a letter to the FBI with a copy for the Greene County Sheriff's Office in Missouri and the Carroll County Sheriff's Office here. Each copy is signed, witnessed and notarized. The letter sets out the details of this crime. It includes dates, names, the amount of the ransom, the participants, this address, your address, cars used—everything.

"I have given a key to that safe deposit box and a numerical code to a person I trust, and I have told him I have reason to believe my life is in danger. I have told him that if I fail to check in with him by nine o'clock each morning, he is to immediately take the key and the code to a person whose name I gave him, a person who lives in another town. I have furnished the second person with a number and instructed her that if someone brings her a key and a code, she is to immediately take the key, the code, and the number to the State Police and tell them to apply the code to the number and it will give them the location of a lock the key will fit. It will also explain my disappearance.

"Do you get the picture? I told you up front this thing was going to be done my way. This girl is not to be harmed! If she is, or if I

am, the whistle will blow. If you think you can do away with me…
just try it. If I don't check in…well, I think you understand. The
ball will start rolling and there is no way you can stop it."

"You bitch. I told Ronnie you were too goody-goody for this
job."

"If you had done what you agreed to do, the way you agreed to
do it, this would not have happened. Now get up. Your head is a
sight. Let me see if I can stop the bleeding."

"Take a look at this arm first. You don't have AIDS, do you, little bitch?"

They heard the automobile arrive. Before they could get the
room straightened and Jenny locked away, Driver came bounding
down the steps.

"God, what happened to you, J.D.?"

"Never mind, loudmouth," he said, cutting his eyes toward the
box. "Did you get the unit?"

"Yep, piece of cake. I dropped it off at the guy's house."

"Will he have it done in time?"

"Yeah. Said he would. I gave him the five hundred. Course I had
already taken the box and Genie by. It'll be another five when we
pick it up. He said don't bring a check. He was concerned about
Ryder, but I told him we had it on a long-term lease."

Lady broke in, "We better have a get-together upstairs, and go
over the ground rules again. Some people have short memories
and others have big mouths."

As J.D. and Driver headed for the kitchen, Lady said, "Are you
all right, Jenny? Did he hurt you?"

"No, I'm all right. I'm just going crazy is all. Can you tell me
what's going on?"

"No, Jenny, I'm sorry. They are making progress though. By the
way, I got that toothbrush for you. I'll take you up in a little while
and let you use it. And tomorrow I'll be here all day. If they are
both gone, I'll let you take that bath. Okay?"

"Thanks, Lady, and thanks for coming to my rescue. I don't know what would…" She couldn't go on.

"Honey, I stooped mighty low when I got involved in this. I thought I had a good reason, but it's not good enough to cover hurting someone. Maybe it's not good enough, period."

The telephone crew arrived at the Kogan residence shortly after 9:00 A.M. to "piggy-back" in the special line for Lance's use. This was a simple procedure that only took about fifteen minutes, but Kogan had time to needle one of the technicians about being a "lazyass union laborer." The poor young man knew nothing about the trap-and-trace or the disappointment from the night before. He had no idea why Kogan was on him and could only shake his head and walk away.

At 9:25 A.M. Lance logged in his first call on the new line. Tim Landry reported on the neighborhood investigation. He had contacted two neighbors on each side of Kogan's residence and two across the street.

A couple of the neighbors mentioned the police car in the drive at Kogan's the afternoon before, but Landry steered them away from it. One, the neighbor to the south on the same side, a Mr. Peter Irwin, said he noticed a car driving by slowly a couple of times. He believed it was on Wednesday. He said he thought it was real estate people at first—there being a couple of houses for sale down the block—but later he noticed it didn't have a sign on the door like most of them do. He still didn't pay much attention. It was a big car like the real estate people use, dark color, two guys in it. He didn't know what kind it was.

Then yesterday afternoon, Mr. Irwin was weeding his garden in the back when he heard a car "squeal its tires." He didn't see it but later noticed the police car in the Kogan's drive and wondered if somebody had made a complaint about reckless driving or something. He said the young lady over there was very nice but her boyfriend, a big guy, was sort of a reckless driver. He had heard him burn out of there several times.

Landry further reported that SAC Palmer and the Kansas City surveillance team were en route. The first contingent was expected at the RA by 3:00 P.M.

Kogan was almost jovial as he prepared to leave for the office at mid-morning. "It seems to me, Barron, that there are really only two choices on the ransom thing. One: Do nothing, just see if we can out-bluff them. Or, two: Pay the damn money, and then follow them with that device you were telling me about until they release Jenny. Then go get the money."

Lance tried to interject a word of caution about underestimating the intelligence of the kidnappers, but Kogan obviously was nearing a decision and did not want to be bothered with any more information.

Kogan went on, "I don't think the dummy thing would work. I guess if they didn't open the case until they got to where they live, it might work. I know I wouldn't go that long without checking the money, and I bet they wouldn't either. I've got my CPA working on it to see what the tax picture would be if we didn't get the money back. I'm going to meet with my lawyer to see about spreading the liability around. I'll let you know as soon as I make a decision."

Kogan headed for the garage but turned around and with a grin said, "It sure is nice, Barron, having you college boys working for me."

THE DECISION

A man cannot live with regret. In making a critical decision, if all else be even, the prudent man looks ahead and chooses the course that, should he be wrong, causes the least amount of regret. Then, he will never have to look back.

—anonymous

At 9:30 P.M. on Saturday April 4, things were getting slow in Springfield, Missouri. In many ways Springfield still had a small town atmosphere. The residents liked it that way. Many of them felt that the Chamber of Commerce's claim of a population of 160,000 must have included a lot of people caught in the motels on their way to and from Branson. That country music mecca had had a definite and positive economic impact on Springfield. Some citizens joked that it would not be long until Springfield was known as "Branson North."

The Battlefield Mall was getting ready to close. The old downtown area was already dead. The winos had found their favorite benches in Park Central Square and were saying their goodnights.

Lance Barron was anxious. He had checked the *Springfield News-Leader* for the third time. The ad he placed was definitely in there under PERSONALS. It read "Jenny, please come home." Lance wondered if there were any lonely souls named Jenny out there who would read the ad and hope it was meant for them. How long would the kidnappers wait? Their call could come at any time.

Lance was wearing black coveralls and a black knit cap. During the drop he would be on the floorboard on the passenger side of Kogan's car. He was armed with a .38 caliber Smith and Wesson snub-nosed revolver. Most of the younger agents carried the Glock 9mm automatic. Barron had qualified with it, but he preferred his old standby.

During the afternoon, Barron had arranged with SAC Palmer to have UPS deliver a package to the Kogan residence. In addition to his coveralls and cap, the package contained Kevlar vests for himself and Kogan. Lance ordered a size small for Kogan, but it still fit him like a trench coat. Kogan insisted on wearing his suit and tie. The vest hung down below the hem of Kogan's suit coat. Barron suppressed a smile and thought, *He's getting a lot more protection than I am. It's almost full body armor on him.*

Barron went over the plan again with Kogan. He was to accompany Kogan on the ransom drop even if the kidnappers specifically instructed that Kogan come alone. It had not been easy to reach an agreement on that plan.

The first proposal had been that Lance Barron, or another agent more nearly Kogan's size, deliver the ransom, alone. Kogan immediately ruled that out. "If I'm going to lose $300,000, I'm damn sure going to know exactly where it goes to, and I'm going to hold on to it as long as I can."

Then, when the current plan was proposed, FBI Headquarters was opposed to it because of a perceived increased threat to the safety of the victim. In a conference call involving Barron, SAC Palmer, Bureau Supervisor Melvin Booker, and Kogan, every likely scenario was discussed. If instructions from the kidnappers called for a face-to-face meeting, an event Barron considered to be most unlikely, Barron would remain in his concealed position during the meeting. The only circumstance under which Barron would reveal his presence would be to terminate a clear and direct threat to Kogan's life. The main question considered in making the decision was, "Would the concealed presence of an FBI agent in the automobile used in the drop increase the threat to the victim's safety?" The consensus in this case was that it would not. It did, of course, greatly enhance the safety of the person—Kogan—delivering the ransom should there be a confrontation with the kidnappers.

Barron had pointed out that the kidnappers had made great

efforts to conceal their identity, both during the abduction and in their use of a recorded ransom demand. It was unlikely they would now chance a face-to-face meeting with Kogan…unless murder was in their plans. If it was, Kogan and his daughter were in grave danger, whether or not Barron went along. If they planned to kill the messenger, why would they hesitate to kill the hostage?

After much discussion, FBI Headquarters approved the plan. Barron would go along in a concealed position on the drop. Kogan also approved. It was a first for him.

The mapcase containing the $300,000 was in a closet in Kogan's office. Barron showed Kogan where the small OAR transmitter was secured under a false lining on one end of the mapcase. He explained that the transmitter was already on and transmitting a signal that could be read by the surveillance aircraft. In its present resting state, the signal would be a slow pulsing on the display in the plane. When the mapcase was moved the rate of transmission would increase and continue in that mode until the mapcase again came to rest.

Lance described the tracking unit briefly to Kogan and assured him that the Bureau aircraft covering the drop could locate and follow the transmitter wherever it went.

Kogan scowled and said, "I just hope you guys know what the hell you're doing. I sure as hell can't come up with another $300,000. You damn sure better get my daughter or my money back. I don't like making deals with these bastards anyway. The way you put it to me though, I would look like a real ass if I didn't put up the money."

Barron started to counter that statement but thought better of it. They both knew that was not the way Kogan reached his decision, but Lance didn't want to re-open that sensitive issue. Paying the ransom was a tough decision for Kogan, and he wasn't going to let anyone forget it. Lance felt confident that he had fully and fairly explained every option. He was surprised when Kogan announced that he had decided to pay the ransom.

The first chink he had seen in Kogan's armor, the very first indication that Kogan had a father's concern, had come on Friday after midnight. Lance was asleep on the couch when he felt someone shaking his arm. He awoke to find Kogan, in his pajamas, bending over him. "I need to talk to someone," he said.

Lance sat up and blinked himself to attention.

Kogan said, "Didn't you say the other day that you have a daughter?"

"Yes, sir. Laura is twelve years old."

"Maybe you can help me then. I haven't been able to sleep. I keep seeing my daughter's face. I don't know what it means. I want you to tell me, Lance...Is it all right if I call you Lance? I want you to tell me how I can be sure I'm doing the right thing? If you had to do it, how would you decide?"

Lance had already thought long and hard about that question although he had certainly never expected Kogan to ask him for advice. As he had explained the options to Kogan, he had faced the decisions himself. He could not rate the options on their merits, on their likelihood of success. The statistics did not support one decision over the others. Lance found his hypothetical choice had to be based on the amount of *regret* he wanted to live with. For him, that made the decision easy.

He said to Kogan, "When you saw your daughter's face, Mr. Kogan, what was her expression?"

"Oh, I don't know. Just the way she has always looked at me." Kogan almost choked up. "She's always thought I could do anything."

"Would you say she looked trusting?"

"Well, I probably wouldn't say that, but I think I know what you mean. She thinks I'll do the right thing."

"Then, Mr. Kogan, I think you have the answer to your dilemma." Lance paused and studied Kogan's face. "You're going to be seeing

Jenny's face for the rest of your life, one way or the other. I don't think you want to do anything you would later regret. What do you think Jenny *expects* you to do?"

Kogan was silent for what seemed like minutes. Lance was surprised and looked away when he saw tears in Kogan's eyes.

Kogan never did answer. He ended the strange interlude by saying, "Don't say anything to my wife about our talk here tonight." He headed for the door and was almost out when he stopped and looked back. His face was pained. "Thanks, Lance."

That was Friday night. By Saturday morning Kogan was back in form. When he walked in with his wife, who was bringing Lance his breakfast, he told Lance he was ready to pay the ransom. Mrs. Kogan almost shouted, "Oh, Charles. I'm so glad; so glad. I know it's the right thing to do." She reached out for her husband's hand but he stepped aside, avoiding her touch.

"I decided to pay after talking with my lawyer early this morning. He said I could sue the FBI for the return of my money if the case wasn't handled to my satisfaction."

Lance tried not to show pleasure at Kogan's decision or dismay at his ignorance of the law. He said, "Then we'll proceed with that plan, sir. I'll have Tim Landry meet you at the bank. He is an accountant, and he will have the mapcase we will be using. He will assist you and the bank in photographing and packaging the money. Will ten o'clock be all right?"

Kogan agreed. He left at 9:30 and was back home by 1:00 P.M. Tim Landry escorted Kogan from the bank. He said the photographing of the bills went without a hitch.

Lance had immediately called the *Springfield News Leader* and placed the ad.

It was now 10:00 P.M. on Saturday. Lance continued to go over possible scenarios with Kogan. It helped to review all the possibilities and to continue to familiarize Kogan with the equipment. It also helped to pass the time.

Lance was making a note in the log about changing the OAR transmitter battery. When he looked up, Kogan was studying him. "Do you really think all of this is going to work, Lance?"

Determined to be upbeat, Lance said, "We are prepared and our equipment is working. We are ready, but we still have to admit that the kidnappers are in charge. You will be interested to know that Mr. Palmer at the command post told me earlier that Idaho Five, one of our surveillance aircraft, made a flyover at 7500 feet this afternoon. They reported receiving a strong signal from the tracking system. The Pilot in Command reported that the OAR unit brought them directly over your residence, and it was as good a signal as he had seen."

Kogan showed no pleasure at this. "What else are they doing out there?"

Lance told him his boss had a full-scale briefing of the surveillance squad members and the aircrew members early in the afternoon. Palmer felt, as Barron did, that the drop would take place tonight. There was no reason for the kidnappers to wait.

Kogan continued to be tense and irritable. Except for the decision that Barron was to go along on the drop, he was not impressed with the efforts of the FBI so far and had continued to make snide remarks about the lack of progress. As Lance tried to continue rehearsal of the various scenarios that could occur during the drop, Kogan's effort was half-hearted at best. Lance surmised that Kogan's lack of enthusiasm was not caused by any fear of what lay ahead or even by his dissatisfaction with the FBI but by anger at having to admit he was not in control.

"You need to practice hooking the tape recorder up to the telephone just as I have it here," said Barron, showing Kogan again where the suction cup had to be placed to get the best recording. "If they send us to a phone booth, I won't be able to get out and help you."

"What the hell good is it going to do us to record another one of Jenny's recordings?"

"We don't know that they will use Jenny again. We want to be prepared if they do. There is the possibility with a tape that the lab can pull up some background noise or some other clue that could lead us to their location or their identity. Also, it will be important evidence in a trial. In some cases the lab is able to make voice prints from the tape and match them with voice prints from the suspects.

"If they send you somewhere other than a phone booth we want to be prepared for that. You must remember to turn on the A-4 transmitter you are wearing. The mike is on your left lapel and is voice activated. Make sure the mike is outside your vest. The switch to turn the unit on is in your right pants pocket. Remember, this is a one-way radio. The mike is very sensitive. You will be able to talk to us, but you will not receive any transmissions. This is for your protection in the event you are confronted. We don't want the kidnappers to know we can hear you...and them. By hearing both sides of any conversation you have, we can take whatever action is appropriate."

Kogan, frowning, said, "You are sure putting a load on a guy. Are you just trying to see if you can make me look bad?"

"Not at all, Mr. Kogan. We are trying to cover as many possibilities as we can. I'll be there to help you. If they send you to a telephone booth, I'll be right there. If they send you to some place away from the phone booth, I won't be able to keep you covered so we must know what you are doing. That's the purpose of the A-4. You just briefly tell us what you see and what you are doing so we will know what action, if any, to take."

Kogan looked down at the wire running under his lapel, the switch in his right front pocket, his body armor, the tape recorder with the suction cup mike. "This is the biggest bunch of shit I've ever seen. If it all works, it will be a miracle."

Barron said, "I know it seems like a lot, but remember you will be using one device or the other. Never both at the same time."

"Well, hell, maybe you better go over that one more time."

"That's no problem, sir." Lance repeated the instructions and, for the first time, he felt he had Kogan's undivided attention.

"I don't like the setup. It looks like we are just playing right into their hands. They can just send me into some alley, take my money away from me, and run. They wouldn't even have to release Jenny if they did that."

"Unfortunately, Mr. Kogan, that is exactly the situation we are in. They are in charge. We must do what they say and hope they release your daughter. We can't force them to do anything. But we must learn all we can as we follow their instructions. That's what this equipment is doing for us. You never know when one scrap of information from the phone calls or something you see and report through the radio might be the thing that leads to the identification of the kidnappers."

Kogan muttered something that Lance didn't understand. Something about making a fine speech but not being out there looking for his daughter. Lance let it pass.

Barron knew Kogan was tired, worried, and frustrated. He understood Kogan's desire to be taking some overt action, but until Jenny was safe, overt activity of any sort, except that directed by the kidnappers, was out of the question. Continuing to prepare Kogan, and himself, for as many possibilities as they could, was the only productive thing they could do.

Barron was again on the phone with SAC Palmer at the command post. He turned the phone speaker on so Kogan could hear their conversation.

Palmer assured Barron that the personnel for the fixed surveillance were in their vehicles and ready.

"Do you have mixed crews?" asked Barron.

"Yeah, two are mixed. One of the others is all female."

"Great," said Barron. "And they are in their sports cars, I guess."

"Yeah. We were able to get SMSU stickers from the college bookstore on a couple of them."

"Good. I hope those rookies don't try to get in too close."

"They won't. We've got them well briefed on that. We don't want them any closer than five blocks away. We have had them studying the city map locating likely places to set up. You give us the drop site and we'll have them in place writing down numbers long before you get there."

"Sounds good, boss. What about the birdmen? Are they set to go?"

"It will be Idaho Five again tonight. They're standing down at the satellite airport with full tanks right now. We've got Lambright and Higgins. They're the best."

Barron said, "If we haven't heard anything by 10:30, I think we should have them get up anyway. I believe tonight is the night. There is no reason for the bad guys to wait. Their other call came in at 1:50 A.M. Maybe they are creatures of habit."

"Maybe so. And I agree on Idaho Five up at ten thirty. They can easily go for five hours, and we have Idaho Three fresh and on standby. We really got a break on the weather. They were forecasting scattered thunderstorms earlier but they haven't developed. We'll have our air cover."

Lance laughed, "Boss, be sure and remind Lambright to keep it high. They don't call him 'Cousin Weakeyes' for nothing."

"What do you mean?"

"Well, ol' Loyal likes to fly the surveillance a little low at times. Just remind him this is not Kansas City with buses and taxis running all night long and all that air traffic. It will be dead quiet here tonight and the kidnappers will probably be outside their car some. We don't want our own 'eye' spooking the deal."

"We've got all of that covered, Lance. Just concentrate on getting the word to us and taking care of Mr. K."

"Okay, boss. We hope to be back in touch soon."

Kogan immediately said, "You can tell your frigging boss that he don't need to worry about anybody taking care of Mr. K. I can take care of myself. And what the hell is a fixed surveillance and mix screws?"

Barron laughed; Kogan didn't even smile. "That's 'mixed crews,' Mr. Kogan. We have a squad from the Kansas City office that is expert in conducting surveillances. They work closely with the aircraft crews. They spend much of their time in Kansas City tailing organized crime figures. In this case, of course, we don't have anyone to follow. They have another technique, however, that has been effective when we can't follow the target. It's called a fixed surveillance—or fisur as we call it. It works like this. The kidnappers will direct you to a particular spot; it might be a park, a specific address, a well known building, probably a telephone booth. Many times the first place will be a test. They will probably send you to a location where they can observe our actions. They want to see if you will follow instructions, and they want to see if we are covering you. They might be parked near the spot, or they might drive by or maybe observe from inside somewhere. So, we can't have units driving by gawking. The spot also has to be one where they can get another message to us. They might leave a note in a mailbox or a telephone booth or taped to the underside of a garbage can lid. Any place they can observe us and still get a message to us will do.

"In a fisur, we surround the area they send us to as quickly as possible. We put vehicles near major intersections on all sides of the designated spot but well away from it. You heard Mr. Palmer say they are to get no closer than five blocks. The surveillance squad uses a variety of sports cars, pickups, motorcycles, as well as unlikely-looking people. They don't use vehicles or people who look like average cops. Even the dumbest criminal can spot a dark colored four-door sedan with black sidewall tires occupied by two middle-aged, slightly overweight males wearing suits and ties."

This brought a smile from Kogan. Barron couldn't believe it.

"We use our younger agents, and we like to have a male-female pair if we can. That is what we mean by a 'mixed crew.' It's the least conspicuous arrangement, particularly in a college town. You heard Palmer say we have one all-female car tonight. That's unusual. We normally don't have that many female agents."

Kogan growled, "One is too many in my book."

Barron, undeterred, continued, "Once in position, their job is simple: log as many automobile tags as possible. One reads the tags into a tape recorder and the other takes notes. If things are slow and they can get descriptions of cars and/or occupants, fine— but the most important thing is the tag."

Kogan smirked and said, "So they are just setting around on their asses, hoping the kidnappers will drive by and they can identify them. Is that it? Sounds like a dumb idea to me."

"It works. We had a case in Dallas a few years ago; a young boy was the victim. The kidnappers contacted the father and kept sending him from one phone booth to another all over Dallas. The surveillance team kept racing ahead, setting up and doing their thing. The drop was finally made and the kidnappers got away clean with the money. We didn't have a suspect until we put all those tags into a computer and printed out the results. One car kept showing up at all the sites. We identified the owner and put him under twenty-four hour surveillance until he started spending ransom bills. We charged and convicted him and his partner in local court and recovered most of the ransom money." Lance didn't mention the fate of the victim. He hoped Kogan wouldn't ask…He didn't.

Instead Kogan asked, "Why was the bastard convicted in local court?"

"There was no violation of the federal law."

"Why the hell not? It was a kidnapping, wasn't it? And you said they paid the ransom."

"One of the elements of the Federal statute is that the victim be willfully transported in interstate or foreign commerce. The law says that if the victim of an abduction is not released within twenty-four hours, we can *presume* they have been transported in interstate or foreign commerce. We are working under that presumption now. We still must prove Jenny was taken outside the state to have a violation of federal law."

"Do you mean if we find out Jenny wasn't taken out of Missouri," Kogan, like most natives, pronounced it *Missouruh*, "you can't prosecute the sons-uh-bitches?"

"Oh, they will be prosecuted, all right. We are working this case closely with the Springfield Police Department. Also the Greene County Sheriff's Office and the Highway Patrol were represented at Mr. Palmer's briefing this afternoon. With the exception of the Springfield PD, we haven't asked for any assistance, but we will probably be seeking their assistance later. If it turns out that there is no violation of the federal law, one of those agencies, depending on the circumstances, will file charges. The State of Missouri has a strong kidnapping law and the armed intrusion into your home would be an aggravating circumstance. We would testify just as we would in Federal Court. When we solve this thing and get Jenny back, and hopefully get your money back, somebody is going to jail. You can bet on it."

"You are mighty damn confident for a guy who's been working the case for three days and, as far as I can tell, all you know about the kidnappers is that they can operate a tape recorder and a telephone. But I'm sure you college boys have got it all figured out, don't ya?"

Barron gritted his teeth. "Let's see if we can get a little sleep."

"Amazing grace, how sweet the sound, that saved a wretch like me. I once was lost but now I'm found; was blind but now I see."

Jenny Kogan was singing to keep from crying. It had been hours since she had heard a sound. She was thirsty, hungry, and badly needed to use the bathroom. She had fought claustrophobia until she became too tired to struggle. Fatigue was a blessing, as she drifted in and out of sleep. When she was awake, the singing took all her energy, but she felt it was the only thing that was keeping her sane. She wanted to scream but would not give in to that urge. During one of her spells of claustrophobia, she had angrily jerked the blindfold off only to find it was totally dark inside the box. She chastised herself for losing control and tried to put the blindfold back in place. *Boss said he would tie my hands if I did that. Oh, God, I know I can't stand that.*

"'Twas grace that taught my heart to fear and grace my fears relieved...yes, yes, thank you, Lord. Please relieve my fears."

Jenny had listened so hard and for so long for the sound of tires on the gravel drive that when it finally came she was afraid to believe it. "Please let it be, Lord. Please let it be Lady. Please, please, please, Lord."

And then it was unmistakable as she heard the sound of footsteps in the kitchen and down the steps and then the creaking hinges on the lid and, "Jenny, I'm sorry to be so long. Ronnie was supposed to come by and check on you, but something came up and he couldn't make it. I know you must be starved."

In spite of her relief and excitement, Jenny became acutely aware of and concerned about the condition of her blindfold. When Lady opened the box, the light from an overhead fixture reached her eyes and brought pain. She tried to reposition the blindfold. "I'm not trying to see you, Lady, honest. It was just so long, and I was afraid everyone had left me locked up in here, and I have to go to the bathroom so bad." Jenny started to cry, "I'm sorry, but I panicked and messed it up. I tried to put it back. Don't tell that man."

"Here, let me help you...Okay, that will do for now. Let's go on up to the bathroom and then I'll fix it back just like it was."

Jenny was weak and dizzy. She almost fell as Lady helped her over the edge of the box. They followed the familiar route up the steps and through the kitchen to the bathroom straight ahead.

"I'll be putting your food out here on the table. You can eat as soon as you're through in there."

"Thank you. I'll be out in a few minutes."

Walking around in the now familiar bathroom and the prospect of eating lifted Jenny's spirit. During her long hours in the box, she had formulated a plan to get a message to the outside. After attending to her needs, she pulled the sagging blindfold down and quietly opened the medicine cabinet. The lipstick was still there. She quickly unrolled a length of toilet paper and spread it on the edge of the bathtub. With the lipstick she wrote, HELP, HELP, PLEASE HELP ME!! JENNY KOGAN. She wished she had more substantial paper. She went to the door and asked, "Lady, did you remember to get that toothbrush for me?" Jenny planned to leave the water running after brushing her teeth to cover the sound of opening the window and tossing the message out.

"Yes, I did. I left it in the car. Just a minute and I'll get it for you."

What luck, Jenny thought. She listened for Lady's departure. She then stood in the bathtub, unlocked and raised the small window. The creaking frame was louder than she had imagined. She unhooked the screen and tossed her message out. The end of the small roll of paper caught on the edge of the screen and unfurled like a flag in the breeze. That was not what she had planned, but it was even better, a banner.

Jenny quickly closed the window. She stepped out of the bathtub and pulled the blindfold back into place just as Lady knocked lightly and opened the bathroom door.

"Here it is, Jenny. There's toothpaste in the medicine cabinet. I'll put some on your brush for you."

Jenny felt panic as Lady opened the medicine cabinet. *Did I put the lipstick back?*

Lady said, "Here you are, but you might want to wait until you have eaten. I have your food set out."

"No, please, I want to brush now and, if it's okay, I'll do it again after I eat."

"That's fine. Come on out when you're ready and I'll redo that blindfold in case J.D. shows up."

Jenny furiously brushed the remains of several hamburger meals from her teeth and gums. She silently thanked the kind lady and again wondered how such a person could be involved in holding her captive.

Jenny crossed the small room and called out, "I'm done now, Lady," as she opened the bathroom door.

"Come on over here, Jenny. I have your food on the table. I'm having a cup of coffee. I'm a little concerned that I have not heard a word from the men since Ronnie called to say something had come up."

Jenny made her way to the kitchen table without assistance. Lady pulled a chair out for her. The smell of the food made Jenny realize how long it had been since she had eaten. She didn't know in hours, but she knew she was hungry.

The food was still warm in spite of her bathroom stay: another hamburger, fries and milkshake. Although she could not see it, she had eaten enough fast food to know it was from Hardee's, and it was delicious.

Lady was quiet as Jenny ate. She seemed to be reading something. Jenny heard the turning of pages, and at one point she heard Lady say, "Be patient, Kevie, it won't be much longer."

Jenny ate every morsel. When she finished, Lady said, "Okay, let's redo that blindfold."

"Let me brush my teeth again, please. Will you put the tooth-paste on the brush?" When Lady left the bathroom, Jenny quickly brushed her teeth so she would have time to check her message. She stood in the tub and leaned her head back. There was her skinny white flag flying proudly from the window screen.

As Lady led her back down the two steps and across to the box, Jenny asked, "How much longer do you think I will be here?"

"All I know, Jenny, is that Ronnie was called away today to do something. He said it was important. I hope it won't be much longer."

THE HIGH EYE

The airplane is just a bunch of sticks and wires and cloth, a tool for
learning about the sky and what kind of person I am, when I fly. An
airplane stands for freedom, for joy, for the power to understand, and
to demonstrate that understanding. Those things aren't destructible.

—Richard Bach, *Nothing By Chance*

The night was clear and cool over Greene County as the Cessna
172, registration number N733FK, completed its climb. "Springfield
Approach Control, Idaho Five is with you, level at seven thousand
five hundred."

"Roger, Idaho Five, we have you level at seven thousand five
hundred. We show no traffic in your immediate area."

"Roger, Approach. We'll be working in your space for several
hours beginning in the southeast sector."

"Roger, Idaho Five. We'll keep you posted on any traffic. Advise
us if you need to change altitude."

"Roger that, Approach. Idaho Five standing by on this frequency."

The Idaho Five Pilot in Command was Special Agent Loyal
Lambright of the FBI. Lambright and his crewmate, SA Harold
Higgins, were old hands at this. The two had a combined total of
more than three thousand hours of aerial surveillance. Most of
that was logged while keeping tabs on Mafia figures in Kansas City.
But they had also covered extortion payoffs, bank burglaries, and
thieves stealing TV's from box cars on rail sidings in rural Missouri.
This was their first ransom drop.

733FK was a high wing, four seat airplane with a 170 horse-
power Lycoming engine turning a fixed pitch propeller. The
registered owner was Palco Aviation, Inc., a front for the FBI. The

aircraft was an ideal surveillance vehicle—quiet, stable, and economical to operate.

Lambright, based in Kansas City, was in the left seat. He had N733FK set up for loitering, waiting for some action on the ground. He had throttled back to 2200 RPM, leaned the mixture, and lowered ten degrees of flaps. The indicated air speed was a crawling seventy-five knots, the fuel consumption a scant 5.6 gallons per hour. Lambright had ensured he had full tanks, forty-three gallons usable, at take-off. At their current power setting they could remain aloft for five-plus hours and still meet the legal fuel reserve for landing. Lambright's endurance would be determined more by his bladder capacity than his fuel supply.

While they waited, Lambright did the flying and handled all communications with Air Traffic Control. He was also primarily responsible for collision avoidance, looking out for other aircraft. They were operating in a radar environment with an assigned transponder code. ATC had them on radar. Although ATC said they would keep him posted on other traffic, under Visual Flight Rules, the primary responsibility for collision avoidance still fell on the Pilot in Command. Lambright was alert.

In the right seat, SA Harold Higgins of the Kansas City Division's Wichita, Kansas RA, was responsible for communications with the FBI command post and FBI ground units.

Higgins was also responsible for monitoring the OAR beacon-tracking unit in the back seat. OAR was an acronym for the agency that developed the device—the Oceanic and Atmospheric Research Agency. They had developed the system to track whales and learn their migratory routes. The agency used a boat to locate a surfacing whale. Then they fired a small harpoon containing a transmitter into the whale's back and used an aircraft and the tracking device to locate the whale and record its position day after day as it followed its migratory path. The FBI had found the unit to be very useful in tracking a transmitter hidden in an automobile or a ransom package.

By turning partway around in his seat, Higgins could see the round black face of a cathode ray tube. Emanating from the center of the display was a pulsating green florescent streak. The streak was the visual representation of the signal from a transmitter the size of a package of cigarettes. Tonight, the transmitter was hidden in the lining of a mapcase containing Charles Kogan's $300,000. Lance Barron was counting on the transmitter, the OAR unit, and the skill of the pilots to lead them to the den of the kidnappers, and perhaps to Jenny Kogan.

If one considered the face of the OAR as a clock, the twelve o'clock position on the display would represent the nose of the aircraft. Six o'clock on the display, the tail. If the florescent streak was pulsing out from the center toward one o'clock, it indicated the ransom package was thirty degrees to the right of the nose. If Lambright turned the aircraft to a heading thirty degrees to the right, the pulsing streak would be at twelve o'clock indicating the ransom package was straight ahead. Using the azimuth information provided by the OAR, Idaho Five could find and fly directly over the ransom package at any time.

The OAR also provided limited distance guidance. If the pulsing streak went all the way to the edge of the display, the transmitter was at a range of about twenty miles. If Lambright turned to put the streak directly on the nose, and maintained that heading, with corrections for drift, the streak would decrease in length until it became a dot at the instant the aircraft flew over the transmitter. If Lambright held that heading, the streak would point to six o'clock and would lengthen as the aircraft flew away from the transmitter.

The aircrew could also tell if the transmitter was still or moving. When the transmitter was stationary and had been so for at least sixty seconds, the rate of transmission slowed to one pulse every eight seconds. When the transmitter was moved, the pulse rate increased to a pulse every three seconds and continued at that rate as long as it was moving, returning to the slower rate when it stopped.

Lambright and Higgins were not monitoring the OAR as they flew a lazy racetrack pattern in the dark sky above southeast Springfield. The unit was on and Higgins made sure they were receiving the signal. The signal was clear and showed the "package" to be in its resting state.

During a test flight in the afternoon, Idaho Five, tracking with the OAR, had been brought directly over the Kogan residence at seventy-five hundred feet. Tonight with the aircraft trimmed and stable and the OAR unit checked and ready, Idaho Five waited.

For some, sitting strapped into the seat of a small aircraft with one shoulder touching the window and the other touching your crewmate, with no possibility of getting up to stretch or walk around, was a boring, almost claustrophobic experience. Harold Higgins sometimes felt this way as he waited. But Loyal Lambright was not bored. He looked across the sparkling panorama that was Springfield, Missouri, spread out in neat squares more than a mile below. The city's adopted name, "Queen City of the Ozarks," seemed especially appropriate tonight.

Lambright looked for and found the rotating beacon that marked Springfield Regional Airport fifteen miles to the west-northwest. To the east he could see the red lights on a group of four radio/TV towers that reached up almost halfway to his altitude. By looking north along Highway 65 and slightly west he could see the rotating beacon at Springfield Downtown Airport, a small, one runway field. Old-timers around Springfield would tell you with immense pride that Charles A. Lindbergh once landed there. To the near west-northwest, Lambright could see the general area of the Kogan residence where Lance Barron waited for a phone call. Loyal's eyes followed the long jeweled row of street lights that was Battlefield Road leading eastward out to US 65 where the Branson show crowd was streaming north toward I-44.

He watched the traffic subside around the motels and fast food restaurants below and the lights diminish as the residents of the upscale housing developments turned in for the night. He listened as Springfield Approach Control cleared the last TWA Express flight for a straight-in approach to runway 19. He looked up and saw a million stars in the cool, clean, black Ozark sky. Bored? No way. Claustrophobic? Not a chance. Lambright was enthralled. He still couldn't believe he was getting paid to do this. He would do it for nothing. *Heck,* he thought, *I would pay them to let me do it!*

To say that Loyal Lambright loved flying was akin to saying Chopin loved music. Flying was his passion. It was his life.

There weren't many like Lambright left: those who grew up in the small towns of the South or Midwest in the forties when flying was still a mysterious, magical thing. The appearance of an airplane overhead had been reason enough to call everyone out to the yard. The appearance of a barnstormer at a pasture near the courthouse square was occasion enough to skip school and watch, hoping to get a ride. Lambright thought, *Here I am, flying, getting paid for it, and maybe helping a father get his little girl back. What could be any better than that?*

Lambright was totally at peace as he completed a visual scan outside the aircraft and then made a check of the engine instruments. *Is it my imagination or has the oil temperature moved up since the last scan? It shouldn't have at this power setting. It must be my eyes.* Lambright had a small problem with the eye examination on his past two FAA physicals. He grinned as he thought of the "Cousin Weakeyes" nickname some of his flying mates pinned on him.

The oil temperature was still well within the green arch. He checked the exhaust gas temperature gauge. It was right on the pointer but he turned the mixture control a half turn to the right anyway, a token enriching just in case. He made his arm movements slow and deliberate. No point in disturbing Harold. *Heck, I'm not even sure it's up, and it's still well within safe territory.*

In the crushing silence of the box, Jenny's thoughts kept going back to the encounter with J.D. *What if Lady had not arrived when she did?* She tried to keep her mind off the possibilities by recalling all she had learned from it. *Lady is a strong person who intends to protect me. Lady has directed letters to the FBI and to two Sheriff's offices, one in Missouri, one in Arkansas. The guy I've been thinking of as Driver is the same as Ronnie. Ronnie has been out of town to get something. Ronnie mentioned Ryder and Genie. J.D. has a bite mark on his arm and a wound on his head. I must remember all of these things.*

Going over the information occupied her for a while but she tired of it. The panic started to seep back in. She reached up and felt the lid. Locked. Her breathing started to become rapid and shallow. Her face felt flushed. "Oh, God. I don't think I can stand this much longer."

She tried to sit up. She knew it was impossible but she tried anyway. She strained her abdominal muscles and pushed against the lid with all her strength, then collapsed and cried aloud, "Oh, God, please help me. I can't stand this." *Is this what going crazy is like? I must think of something else.* "Jesus loves me, this I know, for the Bible tells me so. Now I lay me down to sleep. I pray thee, Lord, my soul to keep." *Think of anything but this box. Slow your breathing.* "Yea, though I walk through the valley of the shadow of death." *No; not that. Think of something else.* "Yes, Jesus loves me." *Yes, and my daddy does, too. And my mother and my brother and my sister and Jason does, too. I must get control. Slow your breathing... That's it. Lady won't let them hurt me. That's it, that's it. I have to remember so many things. Slow your breathing. Relax.*

Jenny gradually regained control of herself. She continued to speak aloud "You must keep your mind on other things, Jenny. Let's see. What are you going to do first when you get out? What are your top ten things you want to do? No, things you *will* do, Jenny?" She found that hearing her voice was comforting. "Let's see…I'll stretch. I want to stand on my tiptoes and reach as high as I can and maybe hang from a bar. I want to run, outside, under the trees. I feel like I could run for hours. I want to throw my head back and open my eyes as wide as I can and see the trees and the sky as I run. I want to hug my mother and tell her how special she is. I haven't done that in a long time. I want to take an hour-long shower. I want to phone everybody I know and talk as long as I want. I want to wrestle with Peaches. I want to kiss Jason the way we did last week.

"Is that your top ten list, Jennifer Kogan? I don't think you have ten. What about brushing your teeth? And your hair. You haven't brushed your hair in…How many days has it been? Three? You haven't even washed your face. I'll bet you have blackheads and zits. But don't forget those other things. Let's go through that list again."

And so Miss Jennifer Marie Kogan fought to maintain her sanity as she waited.

In Idaho Five, Loyal Lambright continued to enjoy the spectacular array of stars above the sleeping city and to feel gratitude for his good fortune.

Loyal thought back to the early days of the FBI's aviation program. In the early 1970s the war against organized crime was in full swing in every major city where a La Cosa Nostra family existed. To identify family members and their associates and to document their illegal activity, the Bureau conducted hours of surveillance, attempting to follow the mobsters to their various meeting places. The mobsters quickly learned of the Bureau's interest. They in turn developed various methods of cleaning themselves of "tails" before proceeding. One method was to drive down a one-way street, stop midway in the block, and back up to send the pursuing agents scurrying. Another evasive maneuver was to turn into an automobile sales lot, drive between the rows of cars and exit the lot going in the opposite direction to confront the embarrassed agents. The encounters usually resulted in a wave and a jeer, but there were occasions when obscenities were exchanged. In any case, the surveillance for that day was over as the mobsters either shook the tail and went on to their meeting, or abandoned their plans until another day.

The FBI clearly needed a better method. Over the years a few enterprising agents had covered an occasional ransom drop or delivery of an extortion payoff from a police helicopter. This was a very unsatisfactory arrangement for several reasons. One, the use of the helicopter depended on personal diplomacy by the agent. Its availability was unpredictable. For another, the helicopter was both the best and the worst of surveillance vehicles. On the plus side, it was a stable platform that could be "parked" at the most advantageous spot for observing the area of activity. On the negative side, it was noisy, easy to spot, and very expensive to operate. Most police departments could stretch their budgets only so far.

The answer to the helicopter's shortcomings lay in the use of fixed wing aircraft. This fact first became obvious to imaginative agents in the field and gradually grew from the field back to headquarters. Each request for use of an aircraft was approved, or disapproved, by FBI Headquarters. There was no overall Bureau aircraft policy or budget. Offices that happened to have a licensed pilot assigned were the first to use the technique. Word of the success of these early efforts in following Soviet Agents in New York and San Francisco and organized crime figures in Chicago and Kansas City led to increased requests for aerial surveillance.

In 1975, FBI Headquarters conducted a survey of all agents to identify those who were qualified pilots and who had an interest in flying for the Bureau on a part-time basis. An Aviation Coordinator was appointed at Headquarters to establish procedures and oversee the program. The use of fixed wing aircraft as a surveillance vehicle grew rapidly. Pilots refined and improved their techniques. Many of the surveillances were conducted in Terminal Control Areas, areas of high density aircraft traffic that exist around most major airports. The FAA and its Air Route Traffic Control Centers were most helpful in working out procedures that allowed the Bureau aircraft to do their job without jeopardizing air safety.

FBI pilots gradually refined a system by which they shared the aircraft controls so that one pilot could keep his eyes constantly on the target and the other could monitor the instruments and keep a lookout for other aircraft. The two-pilot operation had been successfully used numerous times, during daylight and dark, to follow targets all over large cities.

Lambright and Higgins knew their job tonight would be easy compared to following Nick Civella's car through downtown Kansas City at night. With the OAR unit and the sparse traffic in the wee hours of the morning in Springfield, Missouri, it should be a cinch. Exciting, but a cinch.

Loyal Lambright took another look at the oil temperature gauge. There was now no doubt that it was rising. Oil pressure and exhaust gas temperature were still normal. Lambright couldn't resist doing what thousands of pilots have done in similar situations. He reached forward and thumped the oil temperature gauge. There is no documented case since the Ford Tri-Motor that the thump has had any beneficial effect, but pilots continue to do it, and hope.

Harold Higgins, still unaware of the oil temperature problem, was monitoring the FBI channel. He reported any significant transmissions from SAC Palmer or Lance Barron. There had been little to report. He occasionally checked the OAR unit. The pulsing streak told him the package was in its resting state.

Idaho Five was ready. There was nothing to do but wait.

THE DROP

The marvelous richness of human experience would lose something of rewarding joy if there were no limitations to overcome. The hilltop hour would not be half so wonderful if there were no dark valleys to traverse.
—Helen Keller

Barron and Kogan were asleep in their chairs when the phone rang. It was 11:34 P.M. when Lance released the PAUSE button. He fought the impulse to pick up the phone. After the fourth ring, he answered, just as Kogan started to make his way to the kitchen extension. "Kogan residence." He heard only a metallic clicking on the other end. Then a weak voice, "Daddy, I'm okay. Take the money to the phone booth at the side of the Git and Go behind Shoney's at National and Battlefield. No cops. You'll hear from us there." There was more clicking, and then a male voice said "Okay," and the phone went dead.

Barron left the phone off the hook.

Kogan said, "Did you record it? Let me hear it. Was it Jenny? I didn't get to it in time."

Barron was already copying the cassette. "Yes, sir. It was Jenny, and she's all right. We've got to get the surveillance units going."

Barron picked up the other phone and dialed the command post. Palmer was on immediately, "FBI."

"We got the call. We have the spot. Can you copy?" Lance's voice betrayed his excitement. "The phone booth at the Get and Go"— actually *Git* and Go but Lance's childhood training was too deeply ingrained to allow him to pronounce it that way—"behind Shoney's at Battlefield and National. They used Jenny on tape again. They said we would hear from them there. Do you have that?"

"Yes, I've got it. Hold on Lance. I'll flush the surveillance people."

Lance could hear Palmer on the radio giving the intersection to the surveillance crews.

Palmer came back, "They're under way, Lance. Tell me about the call."

"It was much like before. A tape recording by Jenny. She sounded weak but said she was okay. We got a good clear message, but it was short." Lance read his notes to Palmer including the male voice at the end. "That's it, Boss. We'll give your people a good lead, and then I'll give you a radio check from Kogan's car."

"Good luck, Lance."

"Thanks, Boss."

Corporal Don Vickers, Springfield PD, had been assigned as liaison with the FBI for the duration of the case. He was on duty when the call came in. Vickers wrote down the information as Palmer read it back to Barron. He then contacted the PD dispatcher and gave her the location of the phone booth. The dispatcher checked her display board in the area of the drop site and saw she had two units patrolling within a mile of the designated intersection. She gave their locations to Vickers who said, "You'll have to move both of them. I'll give you the word when the package gets near the spot."

The plan was for the PD dispatcher to use a "burglary in progress" report at a warehouse in another sector to send the patrol units out of the critical area. Within the Police Department, only the Chief, Vickers, and the night dispatcher were aware of the plan. Barron had proposed it to Vickers, and Vickers had sold it to the Chief. Lance's concern was based on his study of the Barbara Mackle kidnapping several years before in Florida. In that case the ransom drop had been made as instructed. The kidnapper had retrieved the money, but as he left the area, a police car had pulled into a parking lot nearby. The kidnapper, assuming he had been double-crossed, had dropped the ransom package and fled the area. The policeman had known nothing of the kidnapping.

The Mackle family and the FBI had gone through the arduous process of recovering the money, making a public appeal to the kidnapper, convincing him they were attempting to comply, and setting up another drop. After several harrowing hours a second attempt had been successful. The kidnapper had called the family and told them where their daughter could be located—buried in a ventilated box in a field near the University of Georgia in Macon. Barbara Mackle had been recovered, barely alive. But the accidental encounter on the first ransom drop had nearly cost Miss Mackle her life. Barbara Mackle's story had made a lasting impression on Lance Barron.

Kogan, in his double-breasted suit, elevator shoes and protruding armor, retrieved the mapcase and was headed for his car. He turned back and sheepishly said, "I'd better take a leak."

"We can drag our feet a little. They didn't say anything about hurrying. We can give our people a little extra time."

Barron and Kogan followed the interior hallway to the garage. Kogan was a pathetic sight with the mapcase and body armor dragging him down. Barron suddenly felt sympathy for this tired little man. *Even as arrogant and abrasive as he is, he doesn't deserve this.* The reverie ended as they entered the garage and Kogan gestured toward his Cadillac. "I'll bet not many of you college boys drive one like that."

So much for sympathy, Lance thought as he said, "It's a beauty, Mr. Kogan. Put the mapcase in the trunk. I'll remove the bulb from the dome light. We don't want to light up in here every time you open the door."

Barron took his position in the front floorboard before Kogan opened the garage door in case the kidnappers were watching. He made his first transmission as Kogan backed down the drive. "Tiger One to Den; how do you read?" He was wearing a throat mike and ear piece. Kogan could barely hear Barron's transmission. He could not hear the reply.

"We read you four by four, Tiger One. How you me?"

"Five by five, Den. Is Idaho Five with us?"

"Idaho Five here. We hear you fine and we're getting a good signal on the OAR. We have your car visually."

"Okay, Five, good eye. We are on our way."

"We'll cap you 'til you reach the spot. Once we scope the setup, we'll loiter out east until you get some action. We can be on top of you in two minutes."

"Roger, Five."

Lance thought, *It's hard to believe I'm actually under way on a ransom drop. I'm ready. I hope I've prepared Kogan.*

In Barron's memory two ransom drops had turned into armed robberies at the drop site. The kidnappers simply steered the father into an isolated area and robbed him. In the other case, they shot the father dead at the remote drop site. In that case it turned out that the victim, a young girl, had been murdered within hours of her abduction. The kidnappers never intended to return her. Lance hoped they were dealing with rational people. If they weren't, he guessed his chances of protecting Kogan were less than fifty-fifty. He would only expose himself to save Kogan's life or his own. He prayed he would not have to make that decision.

The drive from Kogan's residence to the drop site was less than three miles. Kogan was observing the thirty-mile-per-hour speed limit. Barron relished these few minutes with no decisions to make. His thoughts turned to his family. He pictured them warm and safe in their beds—his wife, Patsy, daughter, Laura, and son, Barry. The thought gave him comfort, and he smiled and felt relaxed for the first time in days. Abruptly his mood changed; he was overcome with dread, then resentment. *Why me? Why am I here facing this unknown situation when I should be there with them?* It wasn't fear. It was a feeling that he was shirking his responsibility.

The feeling passed as quickly as it came. Lance knew why he was here. He had experienced the battle of wits, the exhilaration of the hunt, and the feeling of victory at the end of a successful investigation many times. There was nothing like it. It was worth some sacrifice. And thanks to an ongoing campaign by his wife, his children were proud of him and what he did. He might not be with them as regularly as the eight-to-fivers were, but he made sure their time together was quality.

Lance's thoughts came back to the present. *Will we be able to outwit these guys? They're smart but they always make errors. The next few hours will be critical.*

His moment of reflection was broken. Kogan said, "The traffic is heavier out here than I thought it would be. It must be the late movie crowd."

"Take your time," said Barron from the floor. "You might try to spot one of our fixed units as we move along."

"Hell, I've seen a dozen already that could be them."

"Have you noticed anyone following us?"

"Are you kidding? I've had lights in my mirror since we left, but I can't say it's anyone following us. A couple of them turned off. I don't know…"

Barron said, "I would bet this is a cleaning operation. I don't believe this will be the drop."

"Why the hell not? We've got what they want."

"Yes, but I don't believe they would have us leave all that money in a phone booth at a convenience store that is open for business. I don't think so. I think these people are too smart for that."

"Yeah, that's what I'm afraid of, and too smart for you college boys, too."

Kogan never misses a chance. thought Barron, *Is this the same guy who was waking me up last night to ask my advice? Or was that two nights ago?*

"Where are we?" Barron asked. His six-foot, two-inch frame

filled the floor space. It was not comfortable. Kogan, of course, had to have the seat all the way forward.

"We're here. I see Shoney's, and there is the Git and Go around the corner. I've caught a red light here. Yeah, there's the phone booth on the near corner of the lot. That would be the southwest corner of the Git and Go lot."

Barron said, "Okay, now remember to pull up close and position the car where I can cover you through your door."

"Okay. Dammit—this guy in front of me's got his turn signal on, but he's settin' there like a damned idiot."

With that Kogan gave a blast on the horn and started gesturing toward the driver ahead.

"Take it easy, Mr. Kogan. For gosh sakes, we don't want to get into an altercation…"

"Okay, the bastard finally woke up." Kogan seemed pleased to have educated yet another dumbshit in the ways of the world.

"I've laid the tape recorder out on the seat. It's ready to go."

"Yeah, dammit, Barron, just wait a minute 'til I get the friggin' car parked."

"Oh, I'm sorry. I thought you were in position."

Kogan appeared almost boyish as he struggled with the steering wheel while pulling himself up high enough to see behind him. He backed into the curb and said, "That's as close as I can get with the booth on this side."

"Careful; don't look down here when you talk. Are you close enough to hear the phone when it rings? Go ahead and look around inside the booth. There could be a message in there."

Kogan got out and squinted at the dark inside of the phone booth. He worked the door back and forth but no light came on. He cursed the "damned younger generation" as he came back and picked up the tape recorder and his flashlight. Barron could hear Kogan muttering as he worked to get the tape recorder hooked up.

Not having the light could be a break for us if they're watching, thought Barron.

Kogan finished his task and came back to the car. He remembered to look straight ahead, "What if somebody comes by and wants to use the phone?"

"Just tell them you are expecting an important call and would they mind using another phone. A five-dollar bill for their trouble would be nice. I don't think it will happen. The way you are parked makes it obvious you are using the phone."

Suddenly a disturbing thought hit Lance. *I hope this is not one of the phone booths that has been converted to making outgoing calls only. A lot of them have been. Surely the kidnappers checked that out. I hope they did. I'm not going to mention it to Kogan, but we might not ever get a call here.*

Barron said, "Tiger One to Den. We're in position."

"Ten-Four, Tiger One. How does it look?"

"We have a good set-up to receive a call, but I can't believe they will have us leave the package here. It's too close to the store, which is open. There's too much light, too much traffic, too many places for one of us to hide and watch."

"I think you're right. We should know soon."

Idaho Five came on, "Tiger One, we had your unit active until 12:27. It's now idle. The signal is strong. Over."

"Okay, Five. Save some fuel. This might be a long night."

"Yeah. We're in good shape there."

"Okay, Five. The wait is on."

Kogan leaned back on the headrest and closed his eyes. He was quiet for several minutes. Barron wondered if the strain was starting to take its toll. But Kogan said, "You know who I wish could see me now? That son-of-a-bitchin junior high principal. When I was in seventh grade he told me in front of the class I would never amount to a thing. The teacher had called him in when I returned a note to her after wiping my ass on it…Yeah. No kidding. I was already a year behind, and it looked like I was going to fail again. The damn teacher, Miss Perkins, had sent the note home for my daddy to sign. The note was telling him that I was not doing my homework, and if I didn't straighten up, I would be retained again. What she didn't know was my daddy didn't give a rat's ass about school, and he wasn't too keen on me going, anyway. He was a "Jake-legged" plumber. You know, unlicensed, which pretty much meant he dug ditches. He worked hard, and he wanted me to help him all the time. I worked for him every day after school and on the weekends.

"I showed him the note. He looked at it, but he had a dozen ways of tricking people into reading things for him. He never admitted it, but I don't think he could read a lick. Anyway, he said something about not having his glasses or something like that, and he said, 'Just read it to me.' I did and he said, 'I'm not going to sign it and as far as I'm concerned you can wipe your ass on it.'

"We both laughed and that got me to thinking. I signed it for him, and when I got home, I smeared some peanut butter on it and put it back in the envelope. I took it back to Miss Perkins the next day. I told her my dad didn't think much of the note, but he sent it back with his signature and a little souvenir. She opened it right there in front of the class and her imagination took over. She screamed and dropped it like it was red hot. The class went wild. That's when she called the principal."

The longer the story went the funnier it got to Kogan. He was barely able to continue. "When the principal got to the room, the note was still on the floor. Ol' Miss Perkins pointed to it and told him I had brought it in. He picked it up by the corner and looked at it with the class roaring. That's when he told me I was a disgrace and would never amount to anything. He was going to paddle me right then and there. He didn't get to though. I took off running and never went back. That was my last day in school, ever. I was not quite fourteen years old."

"You dropped out in the seventh grade?"

"That's right. We moved a couple of times after that. The truant officer threatened us, but we just moved on and they finally left us alone.

"Yeah. I sure wish that old principal could see me now. I'm settin' here with the FBI guarding me. I'm gettin' ready to give away $300,000. That's probably more than he made in his entire life. And he said I'd never amount to anything. What do you think of that, Barron?"

"That's some story, Mr. Kogan." Barron knew that was a totally inadequate response, but what else could he say to this strange man? His only other thought was the old cliché, *It sure takes all kinds,* but he didn't say it.

At 1:40 A.M. the phone rang. Kogan jumped and started for it. Lance said, "Just release the PAUSE and let it ring three times. And remember, Mr. Kogan, listen before you say anything. It might be a recording."

On the third ring, Kogan picked it up, "Yeah." He turned toward Lance and nodded. Lance could barely see him in the darkness. After an excruciating wait, Lance heard Kogan say, "Shit, I hung the sonofabitch up!"

It took all of Lance's self-discipline to remain on the floor. Kogan was mumbling and fumbling with the tape recorder. He finally got back into the car.

"Did you get it?"

"Hell, I think so, but I forgot and hung up. It was hard as hell trying to listen, hold my pen light and write all at the same time."

"Was it Jenny?"

"Yeah, just like before but a lot more stuff. They want us to go downtown. I have the address. There's a rental truck down there. It's locked. They want us to put the money in there. She gave me the combination."

"First let's pull out of this area so I can sit up and help. Just go a block or so north on National and pull into a driveway while I'm calling the command post. You're sure you got the right address?"

"Hell, yes. She repeated that and the combination."

"Okay, let me have your notes and you can start moving."

"Tiger One to Den and Idaho Five."

"Go ahead, One, this is Idaho Five."

"Tiger Den is with you."

"We got the call. We are headed for 404 North Jefferson, repeat, 404 North Jefferson. We'll stop to copy the tape and go over the instructions. There is a rental truck involved. Verify the address and stand by."

"Den verifying 404 North Jefferson."

"Idaho Five verifying 404 North Jefferson."

Kogan said, "I'm pulling into this Medical Arts Center here on the east side. It's closed and there's a lot of parking. I'll pull back here in the shadows."

Lance used his penlight to check his city map. "That address is right down in the old town part of Springfield. It'll be dead. Hardly any traffic."

"Tiger One to Den. What does the city directory show at that address?"

"We just checked. It's a wholesale lumber storage facility. It's right beside the railroad tracks. The nearest business is across the tracks at 330 North Jefferson, Meeks Lumber Company."

"Roger, Den. We ought to pull the fixed units back even more. That's a dead area. There will be little traffic. We'll be looking for a rental truck. It's starting to look like a hold-up. Stand by while we review the tape."

While talking, Lance had made a copy of the tape and now played it, "Daddy, I'm okay. Take the money to 404 North Jefferson. There is a Ryder truck there with a lock on the back door. Turn the lock right to one; then left past eight and around to eight; then right to eighteen, then open. I repeat, right to one; left past eight and around to eight; then right to eighteen and open. There's a box in the back. Put the money in the box. Close and lock the door. You will hear from us."

"Tiger One to Den."

"Go ahead, Tiger One."

"We just ran the tape and verified what we gave you. We are to put the package in a box in the rear of the truck and relock it. They said we will hear from them. We're under way."

"What do you think, Lance? I've never heard of that scenario."

"It's a new one on me, Boss. They could be in the truck and rob him when he gets out or while he's working on the lock. They could be in the truck and drive away when he locks the door, but that yellow truck is a mighty poor getaway vehicle. I would vote for the robbery right now. All the business with the combination lock and the box in the back sounds too complex. It could all be a hoax to get him into an isolated area where they have plenty of places to hide until he gets there, and plenty of places to go to after they rob him."

Lance Barron resumed his cramped position on the floor. As they headed north on National Avenue, he went over other possibilities. Chances that the kidnappers were in the immediate area of the drop were slim unless they planned to jump Kogan. Lance couldn't believe they would be waiting in the truck planning to drive away with the money in the box. Even a loose surveillance could follow a bright yellow truck. Maybe they're gambling that we won't risk following the truck. We wouldn't but Idaho Five would. Lance decided the most likely answer was that the kidnappers were secluded where they had a good view of the truck. They had several hours of darkness left. With the money locked in the truck, they could watch the area for as long as they wanted. Then one of them could walk into the lot, sticking to the shadows, open the back door and walk away with the package without even being seen. The OAR would be our only hope.

Robbery at the site was still a real possibility, however. From the kidnappers' point of view, it gave them the least amount of exposure over time. They would have assured themselves at the first site that Kogan was alone. Why give the fuzz a chance to get a surveillance set up on the new spot?

From the floor Lance asked, "Are you still on National? We will need to go west on Cherry or St. Louis…"

"I know exactly where it is. I used to pick up winos down there and use them as day laborers when I was building my hangar. I'm going west on St. Louis. We're just passing the bus station."

Lance reported their position to Den. Den verified and then Harold Higgins in Idaho Five came on, "Tiger One. We have the package active and a good signal on the scope. We also had a visual on the yellow truck. The lot is well lighted on the west end. The truck is backed in on the east end right by the loading dock. There are deep shadows there. We could barely see it. The only exit is on the west end."

"We copied, Five. Stand by."

"Where are we, Mr. Kogan?"

"I'm turning onto Park Central Square. Jefferson is one-way south, so I'll go past the railroad on Boonville and then get on Jefferson and come back south to the lot."

"Okay, keep me posted."

"We just passed Water Street. I'll be turning right at the next corner. Then one block, and I'll turn right again on Jefferson. Which side is that number on?"

"It'll be on your left."

Lance felt the right turn and then shortly afterward, another. Suddenly he was pitched forward as Kogan stood on the brakes.

"Shit, I passed it," said Kogan.

"Can you back up? How far did you miss it?"

"Just a little. When I crossed the railroad tracks I realized it. We're at 330, Meeks Lumber Company."

"Can you back up? Is there traffic?"

Lance felt the car accelerate in reverse.

As they sailed backward Lance thought, *I hope Vickers did his job. A patrolman couldn't ignore this.* Lance felt the car stop and then pull forward slowly. It was 2:02 A.M.

"There's the damned yellow truck way back at the end of the lot." Kogan's voice quivered with tension. "It's dark as hell back there."

"Is there anyone in the truck?"

"Can't see nobody."

"Okay, do it just like the phone booth. I need to cover you at the rear door. Leave your headlights on. Let me know the instant you see anyone."

As Kogan eased the car down the length of the lot, Lance reported their arrival to Den and added, "We are moving directly toward the vehicle with our lights on. Kogan has not seen anyone. Stand by."

Kogan said, "The lot leads back to that railroad overpass. They could be back there waiting for me. Looks like a hobo camp back in there. You couldn't leave anything here long."

"Did you see anyone in the truck?" Barron asked again.

"Shit, I didn't even look. It's too late now."

"Keep it down." Barron whispered from the floor. "Take your flashlight. Turn on the A-4. Read the license tag into your mike. Ready?"

Kogan didn't answer but took the mapcase and flashlight, slid out of the car, and took cautious steps to the rear of the truck. He put the mapcase down and pulled upward on the heavy rubber strap attached to the rear door. The door did not budge. Then Kogan saw the lock. "Oh, shit, I forgot to bring the combination." Lance winced, knowing Kogan's remark was broadcast to everyone on the surveillance. Kogan shuffled back to the driver side of the car and bellowed, "Let me have that friggin' combination."

"Shhssss, get in and close the door. Here is the card you wrote it on." Lance decided not to remind Kogan that the A-4 mike was voice activated. He had enough to worry about. "Where is the mapcase?"

"Oh, shit. I left it out there on the ground." With that, he was gone, but the entire surveillance heard him muttering as he returned to the rear of the truck.

Kogan held the flashlight in his mouth as he dialed the lock. He got it right on the first try. Then, standing on the ground, he pulled on the strap, and the door slid upward on its rollers.

Kogan saw a large plywood box mounted just inside the door. The box almost spanned the width of the truck. The lid, at Kogan's eye level, was held closed by a hasp. Kogan opened the hasp with his right hand but could only open the lid a few inches from his position on the ground. He grabbed the front of the box with his left hand and pulled himself up onto the bumper, pushing the lid open with his right. A large manila envelope swung down from the underside of the lid where it was stapled. Even in the dim light, Kogan could see the word KOGAN in newspaper headlines on the envelope. "What the hell?" Kogan held on to the edge of the box with his left hand while he reached for the envelope and pulled on it. When the staples came loose, the box's heavy lid slammed down on Kogan's left hand. "Son of a bitch," he broadcast. A moaning Kogan dropped the envelope to the ground and raised the lid enough to free his hand before jumping off the bumper. He grabbed his aching hand and massaged it while doing a lively dance and cursing.

After determining that no bones were broken, Kogan placed the mapcase on the wide bumper, raised the hasp with his injured hand enough to get his right hand under the lid to raise it. He then stepped up on the bumper straddling the mapcase and pushed the lid full open. Once he had both feet on the bumper and the lid fully open he retrieved the mapcase from between his legs and lifted it over the side and into the box where it landed with a solid thump. He reached for the hasp and pulled the lid closed by jumping to the ground. He closed and locked the truck door, picked up the large manila envelope and cursed all the way back to his Cadillac.

Lance was anxious. He whispered, "Close the door. What happened?"

Kogan shoved the envelope across the seat. "What the hell do you think this means?"

Lance held up his hand in a gesture for silence as he pulled his headset off. "Turn your radio off, please. What is it?"

Kogan was still shaking his throbbing hand, "Hell, I don't know. There was a plywood box in the back. That was stapled to the lid. It's got my name on it."

Lance shined his flashlight on the package. It was fastened with a metal clasp. "You say it has your name on it?"

"Yeah, on the other side." When he reached for it, Lance said, "Wait, let's not handle it. He flipped the package over with his penlight and there was the name KOGAN spelled out in newspaper headlines. Lance flipped it back over and asked Kogan to hold his penlight on it. Lance donned evidence gloves and lifted the envelope, touching only the side edges with the palms of his gloved hands. He shook the envelope. A set of keys on a Ryder key chain fell onto the seat. He turned the envelope over. "Shine your light in here. There's still something inside." Lance shook the envelope again. A cloth object fell onto the seat. Lance nudged it with his penlight as Kogan provided light with his. A five-by-seven inch card fell from a pair of pink panties.

"Goddamn!" gasped Kogan.

Lance pushed the envelope aside and carefully picked up the card. It was covered on one side with words cut from a newspaper and arranged to read, "DRIVE TRUCK EAST ON TRAFFICWAY TILL U GET THE SIGNAL. JENNY."

"Goddamn lousy bastards!" muttered Kogan.

Lance carefully scooped the panties and card back into the envelope and put them in his briefcase. "Move the car back as close to the truck cab as you can. We must continue to assume they are watching."

As Kogan moved the car, Lance reported, "Tiger One to Den. The package is in the back of the truck. We have instructions to drive the truck east on Trafficway. Over."

"Roger, Tiger One, Where to?"

"We don't know. Until we get a signal. That's all we know."

Den continued, "Have you seen anyone, anything?"

"Negative. It's been totally quiet here. We're moving to the truck. Out."

Kogan had moved the car back until he was alongside the driver side of the truck.

Lance said, "I have the truck keys. I'll go first so I can get to the passenger side. Put your legs up on the seat. I'll crawl out your side." Lance squirmed out of Kogan's car and crawled across six feet of asphalt to the truck. He glanced around enough to see that the lighting was poor. He concluded a person would have to be elevated and using a night scope to see any activity here. Nevertheless, Lance stayed on his knees while he unlocked the truck. When he opened the door the overhead light came on. He lunged to depress the switch on the door frame. He crawled in, keeping his hand on the switch until Kogan arrived. "Go ahead and get in. I have the light switch."

Kogan, weighted down with his body armor and nursing his bruised hand, took two tries before he made it into the high truck cab. Lance crawled across the floorboards as Kogan pulled the door closed.

"What do you think now, Barron?"

Lance noticed that Kogan had dropped the first name protocol. As Kogan adjusted the seat full forward, Lance replied, "It looks more and more like a hijacking. They can now choose their spot without alerting us in advance to the location. By the way, did you get the tag number?"

"Hell, no! I forgot all about it."

Kogan pulled the truck out of the lot, turned left on Jefferson, crossed the railroad and made an immediate left turn onto Trafficway. Lance thought, *They could be sitting out in the country somewhere waiting for the yellow truck to deliver their money. It gets rural in a hurry out that way.*

"Idaho Five to Tiger One."

"Go ahead, Five."

"Request you flash your headlights high-low for ID," Lance repeated the request to Kogan. Kogan stomped around for the dimmer switch and finally complied.

"Okay, Tiger One, we have you east on Trafficway. We will be the primary eye while you are moving."

"Do you show anyone around us?"

"No, but you'll be picking up one or two when you merge with Chestnut. It's all in front of you now."

Kogan asked, "What kind of signal should I be looking for?"

"Anything unusual. Maybe one of those flashing construction lights. They used that in a case I worked in D.C. In another case they put a log across a country road. They came out of the woods with guns and took the car. They backed up to a side road and took off. Left the messenger in the woods. That could happen tonight if we get far enough out. They must plan to take the truck. It would take some time to get the money out of there…but if they were deep enough in the woods…" Lance caught himself. He was doing more speculating than he meant to. "Where are we, Mr. Kogan?"

"We just merged with Chestnut. There's Fed Ex on the left and a Total station that's still open. We've come two miles."

In Idaho Five, Loyal Lambright was spending more time than he wanted checking engine instruments. The oil temperature had continued to climb, and now there was a decrease in oil pressure. Loyal was flying the pitch, maintaining the assigned altitude and checking for air traffic. But his cross check was centering more and more on the oil temperature gauge and the Downtown Airport which was from two to four miles away, depending on which side of the circle they were on.

Loyal was thankful Harold was busy. He was controlling the ailerons and rudder keeping the headlights of the Ryder truck, more than a mile below, in position on his side window. Loyal wondered if he would ever get accustomed to having someone sharing in the flying, actually manipulating the ailerons and rudder while he took care of the pitch and power, but Harold was so smooth it was almost like having an autopilot, and it worked. Harold occasionally took a peek at the OAR unit, although it had continued to show the package in motion and directly under them since the truck left the lot. As long as he kept those headlights in the same place on his window, there was no way the OAR could show anything else.

Loyal checked the oil temperature again. No better; maybe a little worse. He knew he should land this airplane. It wasn't going to get any better. It could get a whole lot worse. He would never be faulted if he landed right now. But he also knew they were at the most critical point in the drop. Surely the kidnappers would soon execute their plan. Then he and Harold would be the only ones who could follow the package. It was probably too late to scramble Idaho Three. The drop would be over before Three could get in position.

As their target approached Highway 65, Loyal was reminded that their eastward route would start to take them farther away from the Downtown Airport. He took another hard look at the oil temperature gauge, now clearly in the yellow caution range, and said a silent prayer.

Lance, from the floor, asked, "Where are we now, Mr. Kogan?"

"We just crossed the tracks. You probably felt them. There's Sutherland Lumber on the right. US 65 is right up ahead. We've come about three miles."

"Thank, you. Tiger One to Den."

"Go ahead, Tiger One."

"The package is at Chestnut and 65. What's the status of our ground units?" Lance knew the answer but wanted some assurance.

"All four are out there, monitoring your transmissions, attempting to parallel your course, trying to blend in, writing down data on automobiles…"

"That sounds good. Mr. K is looking hard for the signal."

Kogan looked down at Lance, "What did he say?"

Lance smiled into the darkness and said, "He said you're doing a heck of a job."

"Idaho Five to Tiger One! Verify your position!" Harold Higgins's voice was up a full octave.

Lance said, "Stand by, Idaho Five. Where are we, Mr. Kogan?" Then to no one in particular, "They ought to know. They've been on top of us all the way."

Kogan said, "We're still eastbound on Chestnut. We're at farm road 193 about two miles east of Highway 65."

Lance relayed the information to Idaho Five and added, "We're blinking our lights" as he motioned to Kogan to do so.

A disturbing thought started to take shape in Lance's mind. *Could the kidnappers have come up with a way to somehow dump the box out the back of the truck? Could they have had a man hiding in the back? But Kogan re-locked the rear door.* The thought that the package could be gone almost made Lance ill.

"Okay, Tiger One. We're still on top of you but the OAR shows the package stationary and going farther behind us!"

Lance did not want to believe it. "How can that be, Harold?"

"We're going back to do a flyover."

"We're continuing on. Do you concur, Den?"

"Yes, Tiger One, stay on course but it's imperative, Idaho Five, that you resolve this right away…Could it be a problem with the OAR?"

"We're headed back west now, sir, and we show the package dead on the nose and resting."

In the truck Kogan yelled, "What the hell is going on? Remember, I can't hear your goddamn radio."

"Stand by, Mr. Kogan. Keep going east and looking for the signal. The aircraft tracking unit is picking up a signal behind us."

"Hole-E shit. How could that happen?"

"I don't know, Mr. Kogan. Idaho Five is checking it out."

"Idaho Five to Den. We just tracked the signal back and got a reversal at Chestnut and the railroad. There are a couple of businesses there on the south side of Chestnut. You better have someone check them out. There must be some sort of electronic device there, overriding our equipment."

Lance didn't wait for Den, "Tiger One to Tigers Two and Four. Go immediately to the area of Chestnut and the railroad crossing. There are a couple of businesses on the south side. Tiger Two you take Sutherland Lumber Company. I think the other is Western Wardrobe. Tiger Four you take it. Check out the area around those businesses. Be careful. If there are cars in the area, break off until we can assess the situation."

After Tigers Two and Four acknowledged Palmer said, "Idaho Five, head back east toward Tiger One and see if you get a signal there." There was no answer. Palmer repeated the transmission. Then, "Tiger Den to Idaho Five, Den to Five, Come in, Idaho Five. Over."

Finally Loyal Lambright said, "Stand by, Den, we've got a problem!"

Aboard Idaho Five, Harold Higgins left the OAR unit and turned around to face the front. "What's up, Loyal? Do I smell smoke?"

Lambright said, "Yeah, we've been running a little warm for a while and it's just started getting critical." At that moment the engine started to pre-detonate and run rough. The oil temperature gauge was near the redline. When Lambright reduced power, the engine stopped! He immediately went to the Emergency Procedures placard on the instrument panel. He called out each step as he went through the list and headed the aircraft toward the Downtown Airport.

Flaps	UP
Air Speed	75 MPH INDICATED
Carburetor Heat	ON
Fuel Selector	BOTH
Mixture	RICH
Ignition Switch	BOTH
Primer	IN AND LOCKED

The engine was windmilling. That was a good sign. At least it wasn't frozen. It popped and sputtered but Lambright quickly saw that it wasn't going to restart. He told Higgins to switch the transponder to 7700. Lambright switched his radio to the emergency frequency, 126.5, called Springfield Approach Control, "May Day! May Day! May Day! This is an emergency! Approach, this is Idaho Five, we have lost our engine." Lambright's voice betrayed the tension.

"Roger, Idaho Five. We show you squawking emergency. What are your intentions?"

"We will try to make Downtown Airport." Loyal Lambright, in his hours of flight training and his numerous check rides, had made dozens of simulated forced landings. Most had been into the largest wheat field within gliding distance, terminated at 500 feet by powering up the idling engine and climbing back to a safe altitude. All had been in the daytime. This was his first real one.

At night all terrain looks much the same. Trees, ditches, telephone lines, fences and a hundred other unseen hazards can do catastrophic damage to the fragile structure of an aircraft. An off-field landing at night is one of the light plane pilot's worst fears.

Fortunately, engine reliability was such that it rarely happened.

"Idaho Five, your heading to Downtown is 030 degrees, four miles. We show no traffic in your area."

"Roger, Approach. What is the wind?"

"Springfield Regional Airport is reporting surface wind at 085 degrees, 10 knots."

"Can you see the runway lights, Harold?"

"I think I see the rotating beacon, but…"

"Springfield Approach to Idaho Five. Did you read my last transmission?"

"Say again, Approach."

"Idaho Five the surface wind at Springfield Regional is 085 degrees, 10 knots. We don't get a reading from Downtown."

"Roger, Approach."

Single engine pilots who have lost their engines, in recounting the experience, invariably mention how quiet it becomes. Lambright called out, "Harold, call Den and advise them that…" Lambright realized he was shouting and started over, quietly, "Call Den and tell them we're going into Downtown. We are done for the night. Tell them to scramble Idaho Three."

Harold relayed the message in a voice his wife would not have recognized.

Lambright strained, trying to see the dim runway lights. He finally saw the rotating beacon and the lights on the TV Tower near the east end of the runway. He wiped his eyes, "Where are those lights?…Approach, what do you show for Downtown now?"

"Downtown is 040, three miles, Idaho Five."

Downtown was an uncontrolled airport. It had no tower, no instrument approaches, no fire trucks. Lambright was starting to wonder if it had runway lights. Pilots operating into and out of the airport were responsible for maintaining their own separation in the air and on the ground. Separation from other aircraft was not a problem. Lambright had been in and out of Downtown several times but never at night. He remembered the narrow runway and the hill about midway down that hid the far end when you were rolling. *The east wind is a break. I can approach from the near end if I can just see those darn runway lights.*

"If we don't see them pretty soon, Loyal, we better pick out one of those lighted streets."

Loyal didn't answer, but he had visions of telephone poles, electric lines, guy wires and parked automobiles.

Then he saw the lights! He couldn't believe how far out they looked. He quickly checked the altimeter. Thirty-seven hundred feet! He had already used half of his altitude, and the field elevation was eleven hundred so he only had about twenty-six hundred feet left. He corrected the 040 heading to 360 degrees. This put him on a long right base leg for runway 090.

Loyal Lambright recalled the statistics that showed that on dead stick landings most pilots overshoot. He wondered if that included night landings. He deliberately set the base leg early with that in mind. He put down two notches of flaps and re-trimmed. He wouldn't go to full flaps until over the threshold. That would allow him to keep open his option to forward slip if he was overshooting. He shouldn't have worried. As the lights became clearer, he realized overshooting would not be the problem. He would be lucky to make the runway at all! As the altimeter went through 2500 feet, Lambright raised the nose slightly to reduce the indicated airspeed to seventy miles per hour and trimmed.

Harold said, "Tighten your seat belt and shoulder harness. I'm cracking the door latch on my side."

Loyal knew that was good procedure. Critical, if they didn't make the runway. One of the real traps pilots fell into when undershooting was trying to stretch the glide by lifting the nose. That could result in a stall with dire results at low altitude. It took courage, but Loyal actually lowered the nose slightly. He turned on the landing light. He caught a glimpse of the full length of the runway just before the far end disappeared behind the hill. They cleared the fence with inches to spare. Lambright put down the last notch to full flaps and trimmed at 65 mph. He gradually increased back pressure to hold the nose at a constant angle as the Cessna settled. In the silence of the dead engine, Loyal heard the wheels hitting the weeds on the overrun. The tires kissed the asphalt in the first ten feet. Loyal applied back pressure to hold the nose gear off as he raised the flaps to keep the weight on the main gear. The aircraft slowed, and the nose gear eased onto the runway. Lambright started to brake but then saw the angled taxiway ahead. He maintained enough forward momentum to coast onto the taxiway where he allowed the Cessna to roll to a stop. His only comment was, "Whew!"

If it had been daylight, one would have called Harold Higgins's face ashen. "What the hell brought that on?"

Lambright said, "We had been building up oil temperature for over an hour. We finally started to lose oil pressure and…"

"Wait a damn minute! You mean you kept us up there for over an hour knowing we were developing an engine problem? I damn sure resent that, Loyal. *Nothing* is worth that kind of risk!"

Lambright sighed. In the darkness of the cabin he turned toward Higgins and quietly replied, "I disagree with you there, Buddy…a few things are."

"Tiger Den to Idaho Five, Over. Tiger Den to Idaho Five, Over."

Harold Higgins was still shaken, sitting strapped in Cessna N733FK at the Downtown Airport when the voice of SAC Palmer broke through. "Go ahead, Tiger Den," Higgins weakly replied.

"What is your condition, Idaho Five?"

"We are on the ground at Downtown Airport. No harm to us, but we are out of action for tonight. The aircraft will require an inspection and probably maintenance. Send someone over to pick us up when you can. Did you scramble Idaho Three?"

"Yes. They're on the way. Should be in radio contact soon."

"Tiger Den to Tiger One, what is your position now?"

"We are approximately twelve miles east of Highway 65. We have seen nothing that would qualify as a signal." The desperation was obvious in Lance's voice.

"What do you propose on the drop, Lance?"

"We've given it a fair shake. I think we should scrub it."

"I agree, but let's have Idaho Three check you out as they come in. Our problem still could be in Idaho Five's OAR unit."

"Long shot sir, but worth a try. We'll park here and wait."

"Tiger Den, this is Idaho Three. We read that. We are thirty-five miles east of Springfield, climbing. We have our OAR on. We are receiving no signal."

"Okay, Idaho Three. Tiger One, with the package, is stationary, approximately twelve miles east of Highway 65. That puts him about eight miles south of the town of Strafford. He is still west of your position. Let us know as soon as you pick up a signal from his OAR."

"Okay Den, we are looking. Tiger One, verify your exact position in relation to Strafford. We are paralleling Interstate 44 and approaching Strafford."

Lance, growing weary of the attempts to pick up the signal, replied, "We are parked at the intersection of Chestnut Expressway extended and State Road 125 which runs south out of Strafford. Over."

Chuck Kogan was muttering at every transmission. "What the hell is going on, Barron? You said they could stay with the package. Why the hell do we have all this confusion?"

"We're working on it, sir." Lance was up off the floor. He had already disconnected the headset and switched the radio to speaker.

"Idaho Three here. We're at Strafford and I-44. We are receiving a resting signal on the OAR." Lance's heart leaped with joy, but Idaho Three was still transmitting, "Verify Tiger One, that you are south of Strafford?"

"That's correct, on State 125 due south. You should show our signal off your left wing."

"Tiger One, the signal we show is at our eleven o'clock. We're turning thirty degrees left to track it."

Lance, still hopeful, came back, "Are you sure, Three?"

"Affirmative. We have a strong resting signal right on the nose. We're heading 225 degrees and closing."

Kogan was furious, "Where the hell is my money, Barron? It better be in the back of this truck."

Lance Barron did not reply. He grabbed his flashlight, went out the passenger side and headed for the rear of the truck. Kogan bailed out on his side, still muttering, and joined Lance. Lance checked the lock. Intact. While trying to decide what to do, he recalled Kogan's failure to get the tag number. He dropped to his knees and shined his flashlight on the tag. There was a large plywood panel hanging down beneath the truck. He leaned in farther and saw a large rectangular opening in the metal bed, the edges scarred and burned by a cutting torch. The plywood panel was hinged at the front to a plywood box. It was held open by the shining metallic arm of a garage door opener. Lance didn't say a word as he ran forward to the cab.

Kogan said, "Well, I'll be a son of a bitch."

Lance was on the radio by the time Kogan caught up. "Tiger One to all units. The signal at Chestnut and the railroad *is* the package! Repeat, *it is* the package. Back off! If you haven't burned it, back off! Tiger Two and Four acknowledge, back off!"

"Tiger Two in the Sutherland lot, backing off."

Lance yelled, "Tiger Four, do you read, back off!"

After an agonizing pause, Tiger Four came on in quiet contrast to Lance's excitement, "Tiger Four to all units, we just recovered the mapcase…It was empty."

PERSEVERANCE

"Brave admiral, say but one good word: What shall we do when hope is gone?" The words leapt like a leaping sword: "Sail on! Sail on! Sail on! and on!"

—Joaquin Miller, *Columbus*

Lance drove the truck back toward Springfield in silence. Kogan ranted from the passenger seat, but Lance tuned him out as he went over what had happened.

The kidnappers outsmarted me. There is no denying that. Still, the ransom was delivered, in a way—the kidnappers' way. The drop went just exactly the way they wanted. At least nothing happened that would cause any increased danger to Jenny. She should be released soon. Maybe she has been already.

Lance tried to console himself with that, but it was no use. He was sick with disappointment. Kogan had a right to be upset. They had learned practically nothing from the drop. Lance forced himself to think of the things that could still be done.

"Tiger One to Tiger Four, remain at the site and secure the area until we can get enough light and help out there to do a thorough search. And Four, be sure and preserve the mapcase and anything else you find out there for fingerprints. Acknowledge."

"Okay, Tiger One. We'll handle it."

"Tiger One to Tiger Den."

"Go ahead, Tiger One."

"Ask Corporal Vickers to call ahead to the PD and get clearance for us to take the truck to their garage while we are processing it. It's had a lot of work done on it. The public VIN has been removed. Get Castle over there to locate the confidential number. I'd like that done right away. We'll meet him there in twenty minutes.

"And, Boss, the license tag on this vehicle is Missouri Truck tag BSD-769. That's current Missouri BSD-769. It's only attached with one screw so it's probably stolen. Have Vickers get a quick listing on that. If it was stolen in the last few days we need to interview the owner right away."

Kogan sat in the passenger seat listening. He had a smirk on his face and at the first opportunity said, "You should just go ahead and tell your boss that you have screwed up this situation royally, and you and the frigging FBI are going to get your asses sued for sure. You told me that with all that fancy equipment, you could find my money at any time. Well, Mr. College Boy, where is it?"

"I don't know where your money is, Mr. Kogan, but the kidnappers have it. That's what they wanted. Your daughter should be released soon. That will give us another chance to learn more about the kidnappers."

"Where have I heard that bullshit before? You were going to learn a lot about the kidnappers from the ransom drop. Tell me one frigging thing you learned? I'll tell you one thing I learned and it's a fact. The bastards are $300,000 richer than they were this morning."

Kogan was almost screaming. "Don't plan on learning anything about them from my daughter. I don't think I'll even let you talk to her. And I'll tell you another thing. If you and your stupid-ass agents don't get out there and talk to Kline about this, I'm going out there myself and I'll guarantee you it won't be a friendly conversation."

Before Lance could respond, he was interrupted by the radio. "Tiger Den to One."

"Go ahead, Den."

"That tag you gave us, Missouri Truck, BSD-769 is registered to Regent Furniture Company, 4529 West Sunshine in Springfield. It was reported stolen by the driver, Edward Summerfield, at 6:30 P.M.

on April 2. The police report indicates Summerfield stopped at a tavern in Willard, Missouri, on the way home from work. When he came out, the tag was gone. Vickers is running a criminal check on him. We will send a couple of people out to question him as soon as it's daylight. Over."

"What about Castle? Will he be at the PD?"

"He's already there."

"Good, I'll need to use his car."

"Are you coming back to the office?"

"No, Sir. I'll take Mr. Kogan by the lumberyard to pick up his car. I'll escort him home and then join Castle at the PD."

Lance found Castle waiting at the police department. They secured the truck, and Castle began his inspection. Two members of the crime scene team started their dusting.

"Are you ready, Mr. Kogan?"

"You damn right. I've seen all of that truck I want to see, but you ought to like it. It's a monument to your ignorance."

Lance was not sure how long he could bear Kogan. He didn't reply, but he did give Kogan a look meant to convey a message, *There is a limit, Mr. Kogan, and you have almost reached it.* He said, "I'll take you to your car."

As Lance drove to the lumberyard, he realized how close the site was to PD Headquarters, only about five blocks. In view of that and with the knowledge of what happened, he now felt it was unlikely the kidnappers even watched them at the truck site. *They just sat out there at the rail crossing and waited for us to bring the yellow truck out and drop the money.* Lance was irritated to think how concerned he had been about a hijacking. It looked so simple in hindsight.

It was 3:30 when Lance and Kogan arrived at the Kogan residence. Lance parked in the drive and followed Mr. Kogan into his home through the garage. As he walked past Kogan's silver Cadillac he recalled the high expectations he had when they left. Could it have been only four hours ago?

Mrs. Kogan met them in the hall with a broad smile but her expression changed quickly when she saw her husband's face. "What happened, Charles? Is Jenny all right?"

"Hell, I don't know. We don't know a damn thing." He pushed past his wife and went on toward the office.

Lance said, "We followed their instructions, ma'am. They have the ransom. We hope to hear from Jenny soon."

Kogan turned around at full volume. "The damn FBI bungled it again. Can you believe these guys? The kidnappers got the money and got away with it, and these guys don't even know when it happened. I'm calling Gene Taylor in the morning. I'm not going to put up with this. We're going to get somebody on this case that knows what they're doing. My money is gone and we don't even have a clue who got it. *Not a clue.*"

Lance recognized the name of Taylor, the long term Congressman from Missouri, an influential man in Washington and a folk hero here in his district. But if Kogan thought a threat of political inter-ference would affect the investigation, he was badly mistaken. Lance was convinced that one of the principles that had led to the success of the FBI, and one of its most cherished attributes, was its freedom from partisan politics. Any inquiry by a Congressman or Senator from either party into the progress of an investigation would be promptly and courteously acknowledged, but it would not affect, in any way, the manner in which the investigation was being handled.

Lance calmly said, more to Mrs. Kogan, who was listening, than to her husband, "I'm on my way back to the PD. I'll gather up my personal belongings. I believe Jenny will contact you soon. When she does, please call me immediately."

Kogan broke in, "Why? You've fouled up everything so far."

Lance hurriedly shoved items into his canvas gym bag and dropped his razor and toothbrush into the side pockets. "Our interview of your daughter will be critical to the solution of this case, Mr. Kogan. When we take what she has learned about the kidnappers and put it with the other investigation we..."

"What other investigation? You haven't done a damn thing that I know of."

"We still have a trap-and-trace report coming on the call to this phone last night. We are conducting an examination of the rental truck. We expect to learn who rented it and where. We can possibly learn who did the cutting torch job, who bought that new garage door opener. We still have all those marked bills out there. We have agents working on the analysis of the fixed surveillance logs. Add that to what Jenny can tell us..."

"What about Kline and his niggers? I've been telling you all along..."

"I started to tell you earlier, Mr. Kogan, but the radio interrupted. Our agents interviewed Mr. Kline yesterday when he returned from a trip outside the country. He has been eliminated as a suspect."

"Who says?"

"I don't know all the details, sir, but the FBI is satisfied that neither Mr. Kline nor any of his employees—he only has five—were involved in the kidnapping of your daughter. And incidentally, sir, the only employee of Mr. Kline who could possibly be mistaken for an African-American is from India. He was on a charter flight to Minneapolis when the kidnapping occurred. We have verified that through FAA records."

Kogan blushed. "Screw you, Barron. I'd like to see how you'd handle it if some masked bastards busted in and took your daughter."

"I hope I never have to find out, Mr. Kogan. Please let me know as soon as you hear from Jenny. And thank you, Mrs. Kogan for your hospitality. I hope to meet all of your family soon."

As he left the Kogan's, Lance finally admitted he was tired. He thought, *What if we don't get Jenny back? What if we never find out who the kidnappers are? Maybe Mr. Kogan is right. Maybe we don't know what we are doing.* It was rare for Lance Barron to have negative thoughts. He tried to push them out of his mind as he drove north toward the Police Department.

Ben Castle had finished his examination and was busy helping the crime scene team dust the vehicle. "I found two confidential VIN numbers, Lance. They matched and neither had been altered. And, we've already lifted a couple of promising prints from the cab. Our best ones are on the garage door opener. Whoever installed it didn't bother with gloves or even a wipe rag. There are some good ones on the plywood box, too. We're gonna get a break soon, Lance. I can feel it!"

Lance experienced a phenomenon he had often observed. He suddenly felt invigorated, his determination resurrected by Castle's enthusiasm. It didn't take much, just the knowledge that someone believed in what he was doing. That was enough. He recalled reading somewhere *Enthusiasm is the second most contagious of all attitudes. Unfortunately, a lack of enthusiasm is the most contagious.* He had spent most of the past four days being dragged down by Charles Kogan's negativism. Now, just a few words from a right-thinking fellow agent, and he felt he could conquer the world.

"That's great news, Ben. How about the glove compartment? Have you done that yet?"

Castle grinned, "Were you hoping we would find a copy of the rental agreement in there?"

"That would be nice but, no, I'm hoping to find Ryder's twenty-four-hour-a-day assistance number."

"My guys removed the owner's manual and some other material for dusting, but I can tell you what the number is anyway. Haven't you seen that on TV? 'Just call 1-800-Go-Ryder.'"

"You're so smart, Ben. You ought to be an FBI Agent. Now, let me have that VIN you lifted from those secret places that only you and the NATB know about."

"Here it is, Lance. Guaranteed!"

"Thanks, pal…Thanks for a lot of things."

Lance went into the Shift Commander's office. Lieutenant Stan Long was on duty. Lance had met Long once or twice, including one hotly contested skeet session on the PD's firearms range.

"Hey, Lance. What brings an old sharpshooter like you out in the middle of the night? I thought you G-Men only worked eight to five."

Lance laughed, "We decided to move out of this crime-ridden city. We just pulled in here to get our truck overhauled. I understand y'all do good work."

They both chuckled, then Long turned serious and said, "I know you've got something big going, Lance. Two of our units really jumped the dispatcher after she sent them on a couple of wild goose chases. I went in there to check on what she was doing. She firmly told me she was doing exactly what the chief told her to do, and if I needed to know any more about it, I could call him up. You think I'm gonna call the chief at one in the morning? Not me! I just told my guys they were still on the payroll so they should just go wherever she sends them."

"I appreciate that, Stan. We are working a very touchy case, but the most sensitive part is almost over. I just came in to use the phone."

Lance's call to 1-800-Go-Ryder reached the company's twenty-four-hour control center in Denver. After a few minutes of explaining who he was and why the information was needed, the computer operator advised that VIN 1FDHE27Y3PHA56009 was assigned to a 1993 Ford van, the property of Southern View Texaco, 16th and Clark Street, Tulsa, OK 74113, telephone 918-743-7788.

Special Agent Joel Karlis, Tulsa RA was in the office early, dictating a report when the call came from Ralph Berger, the Special

Agent in Charge of the Oklahoma City office.

Berger led right in, "Joel, I don't believe your RA has had any information yet on Kansas City's kidnapping case, have you?"

"No, sir, I haven't seen anything on it."

Berger gave Karlis a brief outline of the abduction and ransom drop. Then he said, "I'll fax you a copy of the information teletype KC sent to all surrounding offices. We haven't had any leads until now. The drop, late last night, involved the use of a Ryder Rental truck. Kansas City agents traced the truck through Ryder in Denver. Are you with me, so far?"

"Yes, sir. I'm right with you."

"Okay. Here's where it involves us. Ryder told KC the truck belongs to the Ryder agency at Southern View Texaco, 16th and Clark there in Tulsa. That's all we know, Joel. We don't know when it was rented, but it was before midnight on Sunday. That's when it was first seen in Springfield. We don't even know that it was rented in Tulsa. We hope it was. We know it is registered there, but that doesn't mean, you understand, that it was rented from there. We need to resolve that right away. You know, of course, that some of their rentals are one-way so it could have been rented somewhere else. The Tulsa franchise should know since it's their truck. Ryder told KC they have a computerized system to keep up with all their rentals at all times. Unfortunately, some of their franchises do not use it. We hope that's not the case this time. You need to get out there and really pump them on this, Joel, but you'll have to be careful about what information you give them. The girl is still missing."

"Okay, boss, I'll get Ed Kelley, and we'll pick up the fax and be on our way. I rented a truck from them a couple of years ago when we moved into our new house. They were nice folks. I'll bet they're still there."

"Okay, Joel, let me know what you find out. I'll phone it to Springfield. You can follow up with a teletype. I hope it doesn't turn out the damn truck was stolen. It had a stolen tag on it. Kansas City ran the VIN through NCIC and didn't get a hit. That's encouraging, but it could still be stolen. If it is, they're back to square one."

Karlis said, "We'll get right on it, Boss. I'll be in touch."

Joel Karlis grew up in Oklahoma. He often said his transfer to Tulsa, after twelve years in the slums of Cleveland and Newark, was like going to hell and then getting a reprieve. He was a conscientious and capable agent and was usually the first to volunteer for any special assignment. The term "laid back" was coined to describe Joel Karlis. If he had one fault, it was that he liked people too much. He liked to visit and people liked to talk with him. He listened. He made them feel important. He remembered their names and how many children they had. They remembered him. He was particularly adept at developing informants. The Bureau required that every agent working criminal violations have at least three confidential informants or CIs. Two of the three could be under development, potential criminal informants, PCIs they were called, but one had to be a CI, fully certified as having furnished valid information in three FBI or local investigations. Most agents struggled to keep the required number. Karlis always had his three, all CIs. In addition, he usually had several PCIs and a half dozen "hip-pocket informants," people who liked to visit with him and share the latest gossip from the street. They were not officially "sources" and would never appear in court as witnesses, but they gave Karlis a lot of good information about general criminal activity in the area. Karlis also had a very close working relationship with several detectives on the Tulsa Police Department. They shared mutually beneficial information on criminal activity.

Ed Kelley was a young second office agent, doing his first stint in an RA after serving his first tour in the Atlanta Field Office. He was not nearly as relaxed as Karlis, but he was learning.

Karlis and Kelley found Wayne Bennett, owner of Southern

View Texaco and holder of the Ryder franchise, in his office. Karlis greeted Bennett like he was an old friend. It didn't take Bennett long to remember Karlis. They laughed over a couple of fishing stories Karlis recalled Bennett telling. Kelley fretted and cleared his throat, hoping Karlis would get down to business.

Karlis finally did. "We're not renting today, Wayne. We want to get some information about someone who did. Our guys recovered a truck over in Springfield, Missouri, where it was used in a caper. We verified through Denver that it is your truck. We hope it was rented from here. We want to get all the information you can give us on the rental. We know it was rented sometime before Sunday. That's when it was first seen in Springfield."

Bennett thought at first that Karlis was setting him up for some joke but soon became serious as Karlis continued. He said, "We'll sure give you what we have, Joel. Which truck was it?"

"The truck is a '93 Ford, VIN 1FDHE27Y3PHA56009."

Bennett was a stocky man in his early forties. He looked younger when Karlis was telling the fish stories. He aged considerably when he realized he might have to go through the paperwork. He relied heavily on his secretary for handling the rentals. He started pawing through a stack of rental contracts he had pulled from his secretary's desk. "My secretary is not in this morning. I don't think we file by VIN number anyway. You don't know who rented it?"

"No, sir."

"It will be a matter of going through these manually. Do you know anything about the person who rented it?"

"No, sir, not a thing." said Karlis, "That's what we hope to learn."

Bennett was not even looking at the contracts. He continued to leaf through them as he talked, hoping perhaps, that one of them might magically jump out and identify itself. He said, "Most of our rentals are local, one- or two-day jobs, people moving across town.

Of course we are also in the long distance, one-way business. The one you're asking about sounds like a one-way. It might have been rented somewhere else."

Bennett was getting nowhere. Karlis finally asked, "How many trucks do you have leased from you right now? You can exclude those rented since Sunday."

Bennett seemed to appreciate this guidance. He calmed down and methodically separated the lease agreements into two groups. He looked up, grinned and proudly announced, "Hey, we only have five out right now that were rented before Sunday!"

"Now," said Karlis, "are the VIN numbers on the contracts?"

"Oh, yeah, there's a full description of the vehicle, including any damage such as scratches, dents, things like that."

Bennett now attacked the small stack with a purpose. Karlis took cotton gloves from his briefcase and asked Bennett to allow him to do the sorting from here on. Bennett was delighted.

With only five contracts, Karlis quickly located the one relating to a 1993 Ford.

As anxious as Karlis was to look at it, he forced himself to say, "Let's not handle that one any more until we get it protected." Kelley put on a pair of gloves. Karlis pointed out the contract and Kelley used tweezers to lift it into the glassine envelope Karlis was holding. Karlis then carefully inserted his pen into the envelope and placed his initials and the date on the corner of the document. He then closed the envelope with evidence tape and asked Bennett to copy both sides.

"With your permission, we will take the original and leave this copy for your files. Now, tell us everything you can about this rental."

Bennett studied the copy and said, "Well, first of all it was rented by a Mr. William A. Patrick, 2880 Calhoun, Apartment #240, here in Tulsa on Thursday, April 2. He rented it for four days. The rental was a local in that he picked it up here and he is supposed to return it here today. He used an Illinois driver's license for identification, but he has a local address and telephone number. His driver's license number is P444-40-8265, issued to William A. Patrick, 935 Walnut Street, Danville, Illinois. He is a white male, six feet, four inches, one hundred ninety pounds, blue eyes, blond hair."

Karlis interrupted, "Do you remember this guy?"

Bennett scratched his head, "No, I don't. Gloria handles most of these. I see she handled this one. I normally see the customers, but unless it is something out of the ordinary, I don't deal with them. I don't remember this guy at all. That probably means I wasn't here...Yeah, let me see. Last Thursday...I think that was the day... yeah, in the afternoon, I had to take a truck to the garage for some work. I was gone for a couple of hours. She told me about it when I got in. Hey, yeah, I remember it now. This guy took the truck right out. He left his car on the lot over there. I didn't see him, but when I got back Gloria was telling me about it. She said he was a really sexy guy with a really sexy car. Me and the guy in the back kidded her about him. The guy in the back told her she better be careful because the guy was a biker. His car stayed over there the rest of the afternoon. It was still over there when we closed at 6:00. It was red. A red Corvette, late model."

"Why did you think he was a biker?" asked Karlis.

"Me? I don't know. It was the guy in the back that started that. He kids Gloria a lot anyway. Maybe the guy had tattoos or a ponytail or something. I don't know. I didn't even see him."

Karlis asked with a grin, "Is the man in the back, in the back?"

Bennett, missing the humor said, "Yeah, he's back there. He does all our minor repairs, keeps the tow dollies in shape, et cetera."

Karlis grinned, "Does he have a name or does everyone just call him 'the man in the back?'"

"Oh, yeah. It's Joe; Joe Dunlop. He's back there. Just go on back."

"Thank you, sir. We'll check in with you before we leave." Even serious Ed Kelley couldn't suppress a slight snicker as they headed for the man in the back.

Joe Dunlop was changing a trailer tire when they entered. He looked up, smiled, but kept working until he finished removing the tire from the rim. He then wiped his hands on a red shop cloth, grinned and said. "This must be important. I can't remember the last time we had a suit and tie back here, and now we get two at a time. You know, I thought at first you was Ed McMahon delivering my Sweepstakes check but you're both too young for that." Dunlop laughed as he put out a still greasy hand and said, "I'm Joe, how can I help you?"

Karlis said, "Mr. Dunlop, my name is…"

Dunlop abruptly turned and looked behind himself, "I don't see any Mr. Dunlop. Mr. Dunlop was my dad. He's dead and gone. I'm Joe."

Karlis smiled and said, "Sorry about that, Joe. I'm Joel and this is Ed."

All three realized the irony at once and burst into laughter. "No not McMahon—Kelley, Ed Kelley. We are with the FBI. We want to ask you a couple of questions about a man who rented a truck here last Thursday."

Joe scratched his head. "Well, we rent a lot of 'em."

"Yeah, I know. We were talking to Mr. Bennett, Wayne, a few minutes ago. He said he heard you kidding Gloria about this guy being a biker. Do you remember that?"

Joe said, "Let's set down over here and let me think about that a minute. Gloria sizes up every guy that comes in here. That was last Thursday, you say? I don't think I saw the guy. If it's the one I'm thinking about, she was talking about how good looking he was and how sexy his car was. Yeah, the guy was gone in the truck, but his car was still out there. It was a bright red Corvette, not more than a year old. It was parked right out there," Joe said, pointing. "It was still there when we closed."

"Why did you think he was a biker?"

"Oh, I was just goin' on with her. She was telling me how good looking he was. I asked her if he had tattoos, earrings, a beard, a ponytail, or if he had his wallet on a chain? Most of those bikers do, you know. She said, 'What are you talking about? This guy wasn't like that at all. What makes you think he was a biker?' I told her to look out there at his car. He's got his Harley Davidson wings in his back window. Gloria looked out there and said, 'I can't believe that! He was so clean and neat. I can't believe he was a biker.' She's so gullible. I got a good laugh out of it. That's all."

"Did he really have Harley Davidson wings in his back window?" asked Kelley.

"Naw. They were some kind of wings but not Harleys. I think they were a different color. I don't know what they were. I've seen others around like that, but I never really paid much attention to them. I wouldn't have even noticed them if he hadn't left his car there for so long and if Gloria hadn't been taking on so about him."

Karlis said, "We are assuming the man didn't rent the truck in his true name and then use it in a crime. We are in the process of trying to sort all of that out. It could be very helpful to us in identifying him if you will remember as much about those wings as you can. Can you remember the color?"

Joe closed his eyes and pressed his temples, shaking his head slightly. He finally said, "Now don't quote me on this, but they might have been blue. Harley's are sort of orange, you know."

Karlis made a note and then asked, "In all the looking at the wings, did you happen to notice the tag on the car?"

"Oh, yeah. It was an Oklahoma tag. I'm sure about that. Uh…I don't mean to be nosy, but I guess y'all figure this guy ain't gonna bring the truck back."

"That's right, Joe. We don't know who he is, but we know he won't be bringing the truck back."

"I wish I could help you out, but all I saw was the car. Have you talked to Miss Gloria?"

"No, not yet, but we're going to as soon as she comes in. Thank you, Joe, for your time and, hey, I hope the next suit and tie you get back here will be the real Ed McMahon."

"Hey, thanks. Man, that would make my day."

Back in the office. Karlis asked, "Wayne, what time do you expect your secretary back?"

"She had some personal business downtown. She left just before y'all came in. She should be back around ten o'clock."

"What is Gloria's full name?"

"Gloria Benson. Miss Gloria Benson, she always says. She likes to emphasize the Miss. She's sort of adamant about that. Most women these days want to be called 'Ms,' but not her. Miss Gloria, she's really something."

Karlis said, "Yeah, I remember her from the last time I was here, but I only remembered her first name. Very outgoing as I recall."

"Oh, yeah. That's her; good as gold and a hell of a secretary."

"Okay, Mr. Bennett, we are going to grab a cup. We'll be back around ten."

Kelley drove. Karlis went over his notes and then stared out the window. He finally said, "This guy Patrick would not have rented that truck in his own name if he knew it was going to be used in a crime. Maybe the truck was stolen from him. I-44 runs right through Springfield, Missouri. That's the route he would take toward Danville, Illinois, until he reached I-70 in St. Louis. But if it was stolen from him, why hasn't he reported it? Maybe the kidnappers took it from him, and he's not able to report it. If that's the case, they're not going to find him in Illinois, and we're not going to find him here. But, if he left here in the truck and headed for Illinois, who moved his car? This should be an interesting afternoon."

Karlis used a pay phone to call Field Office Headquarters in Oklahoma City.

"Boss, the truck was rented from Ryder here last Thursday. We have good descriptive data and an address in Illinois on the guy who rented it. He also gave a Tulsa address. We are going to check that out, but I wanted to get the Illinois information to you as soon as possible so you could get a teletype out."

Karlis gave Berger the descriptive data on William A. Patrick and the red Corvette with Oklahoma tags and the wings sticker in the back window. SAC Berger said he would handle the teletype to the office that covers Danville, Illinois; it would be either Chicago or Springfield, Illinois.

Karlis and Kelley drove directly to Calhoun Street. The number Patrick used on the rental contract, 2880, if it had existed, would have been in the middle of a park. There was a large modern apartment complex right next to the park. Its address was 2830 Calhoun.

On a hunch Karlis decided to check with the manager. Signs pointed the way to a first floor office in the back of the complex. A sign on the door read "Office Hours 8:00 A.M. to 6:00 P.M. Emergency: call 887-8342." Karlis opened the door. The office was small with only one desk. Two walls were lined with file cabinets. A couch and two chairs completed the furnishings. A small, frail young man was standing behind the desk talking on the phone. A sign on his desk read, "Roland Rose, Resident Manager."

The young man, frowning, put his hand over the phone and whispered "Yes?"

Karlis felt compelled to whisper, "We'd like the apartment number of Mr. William Patrick."

The man, obviously annoyed and no longer whispering, said, "There is no tenant here by that name."

Karlis, also at normal volume said, "I'll wait until you finish your phone conversation," and he sat down. Kelley followed suit.

The man, now more than annoyed, quickly hung up. "What is it you want?"

Karlis and Kelley stood. Karlis extended his credentials. "My name is Joel Karlis. I'm a Special Agent with the FBI." Then, nodding toward Kelley he said, "This is Special Agent Edward Kelley. We didn't intend to interrupt you. We would have been happy to wait. We do need some information."

The answer was abrupt, "What is it you want? I'm not sure I can give out information. Do you have a, uh…warrant or whatever it is they use?"

Karlis was patient but he wasn't Job. He said, "We are not asking for any state secrets. Are you the apartment manager?"

The young man pointed to the sign on his desk and replied, "You can read, can't you?"

"Yes, I can, sir. You must be Mr. Rose. Would you please check your records for a tenant named William A. Patrick?"

"I am Roland Rose, but I don't need to check the records. We have no such tenant."

Karlis forced himself to continue through clenched teeth. "Have you noticed a late model red Corvette parked in the lot here?"

"Look, mister, I live here along with a hundred and fifty other tenants. I also work here trying to keep all of them paid up on their rent and happy. I rarely go into the parking lot and I don't know one car from another. No, I don't believe I've seen a red… whatever it was. Why?"

Karlis met too many friendly and helpful people in his work to spend time with a sorehead. One of the most pleasant aspects of his job was the willingness, no, the *eagerness* of most citizens to be of assistance to the FBI. He smiled and said, "I'm sorry we caught you at a bad time, Mr. Rose. Thank you anyway."

As he headed for the door Karlis had a feeling he would see Mr. Roland Rose again. He wondered if it was possible to catch him at a good time.

Karlis and Kelley drove through the parking lot that surrounded the complex on three sides but did not see a Corvette of any color.

Kelley said, "Tell me, Joel, if a guy doesn't know one car from another, what kind of car would he drive?"

Karlis smiled as he pondered that. "Ed, are you becoming a philosopher?"

Because of the unscheduled stop at the apartment complex Karlis decided they better grab their coffee from the drive through window in order to make it back to Bennett's by ten o'clock. They reached the Ryder office and swallowed the last of their coffee right on time.

Miss Gloria Benson, thirty-five, attractive, well dressed, slightly overweight, greeted Karlis by name and mentioned their previous meeting. Before he could respond she turned to Ed Kelley with a radiant smile and extended her hand almost at shoulder level. "I'm Miss Gloria Benson."

Kelley was caught off-guard. In a reflex action, he almost kissed the extended hand before catching himself. He managed to grasp it in a high handshake and mumble, "I'm happy to meet you, Miss Benson. I'm Ed Kelley."

Karlis would have liked to watch the blushing Kelley conduct this interview, but *duty before pleasure,* he thought. "Did Wayne mention that we were by here earlier?"

"Yes he did, and he gave me the copy of the contract you were asking about. He said it looked like our customer is in deep trouble. I just can't believe it."

"Do you remember the man Patrick?"

Miss Benson lowered her eyes and smiled, "Oh, yes, I remember him very well. He was gorgeous." She laughed. "He was so bashful. His hand actually shook when he was signing the contract."

"How about describing him, starting with his age. Please don't look at the data you took from his driver's license. Describe him the way you remember him."

She thought briefly and said, "I would bet he was between thirty-three and thirty-nine. No older than that; deep tan, white teeth, like I said, gorgeous."

"Did he wear glasses?"

"No. He had on sunglasses when he came in, but he propped them up on his forehead. You know; like this," she demonstrated, then smiled. "It would be a shame to keep those eyes covered."

"What about the eyes?"

"Oh, he had the most beautiful blue eyes with little crow's feet in the corners like he was laughing all the time."

"What about his hair?"

"Blond, almost white, parted on the side, the right side I think, medium length on the sides, combed back over his ears, neat."

"How about his size? How tall was he?"

"Oh, he was very tall. Taller than you are and slender."

"I'm six foot two. How much taller was he?"

Miss Benson moved up close to Karlis and looked up into his eyes, smiling. "I didn't get quite this close to him, darn it, but I think he was at least a couple of inches taller than you."

Karlis took notes as she went on. "He was slender; nice, wide shoulders. I don't know how to judge his weight, but he wasn't real muscular; not skinny either; just well-built and tall. He had on khaki slacks and a blue oxford cloth shirt. I don't remember the shoes. Wayne said the truck has been recovered. I hope he's not in trouble. What do you think he's done?"

"Excuse me, let's finish with his description. The data you wrote on the contract; did that come from his driver's license?"

"Yes. Right off the driver's license. Let's see, six feet four inches, one hundred ninety pounds, blue eyes, blond hair and, let's see, date of birth, uh…thirty-six years old."

"And is that what he looked like to you?"

"Yes. I had it pretty close, didn't I?" She smiled and looked from Karlis to Kelley for approval.

Karlis said, "What other identification did you require?"

"He had a local address. He said he had been working here for a few months and was going back to Illinois to get the rest of his furniture. He showed me the lease agreement from his apartment. He put the address right there on the rental contract. And, as I said, he used his Illinois driver's license."

"Did you notice what kind of car he was driving?"

"Oh, yes. It was gorgeous." She paused and Karlis thought he saw a slight blush. "I know; I use that word way too much. But, anyway, he had a really nice car; a red Corvette. Did you ever ride in one? It's like no other car I've ever been in."

"Did you notice the tag on the car?"

"No, I didn't, but it did have a sticker on the back window. The guy in back tried to tell me he was a member of a motorcycle gang. He said he knew he was a biker because of the sticker. I didn't believe it so I didn't pay much attention to the sticker. If he's a biker, I'd like to join the club." She laughed.

"Can you describe the sticker for us?" asked Kelley.

"No, I really can't. It was just some kind of wings."

"Do you remember the color?"

"No…I don't know…maybe gold."

Karlis said, "You said earlier that he was shaking when he signed the contract. Could you elaborate on that?"

"Well, not really shaking, I guess. He seemed to be bashful or timid for a guy that had so much going for him; you know, great looks and the car and all. I kinda go for the bashful type, but you don't find many that good-looking. When I asked him if he needed any boxes, pads, et cetera for the move, he stuttered a little bit and finally said his friend had all of that…A girl friend, I guess. Oh, well."

"Would you recognize this William A. Patrick if you saw him again, or a picture of him?"

"Boy, I sure would like to give it a try," she laughed. "Yeah, I'm pretty sure I would."

"Now thinking back to this transaction, was there anything unusual about it? For instance, the fact he had a local address but an Illinois driver's license. Wasn't that a little odd?"

"No, not at all. Think about it. Most of the people we deal with are in some phase of a move. If they are moving from another state, they don't get a new driver's license right away, or a car license either. Or, in some cases, they live in another state, and they are here to help a parent or a girl friend move. They use the parent's or girlfriend's local address here, but they might live in Alabama and have an Alabama driver's license. No, it's not unusual. If the driver's license appears valid, we accept it. We do require a proof-of-insurance card. If they don't have that we require that they buy a policy to cover the trip."

"Did Mr. Patrick have a proof-of-insurance card?"

"No, and you can see right here on the contract that he paid a premium of $80 for insurance."

"What are the other charges on there?"

"He rented the ten-foot van for four days at $50 per day plus twenty-five cents per mile. Our mileage chart shows the distance from Tulsa to Danville, Illinois as 620 miles, that is 1240 miles at twenty-five cents per mile or $310, plus the $200 for four days, plus $80 for insurance. That is $590. The rental tax here is ten percent of the rental fee, not including the insurance, that's $51, for a total of $641."

Karlis said, "So Mr. Patrick paid you $641 to rent the van for four days? How did he pay?"

"Well, actually we also require a deposit to cover any damage to the equipment. The deposit is fifty percent of the rental fee. It does not apply to the tax and insurance. The deposit is refunded if there is no damage to the vehicle during the rental period. In this case, the rental fee was $510 plus the deposit of $255, plus the tax of $51 plus the $80 insurance premium. The grand total was $896. Of course, he will get the $255 back if he returns the truck undamaged and full of fuel."

Karlis and Kelley were both taking notes. Kelley finally caught up and said, "I believe you've done this before."

Gloria shrugged, blushed a little, "Yeah, a few times."

"How did Patrick pay for it?" Karlis asked.

"Oh, yes, that was the other unusual thing. Most people pay by charge card or check, but he paid cash."

"Cash, huh?"

"Yes, nine one-hundred-dollar bills."

Karlis said, "Miss Benson, I want to ask a favor of you. This telephone number Patrick listed on the contract as his home phone here in Tulsa. How about making a call to that number and asking for Mr. Patrick? If you should reach him, make some pretext about checking on the truck since it is due back today. Can you handle that?"

"Oh, I can handle it all right, but maybe you should tell me what's going on here. Mr. Bennett just told me the truck was used in a crime. Is that right?"

"Yes, that's right. That's all I'm authorized to tell you. We don't know much more than that ourselves. We don't know if Mr. Patrick is involved or not. We only know the truck was used."

"Why don't you just go out and question Mr. Patrick about it, if he's back from Illinois?"

"The address he used on the rental contract is fictitious. It does not exist."

Gloria Benson lowered her eyes and her voice. "Oh…Oh I'm so sorry to hear that. He had so much going for…Sure, I'll make the call."

Gloria paused for a few moments to gather her thoughts and then dialed the number. She waited only a few seconds, then placed the phone on its cradle. The expression on her face spoke louder than her words, "Sorry, that is not a working number."

Miss Gloria Benson almost, but not quite, caught the tear before it ran down her cheek.

THE MARK

If we begin with certainties, we shall end in doubts; but if we begin
with doubts, and are patient in them, we shall end in certainties.

—Francis Bacon

Special Agent James A. Conrad, FBI, assigned to the Danville,
Illinois, RA was at the county jail in Paris, Illinois, conducting an
interview of a suspect in a stale old bank burglary case when he
got the pager message to call headquarters. That was the FBI Field
Division Headquarters in Springfield, Illinois.

Vince Trainor, supervisor of the Major Crimes Squad, got directly
to the point. "Jim, we have just been notified of a kidnapping in
Springfield, Missouri. A 16-year-old girl was abducted from her
home last Thursday. Oklahoma City learned today that a truck
used in the ransom drop was rented in Tulsa by a man using an
Illinois driver's license with a Danville address. His name is
William A. Patrick. The teletype, which I'm faxing to your office,
sets out more details. You need to get Patrick fully identified and
possibly put under surveillance. We'll make that decision after you
have checked him out. He could be one of the kidnappers, but he
does not match the description. Okay?"

Conrad drawled, "We're on the way, Vince. What about the girl?
Is she okay?"

"We don't know. They still have her."

Jim Conrad was a tall, lanky, former basketball coach at a small
college in Mississippi. He had been an agent for fifteen years, and
no one had ever seen him excited. He had arrested armed bank
robbers, fugitives wanted for murder, revolutionaries, prison

escapees, the full gamut. He had led the Division in convictions for three years in a row, but he never seemed to be fully awake. His manner was slow and methodical but those who looked beyond appearances were not fooled. Conrad was, hands down, the best "paper pusher" in the Division. He also conducted thorough and probing interviews. His cool manner had caused more than one bank teller to confess to "tapping the till" after facing Conrad's patient probing and sound explanation of what the bank's records showed.

Conrad was accompanied today by first office agent Brad Gilbert. Graduates of the Academy at Quantico, Virginia were sent out to their first office with a thorough book knowledge of the one-hundred-plus violations investigated by the Bureau. But the jump from book knowledge to practical application was wide for some. Conrad was excellent at breaking in first office agents. He would answer questions when asked, but he'd rather sit back and watch the new agent learn.

Conrad's current trainee had been a San Francisco policeman before getting his master's degree and becoming an FBI Agent. He had been initially assigned to the Springfield Division, but re-assigned to the Danville RA thirteen months ago. He was expecting a transfer to his second office soon. He had complained recently to Conrad that they didn't seem to get many big cases. They did have a full blown bank robbery in Chrisman a few months back. The two robbers shot it out with the Illinois State Police in the afternoon and made good their getaway. Gilbert and Conrad, along with the Danville Police Department located and apprehended the armed pair that night and recovered most of the loot. Gilbert was delighted. Conrad was unperturbed.

But most of Gilbert's work had involved applicant background checks, small thefts from interstate shipments, interstate transportation of stolen motor vehicles, and an occasional bank fraud case. When Gilbert complained, Conrad said, "Just wait 'til you get on an organized crime squad in New York or Chicago. You'll wish you were back here working this easy stuff."

It was 10:25 when Conrad hung up the phone and said to Gilbert, "We might have that big one you've been looking for. Go get the car and meet me in front. I'll tell you about it on our way back to Danville." Conrad's pace approached low-normal. He buzzed the jailer to come get the prisoner. He thanked the suspect for his time and said, "We'll get back to you. I guess we know where to find you."

"Very funny, asshole," replied the prisoner.

Conrad gave him a pained expression and said, "And a good day to you too, sir," as he slowly headed for the door.

Brad Gilbert was double-parked, anxiously awaiting Conrad. Conrad finally strolled out and flopped into the passenger seat.

When they reached the highway, Conrad said, "Use the lights and siren, Brad."

After a mile or so of silence, Gilbert cut his eyes over toward Conrad to see if he might be sleeping. "Are you going to tell me about this big case?"

Conrad gave Gilbert a brief summary of what Trainor had told him and then said, "It seems strange that a person would rent a truck in his own name and then use it in a kidnapping. There has to be more here than that. We'll go by the office and pick up the fax. I hope the Sheriff is in. He knows every voter in Vermilion County. He'll know this guy, voter or not."

The fax was in when they arrived. Conrad scanned it and handed it over to Gilbert.

URGENT

TO: SAC, SPRINGFIELD
FROM: SAC, OKLAHOMA CITY(7-2413)

UNSUBS (3);
JENNIFER MARIE KOGAN - VICTIM
KIDNAPPING
OO:KANSAS CITY(7-2675)

FOR INFORMATION OF SPRINGFIELD DIVISION, VICTIM
WAS ABDUCTED FROM HER HOME IN SPRINGFIELD,
MISSOURI BY TWO UNIDENTIFIED SUBJECTS AT 4:40 PM
ON THURSDAY, APRIL 2. ONE SUBJECT DISPLAYED
SHOULDER WEAPON IN CONFRONTING FATHER OF VICTIM.
VICTIM AND BOTH SUBJECTS DEPARTED ABDUCTION SITE
IN VICTIM'S AUTOMOBILE. AUTOMOBILE RECOVERED 5
MILES NORTH OF SPRINGFIELD, MISSOURI WITHIN HOUR
OF ABDUCTION. RANSOM DROP OF $300,000 MADE BY
FATHER AT 2:00 AM SUNDAY, APRIL 5 USING RYDER
RENTAL TRUCK PROVIDED BY KIDNAPPERS.

TRUCK RECOVERED AND PROCESSED. TRUCK RENTED FROM
RYDER AGENCY, TULSA, OKLAHOMA ON FRIDAY, APRIL
3, BY WHITE MALE USING NON-EXISTENT TULSA
ADDRESS AND ILLINOIS DRIVER'S LICENSE P444-40-
8265 ISSUED TO WILLIAM A. PATRICK, 935 EAST
WALNUT, DANVILLE, ILLINOIS. SUBJECT DESCRIBED BY
RENTAL AGENCY EMPLOYEE AS WHITE MALE, 33-39
YEARS OF AGE, 6'4". SLENDER, BLOND HAIR, CLEAN
SHAVEN, DRIVING LATE MODEL RED CORVETTE WITH
POSSIBLE HARLEY DAVIDSON OR SIMILAR STICKER ON
REAR WINDOW.

UNSUBS WORE BLACK COVERALLS, LONG SLEEVES, SKI
MASKS, AND GLOVES. ENCOUNTER WITH FATHER LASTED
15 TO 20 SECONDS. ONLY WORDS SPOKEN BY UNSUBS
WERE, "YOU WILL HEAR FROM US." UNSUB #1
DESCRIBED BY VICTIM'S FATHER AS BLACK MALE,
6'2", 220 POUNDS. UNSUB #2 IS BLACK MALE, 5'8",
145, SKINNY. NO SUSPECTS DEVELOPED TO DATE.

VICTIM IS A WHITE FEMALE, 16 YEARS OF AGE. 5'4",
118 POUNDS, LIGHT BROWN SHOULDER LENGTH HAIR,

BROWN EYES, SMALL MOLE AT CORNER OF MOUTH, RIGHT
SIDE. LAST SEEN WEARING SHORT RED SKIRT, WHITE
SWEATER WITH GHS AND A MEGAPHONE ON FRONT, WHITE
SNEAKERS.

LEADS:

SPRINGFIELD DIVISION

AT DANVILLE, ILLINOIS

IMMEDIATELY CONDUCT DISCREET INVESTIGATION OF
WILLIAM A. PATRICK, 935 EAST WALNUT TO DETERMINE
HIS DESCRIPTION, BACKGROUND AND ACTIVITIES ON
THURSDAY, APRIL 2, AT 4:40PM, FRIDAY APRIL 3 AT
2:30PM AND MONDAY APRIL 6 AT 2:00AM.

IF PATRICK REMAINS A SUSPECT AFTER ABOVE
INVESTIGATION, PLACE UNDER SURVEILLANCE. DO NOT
CONTACT UNTIL VICTIM IS RECOVERED.

INFORMATION COPIES FOR KANSAS CITY (7-2552),
LITTLE ROCK, AND ST. LOUIS DIVISIONS.

ARMED AND DANGEROUS

Conrad said, "Check Patrick out in the telephone directory and the city directory, Brad. I'll call the sheriff and arrange to meet him in fifteen minutes."

By the time Conrad got off the phone, Gilbert had the information from the directories.

"You won't believe this, Jim. This guy lives in a good neighborhood and according to the city directory, he is on the faculty at Danville High School. I checked back for three years and he's in there as a faculty member every time." Conrad's only "comment" was a raised eyebrow.

Sheriff Walt Wolford was in his third four-year term as sheriff of Vermilion County. He was popular with his employees and deputies. His margin of victory grew in each election. Jim Conrad had been instrumental in getting Wolford selected to attend the prestigious FBI National Academy at Quantico, Virginia during his second term. At the academy career police officers from around the nation received twelve weeks of intensive training in the latest and most sophisticated law enforcement techniques.

An important by-product of the National Academy was the camaraderie that developed among the participants and between them and the FBI. This friendship was reinforced at an annual re-training session for all National Academy graduates within each FBI Field Division. The overall result was a spirit of trust and cooperation between law enforcement agencies that was invaluable in the war against crime. Jim Conrad knew he could count on Sheriff Walt Wolford to give him an accurate evaluation of William A. Patrick if he knew him. If he didn't know him, he would know someone who did.

Jim Conrad and Brad Gilbert were well-known at the Vermilion County Sheriff's Office. They came by at least once a week. Usually it was to run a criminal records check on a suspect in a federal crime or as a part of a background investigation on an applicant for a federal job. They usually said "hello" to the sheriff if he was in.

"Good morning, Mrs. Goldman." Jim Conrad said to the sheriff's long-time secretary. After a hundred attempts, she had given up asking Conrad to call her Phyllis. Conrad retained his southern deference toward women.

"He's waiting, Jim. You don't normally call for an appointment. This must be a biggie," she smiled. "Hello, Brad."

"Hello, Phyllis."

Conrad bowed and said, "We will just go on in then; thank you, ma'am," as he walked around her desk. Gilbert followed.

Sheriff Wolford was a big man. Not quite as tall as Conrad but broad of shoulder with a size eighteen collar. During his twelve weeks at the National Academy he had lost twenty pounds and came back looking younger and feeling better than he had in years. The regular hours and a daily exercise routine did wonders for him, but they didn't change his job. When he returned to his normal routine of twelve to sixteen hour days, eating breakfasts of bear claws and coffee in his car and an occasional chicken fried steak with the boys at the local diner at two in the morning after a stakeout of a suspected burglar, the pounds came back.

"What's up, Jim?" Wolford said as he rose and extended a beefy hand to Conrad and nodded toward Gilbert. The sheriff made friends slowly but solidly. The young agents moved in and out so rapidly he hardly ever got to know their names. Conrad was a fixture.

"Y'all sit down," said the sheriff.

Conrad was happy to oblige. Gilbert remained standing.

"Walt, we have a serious situation that must be handled quickly but delicately. A young girl's life is at stake. I will just hit the high spots here. We had a kidnapping in Springfield, Missouri, a few days ago. They took a sixteen-year-old girl from her home. They later demanded and got a big ransom payment. Our agents in Missouri recovered a rental truck that was used in the ransom drop. It was rented in Tulsa the day after the kidnapping by a man using a Tulsa address but an Illinois driver's license. The license is listed to a man who lives here in Danville."

That was all Wolford needed. "Who the hell is it?" he growled.

"Walt, you understand we must keep this tight until we learn the status of the girl?"

"Yes, dammit, Jim, I understand that. Tell me who it is and I'll help you."

Conrad paused and then almost whispered, "The driver's license is issued to William A. Patrick, 935 East Walnut Street here in Danville."

Even before Conrad finished his sentence, Wolford was out of his chair. He said, "I know you're not kidding me, Jim, but there's got to be some mistake. That guy is Mr. America around here. His driver's license must have been stolen."

"We checked NCIC by name and number. The computer has no stolen report on it. It's not in there."

Wolford, still standing, said, "Do you know who William A. Patrick is?"

Gilbert spoke up, "We looked him up in the city directory. It shows him as a member of the Danville High School faculty for the past three years and…"

"You damn right. He is one of our fair-haired boys here. He was a great athlete in high school. He went to college at Drake University on a track scholarship. His family has been here forever. He goes to the same church I do. I think he was an Eagle Scout. He almost made the Olympic team. He married his high school sweetheart. His parents are upstanding people. I just know, Jim, that there is a mistake here somewhere. Next to Dick and Jerry Van Dyke, he's the most famous person Danville has ever produced, and on top of that, he is a hell of a track coach."

"Okay, Walt, I believe you. That's the reason we came to you. I figured you would know him. We need to figure out a way to verify where he was on a couple of key dates without contacting him. We just can't take a chance on talking to him until we know he was not involved. By the way, the father of the girl is the only one who saw the kidnappers. He thinks they were black men. Is this guy black?"

"Hell, no. That ought to be good enough for you right there."

Conrad continued, "But the people in Tulsa, where he rented the truck, described him as a white male, 6'4", slender, blond hair, thirty-three to thirty-nine years of age."

As Conrad read the description from the fax, Wolford sank back down into his chair, "By God, Jim, you have described Billy Patrick to a T. I just can't believe that boy would be involved in anything like that. Let me think here a minute. I know his wife's folks real well, but they might not be able to keep it quiet if I started asking about him. They might not even know where he was anyway.

"Let's see, a couple of those days were school days. They would sure know in the school office if he wasn't at school. They would have had to hire a substitute. The principal out there is new. I know him, but he hasn't been around here long enough for me to know how he thinks. I don't want to get Billy Patrick in any trouble just by asking about him…Hey, I know how I can find out! The wife of one of my deputies works out there in some clerical capacity. I'll bet she could find out if he was out of school on any of those days. What do you think?"

"Is the deputy on duty?"

"No, he works nights. He would be at home now, but he's probably asleep."

"Do you know his wife well enough to call her at work? I'd like to involve as few people as possible."

"Yeah, I know…he, the deputy, has been with me since the beginning of my second term…Yeah, I could talk to her. I'll tell her it's important that she keep it quiet. Let's see now, all we need to know is if Bill Patrick was at school on Thursday and Friday of last week. That's April second and third, is that right? That's all we need to know?"

"Yes, that's right, but please impress upon her that the information must be accurate. We're going to base our next action on what she tells you. We must not make a mistake."

The sheriff got through to Debbie Sue Gardner without identifying himself to the switchboard. Debbie was cordial and after a bit of small talk about her husband, the sheriff explained what he needed to know. He put heavy emphasis on the need for accuracy and confidentiality.

Debbie said she knew where the information was filed, but it would take her a few minutes to look it up so she would call back when she had it.

While they were waiting Conrad asked, "By the way, Walt, what kind of car does Patrick drive?"

"I don't know off-hand but we can look it up. It won't be any-thing too fancy. He's a low-profile guy. Why do you ask?"

"The people at the truck rental said he was driving a red Corvette, late model."

"Naw, I can't believe that."

Wolford picked up his phone and pressed intercom. "Phyllis, get me a DMV check on William A. Patrick. Thanks."

"Did you ever know him to be a motorcycle enthusiast? Maybe a Harley Davidson man?"

"Hell no. I'd almost bet you on that. For one thing, he's never had enough money, and he was always so involved with sports. Maybe when he was in college, but I doubt it. He's just not the type. The DMV report will show it if he has a motorcycle but I'd sure be surprised. Why?"

"The people at the truck rental said his Corvette had some kind of sticker on the back. Maybe a Harley Davidson sort of winged thing."

Wolford chuckled and said, "I don't know about any winged thing but I can just about guarantee you he doesn't have a Corvette to stick it on."

Phyllis Goldman tapped lightly on the door and entered with the DMV report. She handed it to Wolford without a word and departed wiping her hands in an unconscious gesture that said, "I deny any knowledge of this."

Wolford looked at the report and said, "One 1988 Chrysler LeBaron, VIN such and such registered to William A. and Sarah L. Patrick. One 1985 Nissan pickup registered to William A. Patrick." He looked up, "No Harleys, no Corvettes."

The intercom clicked and Phyllis said, "Debbie Gardner for you on line one."

Debbie reported that Billy Patrick was in school and on duty on Thursday, April second and Friday, April third. There were no sub-stitute teachers in any classroom at the high school level on those dates. Wolford felt compelled to ask her if she was certain the info was accurate. She simply said, "Yes." Then she followed up with, "I also clearly remember we had a track meet here last Friday. He was in here a couple of times during the morning trying to line up people to be finish-line judges and timers."

Sheriff Wolford said, "Tell your husband you have been doing his work while he was sleeping. Thanks, Debbie."

"Gentlemen, if I understand the situation, Billy Patrick couldn't be one of your kidnappers because he isn't the right race, and he wasn't in Springfield, Missouri, on the day in question. And, he didn't rent the truck because he wasn't in the State of Oklahoma when it was rented."

Conrad said, "But his driver's license was there. Why? I think we need to talk with Mr. Patrick right away, but I'll have to let the big wigs make that decision."

Conrad and Gilbert headed back to the RA to call Vince Trainor. While en route, Conrad, in his teaching mode said, "It's impossible to estimate the value of a contact like Walt Wolford. With one phone call he resolved most of the questions about William A. Patrick. Only a local law enforcement man who knows his constituents could have done that. Whatever it costs us to send people like him to the National Academy, it pays off many times over. They learn we are all in this fight together. Some agents never learn that. I know you can see it, Brad, because you used to be on the other side of it."

Vince Trainor, on the phone, agreed with Jim that Patrick could not be directly involved in the kidnapping. He said, however, that the decision on whether or not to contact him must be made by the Office of Origin, Kansas City, "I'll get the answer and get back to you."

"In the interest of time, Vince, Brad and I will head on out toward the high school. We will stand by on Channel Two. The radio is not always reliable at that distance. If I haven't heard from you in thirty minutes, I'll land-line you."

Conrad and Gilbert were only three blocks from the office when the dispatcher came on. "SI-24, SI-3 requests that you land-line him for instructions."

"Ten-four, Springfield."

"Damn that was quick," said Conrad, "but the answer must not be a no. He could have said no on the radio."

Conrad found a pay phone at an Exxon station. He called collect and was transferred to Vince Trainor.

"Yeah, Vince, what's up?"

"Jim. I talked with the Kansas City SAC, Paul Palmer, who is running the show down in Springfield, Missouri. He is naturally concerned about this lead because it's about all they have going. He agreed with your reasoning that Patrick could not be one of the kidnappers, nor could he have rented the truck. But he wants to make sure you pursue the angle that Patrick might have let a friend use his driver's license. Pin him down on that. If Patrick doesn't have a solid reason as to why that license was being used by someone else, have him sign a polygraph consent form. We want him on the polygraph today."

"Okay, Vince, I see their point. It's all they have, so they want to get something out of it one way or another. We'll do our best. Course the guy doesn't even have to talk to us."

"Right, but I told Palmer we had the best man in the division on it, and if the guy knows anything, you'll get it."

"Get out of here, Vince."

School was just letting out when Conrad and Gilbert arrived at the campus. Both had been here before to check high school records on applicants for employment with the Bureau in clerical positions. Gilbert had recently interviewed a teacher whom an applicant had used as a personal reference. When a teacher had to be interviewed during the school day, it was Bureau policy to go through the principal's office and conduct the interview during the teacher's break so as not to disrupt the school routine. Since school was out, Conrad decided to go directly to the field house at the stadium located at the back of the parking lot. They found a door labeled office. Conrad knocked. There was an immediate, "Come on in."

Conrad entered, followed by Gilbert. The office was small. A man was sitting behind the only desk talking to another who was squatting beside him, taking notes. Neither looked up.

The walls were lined with bookcases with a filing cabinet between two of them. Every inch of the space above the bookcases and filing cabinet was covered with pictures of football and track teams sitting, kneeling, and standing in neat rows. There was an open door behind the desk leading into a noisy dressing room. Much of the noise was spilling into the office. There was a sign on the desk that read "Coach Patrick."

After several seconds the man behind the desk looked up and saw the suits and ties. "Oh, I'm sorry gentlemen, I was just going over the…"

Conrad broke in, "No problem. We didn't mean to interrupt. Are you William A. Patrick?"

"Yes, and this is Coach Taylor, Lyndon Taylor."

The office was so small there was no way to avoid introductions and handshakes all around. Neither Conrad nor Gilbert used their title or showed any identification.

"We need to speak with you, Mr. Patrick, on a personal matter. If this is not a good time, we can make it a little later, but we want to do it as soon as convenient."

"No, it's no problem. I was just going over the track practice schedule with Coach Taylor. Coach, you can go ahead and get them started. How long do you think this might take?"

Conrad could detect no anxiety in Patrick's voice or demeanor. He seemed relaxed, composed. *He probably thinks we are insurance salesmen,* Conrad thought. His answer was a vague, "I don't think it will take long."

Coach Taylor departed through the door behind the desk and closed it, shutting out most of the noise. Patrick was still standing. Conrad noted, *He's tall, at least six foot four, slender, blond hair, smiling. I can see why Wolford referred to him as their All-American boy or whatever it was.*

"How can I help you, gentlemen?" asked Patrick.

"Mr. Patrick, we are with the FBI. I am Special Agent James A. Conrad. This is Special Agent Brad Gilbert." Both agents pulled and showed their credentials.

Patrick was still standing and smiling. He said, "I thought Mr. Gilbert looked familiar. Weren't you out here a few weeks ago to talk with one of our teachers?"

"Yes. In the teachers' lounge." said Gilbert.

"Yeah, I saw you in the hall. We kidded her about that…asking her what kind of trouble she was in…you know. It's hard to keep a secret around the campus here," he laughed.

Conrad was observing Patrick during this exchange and thought, *This guy doesn't seem to have a worry in the world. But I've been fooled before.*

"May we sit down?"

"Oh, sure. Let me get another chair out of the dressing room." He disappeared.

Conrad looked at Gilbert, raised his eyebrows, and shrugged as if to ask, "Well, what do you think?"

Gilbert, still clinging to his hopes of a big case, said, "He sure fits the description of the guy that rented the truck."

"But we know he didn't do it. Right?"

"Yeah. Unless somebody messed up somewhere."

Patrick came in with a metal chair. He was still smiling. "I don't get too many visitors out here. It's a good thing. This is the world's smallest office, but it could be worse. I only have one assistant in track. Can you imagine what it's like during football season? There are four men on the staff, and we all use this same office."

Conrad was the first to sit down. He said, "We better get going on this so you can get back to your team. Mr. Patrick, do you have any idea why we are here?"

"No, sir," as he followed Conrad's lead and sat down. "I would guess it's about a former student that wants to go to work for the FBI."

Conrad said, "We want to question you about the kidnapping of a sixteen-year-old girl in Missouri."

Conrad studied Patrick as he said it. Patrick seemed genuinely shocked. *Was that the reaction of a person who had nothing to do with it?... Yes. But wasn't it also the reaction of a person who thought he had committed the perfect crime, only to realize the FBI suspected him?... Perhaps.* Conrad had learned long ago not to jump too soon. He continued, "Before we ask you any questions, I am required to remind you of your constitutional rights. I have a form here that sets out those rights. I want to read it to you, and I want you to follow along on the form as I read it. Okay?"

Patrick was no longer smiling. He looked perplexed as Conrad laid out the form on the desk and read the standard Miranda Advice of Rights form that anyone who has ever watched television has memorized. "Do you understand your rights?"

"Yes, sir. Did you say a kidnapping?"

"Yes. We'll get to that."

Conrad continued to read from the form, "Are you willing to answer questions now without an attorney?"

"Yes, but I sure won't have much to say. I don't know a thing about any kidnapping."

"All right, Mr. Patrick, this is the form we have both just read together. Here at the bottom is an acknowledgement that you have read this statement of your rights and had it read to you. And further that you understand your rights and are willing to answer questions. If you do understand your rights and are willing to answer questions, I would like for you to sign on this line and date it."

Patrick took the offered pen and signed without hesitation. Conrad signed as a witness and passed the form to Gilbert who also signed. "Agent Gilbert will first ask you some questions about your background and description."

Conrad hated this routine of following a form, asking questions about date of birth, residence, color eyes, color hair, height, weight, wife's name, children's names, etc. etc., ad infinitum, and he always let the first-office-agents do it. He knew it was valuable information for later reference, but that didn't make it any more interesting to him. The new agents loved to do it, and it gave him a chance to observe the suspect and to formulate the key questions he would ask when it was his turn. Gilbert went through the form item by item.

Conrad was starting to sprawl in his eyelids at half-mast mode as he observed Patrick. *Could this man be involved in a kidnapping?* He doubted it. But he learned long ago that, although there are many things you can learn about people by talking with them, you can't base any of it on their looks. He had interviewed child murderers who looked like choir boys, serial rapists who looked like the boy next door. He once interviewed a bank robber who looked exactly like his own brother.

When Gilbert finished with the background and description form, Conrad asked, "What kind of cars do you own?" He always liked to start with a question that he knew the answer to.

"I…we, my wife and I, own a 1988 Chrysler LeBaron and a 1985 Nissan pickup."

"What color?"

The LeBaron is white, the pickup is red. What is this all about?"

"Do you own a motorcycle?"

Patrick laughed and said, "Heck, no. I've only been on one once. I rode double with a guy in college and every time he turned I thought the thing was going to skid out from under us. No, I think too much of my legs to ride one of those death traps."

Conrad moved his chair a little closer to the desk and asked, "May I see your driver's license?"

Patrick reached for his billfold and said, "I'm carrying a temporary. I'm waiting for mine to be reissued."

"Reissued? What happened?"

"Well, it's kind of a strange story. My wife and I went to Branson, Missouri—you know, the country music place—a couple of weeks ago on the long weekend we had. On the second night we were there we went to the Shoji Tabuchi show. The place was packed. It was a great show. Did you ever see that guy? He is fantastic.

"Well, after the show, Shoji invited anyone who wanted an autograph to hang around. My wife wanted to get his autograph so we waited around, and he came right down to where we were and we got his autograph. He is a super guy. We were just about the last to leave. There was one guy hanging around just watching. He didn't even ask for an autograph. He looked kind of familiar. I thought maybe he was a bodyguard for Shoji.

"When we got outside the theater, the parking lot was still emptying. We had parked way in the back. As we neared our car, a big blue Cadillac drove up behind us and sort of pinned us in the corner of the lot. I turned toward it and this man, the same one I saw hanging around inside the theater, jumped out and grabbed me. He was a big burly guy, strong. He said, 'Give me your billfold.' I remember thinking that he didn't look like a robber. He said it again, 'Give me your billfold.' I was saying, 'Okay, okay' but he was bear-hugging me so hard I couldn't do anything.

"My wife was petrified. She didn't scream but kept saying, 'Please, please don't hurt us.' The driver finally got out and reached in my back pocket and got my billfold while the big guy held me. The big guy sort of threw me down by my front bumper. The little guy said, 'Come on. I got it.' They jumped in their car and left. They didn't look like robbers, and you know the funny thing? I don't carry any credit cards, and I only had about ten dollars in my billfold.

My wife handles all the money and makes all the major purchases. She had a Visa and a Discover card and about two hundred dollars in her purse, and they didn't even go near her."

Conrad, who had been taking notes, asked, "How did they get away in all that traffic?"

"You know, that's another thing. If you've been there, you know how Branson is just scattered all over everywhere. Well, they just drove off across the back of the lot, not in a real hurry, and they drove across a small ditch in that Cadillac right out into this sort of field. Then they turned and went behind a restaurant next door and disappeared. They knew their way around."

"Did you call the police?"

"Yeah…Well, I didn't, but a guy waiting in line to get out of the parking lot saw what was happening. He called 911 on his car phone. He came over and got my name to give to the police. I don't know who he was. He didn't wait around. Nice guy, though."

"Did you make a report to the police?"

"Yeah, finally. It took the police twenty-five to thirty minutes to get there. You know how that traffic is in Branson if you've ever been there."

"Did you get a tag number?"

"All you policemen ask that," Patrick chuckled. "They did, too; in Branson, I mean. My wife is a license plate watcher. She likes to see how many different states she can see as we drive along. She keeps a list. Branson is a good place for tag watching. She got about twenty-five on that trip. Well, anyway, my wife said the car didn't have a front tag. As they drove off she saw a tag on the rear."

Gilbert couldn't wait, "Did she get it?"

Conrad scowled.

Patrick grinned, "Yeah. Arkansas."

"Did she get the number?"

"Naw. Just the state. Arkansas."

Conrad said, "Tell us again about the car. How sure are you about it?"

"Well, it was definitely a big, dark blue, four-door car and… yeah, it was a Cadillac, late model. I just can't see it being anything else."

"All right. Now let's have a good description of the men."

"I gave all of that to the Branson Police, but I'll tell you again if it will help. The main man, the one that grabbed me, was a big burly guy. He looked like a shot putter. Know what I mean? He was about six foot even, two hundred thirty pounds, dark hair, no facial hair but a five o'clock shadow. Big strong arms."

"How old?"

"Oh, I'd say he was about forty. By the way, he had a deep strong voice. 'Give me your billfold.'"

"How was he dressed?"

"I'd say nice. He didn't look like a robber. Maybe a business man. He didn't have on a tie but a nice suit, open collar. My wife said he had those tassels on his shoes. She notices things like that."

"What about the other guy?"

"The driver? Well, I didn't see as much of him, but he was a much smaller, wiry guy; a pole vaulter, maybe. Know what I mean? Five foot eight, 145 pounds, black hair, also about forty, maybe a little younger I guess, but I really don't know. He had sort of a high-pitched voice, 'Let's get out of here.' He seemed more nervous than the big guy."

"These were white guys?"

"Yeah, sure. You don't see any blacks in Branson. It's not their kind of music I guess, but Charlie Pride has a theater there, and he does all right. I like his show."

Conrad said, "Do you think you could pick the two men out of a line-up?"

"Gosh, I don't know. Maybe the big guy. I'd have to see. I didn't see them for long, but I was sure close to them."

"What dates were you in Branson?"

"Well, let's see. Here's a calendar. It wasn't this past weekend but the one before that. That would have been...We had Thursday and Friday off for Spring break. We, my wife and I, drove to Branson on Thursday. We spent Thursday, Friday and Saturday nights. We had a package deal at the Grand Palace Hotel down there, including some show tickets. We came home on Sunday."

"So this robbery took place on what night, Saturday?"

"Yeah, that would be right. It was our last night there. Let's see on the calendar here. It would have been the twenty-eighth, March twenty-eighth."

Conrad said, "Look at your calendar there and tell me where you were on Thursday, April second."

"That was just last Thursday." Patrick looked at the calendar. "Well, it's not on here, but I know I was here because we had our first dual track meet here against Kankakee. They came down here and whupped us good. We've got a long way to go. Oh, by the way, there's the track schedule up there on the bulletin board."

"Okay, I see it. What about Friday afternoon; last Friday afternoon. Where were you?"

"Just this last Friday afternoon? Let me see. This is Monday. Well, I was here at school. We had a light track workout after school. Oh, I know, my wife and I went over to Coach Taylor's place that night to play Canasta. We got in late. I was almost late for my Boy Scout troop meeting the next morning."

Conrad started putting his note pad away. "Thank you for your time, Mr. Patrick. We will check out your story with the Branson Police Department. You wouldn't happen to remember the officers' names would you?"

"No, sir, I don't...Uh, is that all there is to it? I mean, surely the FBI is not investigating a ten dollar robbery. You said something about a kidnapping."

"Mr. Patrick, your driver's license was used to rent a truck. The truck was used in a kidnapping. If the story you have told us is true, and we will check it out, then the two men who robbed you were probably the kidnappers."

"Holy cow. Well, I told you they didn't look like robbers."

Conrad couldn't resist, "Did they look like kidnappers?"

The sarcasm went over Patrick's head and he answered seriously, "No, like I said, they looked, well the big guy anyway, like a businessman."

"May I use your phone to check in with our office?" asked Conrad.

"I'm sorry, sir, we don't have a phone here anymore. We used to, but we couldn't get anything done for having to answer it. You know, parents calling about when Junior would be home, girlfriends calling during team meetings, prank calls. You name it. It was a mess."

"Okay, we will be on our way then," said Conrad.

Patrick followed them out of the office door and said, "You guys are lucky. I'll bet being an FBI Agent is exciting work."

Conrad answered, "Well, yes it is at times, but there is a lot of routine, even boring, work too, and a lot of paperwork. We've generated enough paperwork today to keep us dictating until late tonight and most of tomorrow."

Gilbert joined in as Patrick walked with them toward their car, "I'll bet coaching track is pretty interesting too, and I've heard you are good at it."

"Naw, there's nothing to it if you have the right athletes. I just put them out there on the track and tell them, 'Keep to the left and get back as soon as you can.'" Patrick laughed so hard at this that even Conrad finally joined in.

They shook hands. Gilbert gave Patrick his card and said, "If you think of anything else that might have a bearing on this, give us a call. Agent Conrad can be reached at the same number."

Patrick said, "Well, there is one more thing. I wasn't going to mention it because when I told the policemen in Branson they scoffed at the idea."

Gilbert said, "What's that, Mr. Patrick?"

"I believe those guys that robbed me had been following me earlier in the day."

Conrad joined in, "Why do you think that?"

"My wife and I had been going through those shops in the Grand Palace shopping mall. It's not really a mall but a bunch of individual shops right next to the Grand Palace Theater and Hotel there in Branson. You know, we were in one shop for a few minutes and then into another. After a while, I noticed these two guys because they kept looking at us and not buying anything or even looking at any of the merchandise, you know souvenirs and things. I thought maybe they were, maybe, you know, scoping out my wife; she's a real looker, you know. But they seemed to be looking more at me. Well, anyway, I didn't think too much more about it until the robbery, and I believe it was the same two. Like I said, I told the Branson police, but they didn't seem to think too much of it. It seemed strange to me too, but I wanted to let you know."

Conrad said, "It does seem strange. From what I've heard of Branson there would have been thousands of marks to choose from, many of them senior citizens and some flashing big bankrolls. Why did they pick you out? How long after you spotted them at the Grand Palace did the robbery take place?"

"Well, we went to eat right after we left the shopping area. We walked over to McGuffey's. Boy is that good food! That took a little over an hour. Then we came back and got the car and drove out to the theater. I think the show started at 8:00 P.M. and, counting the intermission and the autograph session, it was a good two hours. I would say that it was three and a half to four hours from the time I noticed them watching me until the big guy jumped me in the lot."

Conrad thanked Patrick again as they reached their car. Conrad made notes on the last revelation before starting the car. They watched Patrick jogging toward the track to join his team. Conrad said, "Brad, I'll bet my badge Mr. Patrick is not involved in the kidnapping, but I'll bet you a hundred dollars the guy who rented the truck looks a lot like him. Here's what we want to do, I'll drop you at your car and I'll go on to the office and get started on a teletype to Kansas City. I want you to go directly to Patrick's house and interview his wife. Just hit the high spots. Ask her first about the robbery. Get everything she can remember about the two guys. What they looked like. What they said. Ask about the car and tag. Ask about the police report. You know what we need. Enough to verify his story about the driver's license. Her description of the guys and the car are the most important things, of course." Conrad then grinned and said, "If she says, 'What trip to Branson? We didn't go to Branson! What robbery are you talking about?' If she says that, Brad, just come on back here. I'll turn my badge and gun in to you and hit the road for Mississippi."

They both laughed. Gilbert said, "I do believe, old buddy, that I detect a bit of excitement in your voice."

Conrad said, "I'm just thinking about those guys in Springfield, Missouri. They have a missing girl. Her father is out $300,000 and is probably raising hell. They don't have any idea who the kidnappers are. Now, think about this, Brad. We are about to send them what is probably a description of the kidnappers, a good description of their car, and a likely description of the guy who rented the truck. It's not a lot, but when you don't have anything else it doesn't take much to revitalize the whole investigation. I am a little excited."

As Gilbert left he heard Conrad say, "I wonder how many dark blue four door Cadillacs there are registered in Arkansas?"

THE SUSPECT

Courage is not the towering oak, that sees the storms come and go; it is the fragile blossom that opens in the snow.

—Alice M. Swaim

The surveillance team's coverage of Tiger One's hour and fifty-one minute wait at the convenience store and their brief stay at the lumberyard produced an enormous amount of automobile tag information.

Second office agent Amos Trout, a member of the Kansas City surveillance team, was in charge of getting the data entered into the computer and analyzed. He was assisted by SA Lucille Baldwin, a first office agent who was his partner on the fixed surveillance.

SA Leland Fain from the Joplin RA was seated next to Ben Castle. As Trout set up his display Fain asked, "Have you worked with this guy Trout?"

"Naw, but I hear he's good," replied Castle, "He's as close to being a computer geek as you will find in the Bureau. He knows just about all there is to know about computers, but he has a tendency to flaunt his knowledge, particularly around the older agents, and sometimes he is a little long-winded. He's a hard worker though."

Trout had picked up the fixed surveillance reports and tapes from the other units when the mapcase was found. He and Baldwin returned to the office where he had his computer set up. SAC Palmer wanted the report ready for the all-agents' meeting scheduled for 8:00 A.M. Trout knew that if the data was properly entered on the preprinted forms he could scan it into the computer. He hoped he wouldn't have to make many manual entries.

Once he got the data in, the analysis was a cinch. The computer program only accepted time, tag number, state, site number and team number. After the data was entered, it was simple to set the desired sort criteria and let the computer do the work. Once the final sort was made, Trout had to look up any comments made by the crew, either on the written forms or on tape. He only had to find the comments on the sightings that met the sort criteria.

Trout and Baldwin got no sleep, but by 8:00 A.M. when SAC Palmer called the sleepy group to order, Amos and Lucy were ready. They had prepared an impressive chart showing all major arteries of the city, the two sites where Tiger One had been sent, and the position of each of the fixed surveillance vehicles in relation to those sites. They had prepared a handout for each agent showing the results of the computer analysis. Trout was eager to make his presentation. He was a little disappointed when he was not first on the agenda.

SAC Palmer opened the meeting by reporting the results of the trap-and-trace on the Kogan home phone. "Southwestern Bell security reported on the call received at 11:54 last night at the Kogan residence. They traced the call to a pay telephone in Berryville, Arkansas. The Little Rock office is sending an agent from Fayetteville over there this morning to check it out. For the information of agents not familiar with that area, Berryville is about thirty-five miles southwest of Branson, about seventy miles southwest of us here in Springfield. The call came through the same trunk as the first call. Any questions or comments?"

Amos Trout was immediately on his feet, heading for the charts. SAC Palmer said, "Just a minute, Amos, I know you are ready to go, but I have a few more remarks.

"We have been so scattered, some of you young people haven't met Lance Barron, the case agent. He's been living with the victim's parents since—when was it, Lance—last Thursday?"

"Right, Sir."

"I'm going to turn the briefing over to Lance. He'll be assigning leads and supervising the investigation from here on. He's been calling most of the shots, anyway. I have several things going in Kansas City that need my attention. I want to emphasize, however, that this case still has the highest priority, and we will commit whatever manpower and resources it takes to see it through to a successful conclusion. Okay, Lance."

Lance began, "I know all of you are tired after last night, but I haven't heard anyone complain. I appreciate that. I know all of you are concerned about the welfare of the young lady. More on that a little later.

"I will summarize the results of what little overt investigation we have been able to conduct. Unfortunately, at this point we have no suspects. Mr. Kogan's rival, Kline, and his employees, have been eliminated as far as being involved in the abduction. Leland and Larry handled that aspect, and did a good job of verifying alibis without causing too much speculation.

"We have looked at several disgruntled ex-employees of Kogan Air, some of whom have more than ample reason to retaliate, but, after checking work schedules, personnel files, criminal records, and credit reports for debt problems, no one has stood out as a suspect. Because of our belief that it would further endanger Jenny to have word of the kidnapping become generally known, we have not yet interviewed any current Kogan employees.

"As far as physical evidence, the police found a few fingerprints of value in Jenny's car. Unfortunately, she has never been fingerprinted so we don't know if all the prints are hers.

"The search of the area where Jenny's car was recovered was void of any physical evidence. However, its proximity to the area where a state trooper saw a dark blue Cadillac parked at about the right time, might be significant.

"We have three excellent tape recordings of incoming phone

calls, two to the Kogan's residence, and one to the pay phone last night. The originals are on their way to the lab for analysis. All three recordings are of the voice of Jenny Kogan, apparently reading from a script. The one exception was a man's voice on last night's tape. It was only the one word—'okay'—but the quality is good. I listened to copies of all three tapes, back to back, earlier this morning. I could hear no difference in voice quality or background noise. The three were probably recorded from the same place and, possibly, at the same time.

"I am concerned that they have not released her. They have had the money for, what, seven or eight hours now. They got away clean. I don't know why they would continue to hold her.

"We got no footprints or tire prints at the drop site last night. There were no fingerprints on the mapcase even though Mr. Kogan handled it several times without gloves before the drop. They must have wiped it clean before abandoning it.

"We did find six cigarette butts at the drop site, right in the northwest corner of the Western Wardrobe lot, all on the pavement within a four-foot radius, all Marlboros. Those will go to the lab for fingerprint and DNA testing.

"The crime scene fellows raised several good latents from the truck, and there were prints all over the garage door opener. The opener is new and a late model. I'll be assigning leads this morning to have it traced from the manufacturer.

"We had a professional welder look at the cutting torch job on the truck. He said it wasn't a difficult job, but in his opinion, it was not done by an amateur. I have assigned leads to contact every welding shop within a ten-county area. There were some good prints and numerous toolmarks on the plywood box. It was not professionally constructed.

"Ben Castle located the confidential numbers on the truck in record time, and we learned from Ryder that the truck belongs to one of their agencies in Tulsa. We anticipate Oklahoma City having the rental information soon…Those are the highlights so far. Are there any questions?"

Lance was forcing himself to be upbeat. He hoped his fatigue didn't show. There must have been questions, but no one wanted to be the first to speak. Finally, Corporal Vickers, who still felt a little out of place, spoke up. "That guy Summerfield, the driver for Regent Furniture that reported his tag stolen; he's a bad actor."

"Oh, yes, I overlooked him, Don. What did you find out?"

"He did some time for burglary. He walked on a couple of possession of stolen goods charges. He also has some DWIs. I've got his picture and rap sheet here."

"Good. Thank you, Don. Let me have that and I'll assign it. We do need to get him interviewed."

Lance looked around, "Anything else?…Okay, show us what you have, Amos."

Agent Trout was offended to be so far down on the agenda, but he approached the chart with a pointer in his hand and a spring in his step. He first pointed out the Kogan residence, and the location of the Git and Go at Battlefield and National, "To get you all oriented," he said. Then, referring to his report, he proceeded, "During coverage of the first site, Tiger Six, the team of SA Linda Loring and SA James Bently, was positioned here, in the Battlefield Mall parking lot, across the street from the Bombay Restaurant. Their position was just west of the intersection of East Battlefield Road and South Glenstone Avenue; one of the busiest intersections in Springfield, and barely five blocks from the drop site. From the time of their arrival at the location, at 11:39 P.M., until their departure for the next site at 12:40 A.M., the team recorded 106 tags, with some automobile and/or operator descriptive data on approximately half of them. Most of the cars they spotted were moving westbound on Battlefield road."

Trout, known by his fellow agents as having a flair for the dramatic, was making the most of this opportunity to address the whole contingent. He was openly ambitious, and since his selection for the surveillance team, he had become the unofficial leader and spokesman for the group. He took advantage of every opportunity to trumpet their accomplishments which were impressive. Amos was popular with the young agents, but a little too eager for some of the seasoned heads.

Trout said, "I found it interesting, and proof of the effectiveness of the system, that one of the cars Tiger Six logged in during their first ten minutes was a silver Cadillac, Missouri tag number SPT-909. This was only one of the 106 tags they recorded, but if they had run a registration check on it, they would have found it registered to Mr. Charles Kogan, 2868 South Martin, Springfield, Missouri, the father of the victim."

SAC Palmer, who had had only three more hours sleep than Trout, said, "Okay, Amos, let's get on with it."

"Yes, sir. Sorry, I just wanted to…"

"Okay, Amos, we know your group did a great job. Let's just get on to the numbers that mean something."

Trout, unfazed, plowed on, "Tiger Three, SA Judith Meyers and SA Gretchen Gould, operating a 1988 Nissan Pickup, Ozarks Edition, complete with SMSU Bears stickers, positioned themselves here, west of the convenience store. Their site was in a strip mall which featured a late-night bar and restaurant on the south side of Battlefield Road just east of its intersection with South Campbell Avenue."

Trout pointed out each location as he mentioned it. "During the fifty-eight minutes they were in position, they recorded ninety-one tag numbers, most of them eastbound on Battlefield Road."

Amos couldn't resist another aside, "Their tape-recorded information included, in addition to the ninety-one tag numbers and some descriptive data, a recording of their conversation with two slightly inebriated and high-spirited college lads who tried to pick them up. Gretchen finally had to leave the vehicle, show her credentials, and create an instant story about an impending rendezvous with the Springfield Police Department on a drug case. The two young men were drunk enough to buy the story, and sober enough to realize it was a no-win situation. They left laughing."

This brought a laugh, and a little applause, from the sleepy group. Palmer smiled, "You're not required to be entertaining, Amos, just informative."

Trout went on, "The third surveillance unit, Tiger Five, was assigned to the south quadrant. SA Lucille Baldwin and yours truly picked a spot at the intersection of South National Avenue and Primrose Street. This stretch of National Avenue is called the Medical Mile for reasons that became obvious when we saw the buildings on either side of the broad thoroughfare. The intersection we chose adjoined the parking lot of Cox Medical Center. The other three corners of the intersection were also occupied by clinics or other medical facilities. We chose this spot because of its proximity to the James River Expressway, and because it was controlled by a stoplight. We could read tags from cars going north on National and east on Primrose. From our arrival at 11:45 P.M. until our departure for the second location, we recorded a total of forty-six tags with some descriptive data on most."

Palmer stirred, cleared his throat and frowned, but didn't say anything.

Leland Fain turned again to Castle and whispered, "I see what you mean. Wake me up when he gets to the good part."

"The fourth surveillance unit, Tiger Four, covering the north sector, chose a location right about here, at the intersection of National Avenue and Sunset. Robert McMahen was in this unit with Mike Toliver. They backed into the driveway of a vacant house. With binoculars they could read the tags of southbound cars that stopped at the intersection and some northbound cars. They could not read eastbound or westbound cars on Sunset unless they turned northbound. During the 115 minutes they spent there they recorded fifty-three tags."

Palmer, seated on the back row, cleared his throat again, and when Amos looked his way, Palmer gave him a circling forefinger in the air. Amos started to get the word.

"At 1:40 A.M. all four units moved toward the second site, here. By prior agreement they took up the same relative positions, that is, the same quadrants, as at the first site." Amos decided he better forego pointing out each location.

"Tiger Three, which had the west quadrant, was in position for twenty-nine minutes, and only recorded three automobiles. Tiger Four, in the north quadrant was the busiest, recording fifteen automobiles in twenty-three minutes. Three of the cars they recorded were police cars."

Palmer sprang to his feet. "Okay, Amos, we appreciate all the extra detail, but we have a lot to cover. Let's get to the analysis."

Amos got the point. "The other two units also recorded low numbers. The fixed surveillance ended at 2:17 A.M. when the rental truck left the lumberyard and went east on Trafficway.

"Now, if you will check your handout, you will see that the surveillance teams logged in 328 vehicles." Famous Amos was finally getting to the good stuff.

"On our first sort, we eliminated all automobiles that were only logged in one time. That left us with seventy-four vehicles that were seen two or more times. As you can see on your analysis sheet, ten cars were logged in four or more times, thirty-five were logged in three times, and forty-nine were logged in two times. Because of the distance between the two sites, and the vast difference in the type of neighborhoods represented, we decided that the most significant factor was those cars that appeared at both sites. We sorted for that factor, and found, as you can see..."

"Excuse me, sir." It was Millie Morgan, Lance Barron's secretary, "I'm sorry to interrupt, Mr. Palmer, but SAC Berger from Oklahoma City is on the phone for you. He said it is urgent."

"Okay, Amos, let's all take a short break, and we will pick up right there."

Lance decided this was an ideal time to rescue Amos from himself. He found him, and complimented him on his detailed analysis of the fixed surveillance. "You were just getting to the cars that were spotted at both sites. How about going on with your report so I can get the assignments made, and we can start getting those people identified and interviewed."

"Okay, Lance, sure, if you think the boss won't mind."

"He won't mind, Amos…I guarantee it."

Lance motioned, and the other agents followed him and Amos to the chart. Amos said, "There were only six cars that were seen at both sites. I reviewed the tape and written records for comments on those cars. The most promising one is Missouri tag ERT-768 which was seen a total of four times, twice at each site. At all four sightings the comment was 'Red Corvette.' At one sighting the comment also included, 'White male.'

"The second vehicle, Missouri tag PAC-690 was seen twice at the first site and once at the second site. The only comment was 'Gray, Sports Utility Vehicle.'

"Missouri tag BIP-324 was seen once near the convenience store and twice at the lumberyard. The comment was 'old model Chevy, black.'

"Arkansas tag YYT-901 was seen once at each site. The comment at the first site was 'blue, Cad, two people.' At the second site 'Caddy, dirty, dark color.'

"Missouri tag DOS-486 was seen once at each site. The comment at one site was, 'small pickup; two guys.'

"The final vehicle, Missouri tag MAC-485, was also seen once at each site. The only comment was 'big green, four-door.' Those are the six, Lance, that were seen at both sites. If I might make a suggestion," he said, turning to address the congregation, "the persons doing the investigation on these six cars should review the original surveillance logs, and take notice of the times and places where the sightings were made. That is not shown on my chart, and it is important. If the suspect says he was just passing through, and the log shows him south of the site at a specific time and north of the site five or six minutes later, he probably was just passing through. But, if the times and places he was sighted show that he was driving all around the place, he should have some explanation for that."

Lance agreed, "That's a good point, Amos. Let's all make sure we get that information from Amos before we go out. Amos, how about you and Lucy taking that one on the red Corvette. He seemed to be getting around a lot." Lance knew Amos would be flattered to get the assignment on the most promising car developed by "his team."

Lance made the other four Missouri tag assignments, and reminded them to check with Amos for the additional time and quadrant information before going out. Finally he said, "Corporal Vickers, how about you taking the Arkansas tag? You people have a more direct contact with the out-of-state DMVs."

Lance was assigning welding shop leads to other agents when SAC Palmer came back all smiles. When the group had settled down, he said, "It looks like we might have gotten a break. That was the SAC from Oklahoma City. The truck was rented in Tulsa by a William A. Patrick, using an Illinois driver's license and a local Tulsa address. Oklahoma City has already set a lead in Illinois on the driver's license, and they are checking out the Tulsa address. The driver's license is not in the computer as stolen.

"The people at the Ryder agency gave a good description of the guy's car. It was a late model red Corvette…" Palmer paused as a rumble went through the group, "What's up?"

Lance said, "One of the vehicles we picked up on the fisur was a red Corvette. We have the tag, but we haven't run it yet."

"Was it an Oklahoma tag?"

"No. Missouri."

"The Ryder people said Patrick's car definitely had Oklahoma tags. That is a real coincidence, though. They went on to say the car had some sort of wings sticker on the back window. They made a big deal over it being a Harley Davidson sticker, but it wasn't the right color, and the guy, Patrick, wasn't the biker type. They said it was a blue or gold set of wings of some kind.

"OKC already set an urgent lead for whoever covers Danville, Illinois, to locate Patrick and put him under surveillance. The secretary at the Ryder Agency thinks she can identify him.

"Now, let's get back to the fixed surveillance. Go ahead, Amos."

"Just a minute, Mr. Palmer, before we go on." It was Loyal Lambright in the back of the room. "That sticker on the fellow's Corvette; what color did you say it was?"

Palmer checked his notes. "One guy, the mechanic, said he thought it was blue. The secretary said it might have been gold. What's your thinking, Loyal?"

"Oh, it's probably nothing, Boss, but I've got a sticker on my car, and at least a dozen times some smartass has asked me if I was a 'Sky Biker.' It looks enough like a Harley sticker to draw remarks, but it's blue and gold. Harley's are orange. Mine's from the AOPA."

"AOPA—what's that, Loyal?"

"The Aircraft Owner's and Pilot's Association…Here, I've got a set of their wings here on my navigation kit."

Lambright held the kit up so everyone could see the down-turned gold wings mounted on a dark blue background with a shield in the center, reading "AOPA since 1939."

A slight murmur went through the group. Palmer said, "By gosh, Loyal, you might have something there. You know what it makes me wonder?"

Lance and several others said, "Kline!"

"Right. I hope we didn't clear him too early."

"Or, one of Kogan's ex-employees," said Lance, "he's fired several pilots. I wonder if any were named Patrick? We need to check that out. I'll add that to the list."

Palmer asked, "Where is AOPA located, Loyal?"

"In Frederick, Maryland. I attended a survival course for Bureau pilots there several years ago. They have a nice facility. It's a fine organization. Most pilots are members."

"Frederick is just north of Washington, isn't it?"

"Yes, sir. It's closer to Washington, but it's covered by Baltimore."

Lance said, "We need to get someone out there right away to see if Patrick is a member. I still can't believe he's the guy, though. How stupid can you get? He didn't rent that truck with his own driver's license, and plan to take it back with a hole cut in the bottom. We might find Patrick dead somewhere, or else why didn't he report the truck stolen?"

"Or if someone stole Patrick's driver's license to rent the truck, why wasn't it in NCIC?" someone asked.

Lance continued, "Loyal, do you know anyone at Headquarters who would know someone at AOPA? We need to check out Patrick right away, and maybe get a list of their members."

"Well, George Ahrens is the Aviation Coordinator at FBIHQ. He hasn't been there long. He used to be in Kansas City, you know. He has set up a couple of training schools with AOPA."

Lance continued, "How about getting Ahrens on the phone, Loyal. See if he can get someone at AOPA to help us out. Follow up with a teletype if they need it. You know what we want."

"Yeah; do they have a member named William A. Patrick."

"Right. And a list of all their members in Oklahoma or maybe just the ones in the Tulsa area. I'm sure they can sort that way."

"Okay, Lance, I'll see what I can do…Should I tell him there is a life at stake?"

"I think that would be quite appropriate, Loyal."

Things had changed for Jenny. Yesterday she had spent several hours outside the box. Lady had brought her warm raisin biscuits and coffee for breakfast, and let her sit at the kitchen table while she ate. Lady mentioned the weather, and made small talk, asking Jenny what it was like being a cheerleader. She also asked about Jenny's brothers and sisters, and about her boyfriend. Jenny sensed that Lady was preoccupied, and not interested in the answers, but Jenny liked being out and talking, anyway.

At one point Lady said, "I wish my son could meet a girl like you, but..." she sighed, "that will never happen."

Lady left the table. Jenny heard her pacing behind her chair. "I'm afraid I have been played for a fool. I wish I had never gotten involved in this. It seemed like the only way..."

Jenny, uplifted by being out of the box, and emboldened by Lady's conversation, tried to keep it going. "Tell me about your son."

Her attempt at expanding the conversation had the opposite effect. "I'm not going to talk about it. I've said too much already."

A long silence followed. Lady got up several times, and went into what Jenny pictured as the front room. After a few minutes there, she would return to the kitchen and sit. Jenny thought of escape but she was still blindfolded. *Is Lady watching? I don't know where the back door is. Is there one?*

Finally Lady said, "I don't know what's going on. They were supposed to call Saturday, but they didn't. One was supposed to stay with you yesterday while I went to church and to visit my son. I made it to church, but I had to skip visiting my son and get back here."

So now it's Monday, Jenny thought, *Monday.* Jenny could not believe she had been locked up for only four days. It seemed so much longer. But she was encouraged by what Lady had said. Something must be happening. Maybe the end was in sight. She thought, *Freedom is relative, I guess. Being outside the box, and hearing someone talk, even Lady's guarded conversation, makes me feel like I'm already free.*

The freedom ended abruptly when Lady apologized, put her back into the box, and left.

When Jenny heard the departing automobile, she opened the lipstick she had been concealing in her hand since her last trip to the bathroom. She turned onto her left side, and in the darkness slowly printed along the joint where the left side of the box joined the bottom, "JENNY KOGAN, MONDAY." She wanted to add the date, but couldn't figure it out. Besides, the rough wood wore rapidly into the lipstick. Three words, printed small, used nearly all of it. *Why print another message, anyway? If I can't escape I, at least, should try and let someone know where I am. I have so much time to think, that's all I can think of to do. That and trying to remember as much as I can.*

For Jenny, these were small victories, but victories nonetheless.

Lady was not gone long this time. She came directly to the box and raised the lid. "Let's go to the kitchen, Jenny. I have your lunch. Did you hear the phone ring while I was away?"

"No." The question surprised Jenny because she had only heard the phone ring once the entire time she had been here. Maybe she couldn't always hear the phone from the box, or maybe Lady didn't get many phone calls.

Lady helped her up the steps. "Do you need to use the bathroom before you eat?"

"Yes, please. I'll only be a few minutes." Jenny returned the lipstick to the medicine chest, and then lifted her loosened blindfold enough to see her banner still flying from the window screen.

When Jenny finished she called to the lady. She was surprised when Lady said, "Come on out, Jenny. Let's take our food into the living room. There's a program on television I want to see, and I want to be close to the phone in case he calls. I'll have to leave your blindfold on, but you can at least listen to the TV, and maybe follow the program."

Lady guided Jenny to a sofa and eased her onto it. She moved a TV tray close and placed the food on it. Jenny recognized the usual

Hardee's burger, fries and milkshake. Not much variety, but she was happy to get it.

Jenny identified the TV station as KY-3 Springfield. She wondered if her story had made the news. She became excited when the station announced a "Newsbreak on the Hour," but the top story was about a Mafia figure being transferred to the Medical Center for Federal Prisoners so he could receive treatment for kidney stones. The announcer then went on to the accident reports. Jenny was trying to establish the time by what the announcer said when the phone rang. Lady turned the TV volume down.

Jenny didn't like eavesdropping, but she remained determined to learn and remember all she could.

Lady said, "Yes, sir. Yes I left the message. I had hoped you would call back yesterday. I'm sorry I bothered you on the weekend, but I had to let you know that we can't make it there Tuesday for our appointment…Well, I haven't been able to make the money arrangement I thought I would…I know, and I appreciate that, but that amount of money is, well, I don't…

"No, I haven't told him yet, but, well…he'll understand…No, he's had it since birth…He's fifteen."

"…That's kind of you. Let me get a pencil…Now, go ahead. One, eight hundred, seven, two, five, one, five, six, four. Yes, I've got it. Thank, you, I'll let you know. Bye."

Jenny heard Lady say, "I don't know how he thinks I will ever get twenty-five thousand dollars together."

Jenny tried to visualize the number, *1-800- no, forget that part! What was the rest of it? 725-1564. Was that it?* She realized Lady was talking to her.

"I'm sorry, Jenny, but I'm going to have to put you back in the… back downstairs. I hate to, but I've just got to go see my son. I can't keep this from him, and I'm not going to give him the word by phone. The trip is less than an hour each way, so I won't be gone too long."

Jenny said, "Before you take me down there, could you let me do some exercises here. I can do them with the blindfold on. I just need to do something physical. I feel so stiff and cramped up."

"Sure, honey, go ahead. You should have told me sooner."

And so Jennifer Marie Kogan, age sixteen, wearing her Glendale High School cheerleader uniform, did jumping jacks in the living room of her captors, and repeated to herself, time after time, *Seven, two, five, one, five, six, four. Seven, two, five, one, five, six, four. Seven, two, five, one, five, six, four.*

Jenny kept at it until Lady said, "Don't overdo it, Jenny. You don't want to hurt yourself. Besides, I have to go. I don't want to be out too late. I have to work again tomorrow."

"You're not going to leave me locked up all day again, are you? I don't think I can stand that." Jenny felt the panic returning for the first time today.

"It wasn't supposed to be this way. One of the guys was supposed to be here. I don't know what's happened to them. I'll tell you what. I'll stretch my lunch hour tomorrow, and come out to check on you, and I'll bring food."

In Tulsa, things were moving rapidly for Joel Karlis. Most investigators, sooner or later, have a case in which things almost magically fall into place. It is a rare occurrence, and should be enjoyed, because there might be a hundred dead-end leads before you get the magic again. Karlis was starting to believe his turn for the brass ring had come.

The Aircraft Owners and Pilots Association, in Frederick, Maryland, had faxed directly to the Tulsa RA, a list of all AOPA members in Tulsa County, Oklahoma. There were 348 members, active and inactive, on the list. Karlis scanned the alphabetized list, but found no William A. Patrick. Only then did he read the disclaimer in capital letters at the top of the message.

THIS LIST IS FURNISHED TO THE FBI FOR LAW ENFORCEMENT PURPOSES ONLY. IT IS NOT TO BE USED FOR ANY COMMERCIAL PURPOSE OR ANY PURPOSE OTHER THAN THAT NARROW PURPOSE SPECIFIED IN FBI LETTER TO AOPA DATED APRIL 6TH. AFTER BEING USED FOR THE SPECIFIED PURPOSE IT IS TO BE DESTROYED, AND THE AOPA IS TO BE SO ADVISED.

Karlis had been waiting for the list since being alerted by Lance Barron in Springfield that it was on the way. Karlis had already obtained a list from the local office of the Oklahoma Department of Motor Vehicles listing all Corvettes, two model-years old, or less, registered in Tulsa County. There were 175 Corvettes on the list. He quickly determined that none was registered to William A. Patrick.

Karlis then started to go through the list looking for red Corvettes only to find that the color was not one of the fields on the printout. He called back to the DMV, and reached the clerk he had dealt with, "Say, on this list I picked up down there a while ago, is there any way I can determine the color of the vehicles?" He was hoping there might be another field in the data base that was not printed out. The clerk, in all seriousness said, "Well, I guess you could call up the owners and ask."

Karlis bit his tongue and said, "Thanks." But to himself, *Gee, I wish I had thought of that.*

Karlis recalled an auto theft ring case he worked in conjunction with the Tulsa Police Department two years ago. In that investigation he learned that the Tulsa PD kept a computerized list of every car they encountered in their various law enforcement functions, whether for a parking violation, speeding ticket, automobile accident, tow-in, suspected use in a crime, suspected drug dealer, suspected hooker or a dozen other categories. In that data base, of course, the color of the car was a vital part of the record. Karlis called one of his main PD contacts, Corporal Bert Brucifer of the Major Crimes Unit, and asked him if he could check the PD base for late model Corvettes—red. Brucifer reminded him of the limitations of the list. "You recall, don't you, Joel, that it's not a complete list? It only contains those cars we put into the computer…"

Karlis interrupted, "Yeah, I know, Bert, but I feel lucky. I have a long list of possibilities. If I don't get a hit from your list, I can always go the long way around."

"Okay, Joel, I'll get right back to you. Are you in the office?"

"Yeah. Thanks, Bert."

Karlis was scanning the long DMV printout, wondering how many of the qualifying Corvettes were red when Brucifer called back. "Hey, Joel. I got that info. We only have seven red ones in our base, and one of them is five years old."

"Okay, Bert, give me the tag, owner's name, and address on each of them, please."

As Brucifer read the data, Karlis wrote it down, then checked the name against the AOPA members list. The fourth entry on the PD list was Oklahoma Tag BRD-943, Eldred James Scott, 2830 Calhoun Street, Tulsa, Oklahoma. Something in that information stirred Karlis's memory, but he couldn't quite pull it up. His mind was racing, and his breathing was shallow. He felt a tingling in his chest as he went down the AOPA list to the S's. And then, there it was! "E.J. 'Jack' Scott, AOPA member OK-#56345, 2830 Calhoun Street, Apartment #420, Tulsa, OK 74103." Karlis's mind flashed back to yesterday—the park at 2880 Calhoun and the rude little apartment manager at 2830. He could barely continue.

"What else do you have on that…that last one, Bert?"

"Let's see. On last December 23, the apartment manager at 2830 Calhoun, a Mr. Roland Rose, wanted the vehicle towed for illegal parking. An officer responded, but he took no action. His comment was, 'parking spaces inadequately marked.'"

Karlis forced himself to continue with the data on the other three red Corvettes. None of the names were on the AOPA list. He contained himself long enough to thank Bert Brucifer for his help. He also asked Brucifer to extend his compliments to whomever came up with the idea for the database. He then hung up the phone, and startled everyone in the squad room by yelling, "Yaaahoooo! Get your coat, Ed. We've got us a suspect."

Jenny was still asleep when Lady opened the lid. "I was late getting in last night, and I didn't want to wake you. That exercise must have done you in. I'm running late for work, but I'll take you up to the bathroom before I go if you'll hurry." Jenny couldn't believe she had slept until morning. She seemed to be sleeping more all the time. She wondered if that was a sign she was giving in. She fought that idea. *I must remember all I can. I must remember.*

She wanted to take time on her bathroom trip to check her window banner, but Lady was hurrying her. As they went down the steps to her cubicle Lady said, "I don't know what's going on with the guys, Jenny, but it's not going to go on much longer. I'm afraid I've been used and made a fool of, and I'm not going to take it. I'll decide what to do tonight, one way or the other."

Jenny felt a little excitement as she took her familiar position in the box, and heard the closing and securing of the lid. She started reciting her mantra of all the things she was going to remember, but in spite of her resolve, she soon fell asleep again.

Jenny did not hear the car arrive. She awakened to the sound of heavy footfalls and the banging of a screen door. There was a flurry of activity with a lot of walking around and going in and out. There was more than one person. She prayed it was not J.D. She struggled to get her blindfold tightened.

At last, after what she estimated was more than an hour, she heard the now familiar sound of tires on gravel subsiding as a car left. She was relieved at first, but then the old feeling of being trapped and alone returned. She fought it. *Lady would not run out on me. She would not leave me here alone…would she?* For the first time in her young life, Jenny thought about dying. *What if something went wrong and they thought they were set up, double-crossed?*

What if Daddy wouldn't give them what they wanted? Lady said she was going to end it one way or the other. Is this what she meant? No, she wouldn't do that. She's been kind to me...You fool! Don't forget, she's one of the kidnappers.

If they left me here, locked up, how long would it take to die? Does it hurt to die? I never thought of that before. If I'm going to die, I hope it doesn't take long. I'd rather die right now than to stay here alone any longer. At least I would die with my sanity.

Then Jenny sobbed out, "No, no, I don't want to die. Please, please, Lord Jesus. Don't let me die here in this box."

Jenny fought to control herself. *I think it has been two days since I cried. Let's see, Lady said yesterday was Monday so this is Tuesday. It was Thursday when it happened, wasn't it? So that would be...I've been here five days. That would be, let's see, Thursday, Friday, Saturday, no surely it wasn't Thursday. Yes it was, and today is Monday. Lady said it was Monday. No, that was yesterday when she said it was Monday? How many days?* She heard tires on the gravel again.

Lady came straight down to her. "Are you all right, Jenny? Did anybody bother you?"

Jenny sat up and Lady hugged her. "Are you all right, honey? They were here, weren't they? They didn't hurt you, did they?"

Why is Lady crying?

"I heard someone upstairs. They were here for a long time. I don't know who it was."

"They didn't hurt you?"

"No. They didn't come down here. I could hear them walking around, going in and out. What happened?"

"I've been such a fool, Jenny, and this proves it. I should never have listened to them. They have run out on me and I'm halfway glad. Ronnie, or someone, moved all of his stuff out today and they took a lot of my things, too. My TV, my stereo, a couple of my chairs. He even cleaned out the refrigerator. It serves me right. I never took a shortcut before, but Ronnie made it sound so easy.

But no matter what you think, Jenny, what anybody thinks, I didn't do it for myself. I don't want you to think I did it for myself, Jenny."

Lady was crying and speaking faster and faster. "I know I'm in bad trouble and I don't know what to do, but I'm so glad, Jenny, that they didn't hurt you. I'm going to start making up for my wrongs by letting you go. Jenny, you're going home!"

Jenny couldn't believe what she heard from this lady she had never seen. Just a little while ago she was ready to die and now she was going home? *Please don't let it be a cruel joke.*

"Did my daddy give them what they wanted?"

"I don't know, Jenny. He must have. But you're going home anyway. I'm going to see to that. Come on."

Lady helped Jenny over the side of the box. "I hope you will understand this, Jenny. I have to leave the blindfold on, but it won't be for long."

"We're leaving right now? Do you mean it?"

"Sure I do. Come on." Lady seemed to be more excited about this than Jenny, who was still afraid to believe it.

Lady helped her up the steps. Jenny declined the use of the bathroom. They made the right turn out of the kitchen and across the carpet to the front door just like Jenny remembered. Then they were on the porch and down three steps. Then through the sniffing dogs and across the gravel where Lady opened a car door and helped her in. Jenny thought, *This is a different car. She's using a stick shift and these are bucket seats.*

Jenny started to believe it was going to happen. She was going home. Her determination to remember all she could returned. She even predicted, in her mind, when the car would stop and Lady would get out to open the chainlink gate. Jenny smiled as the Lady got out again to close the gate after they had gone through. *So her goats wouldn't get out,* thought Jenny.

Jenny forced herself to try and remember the turns and the

times between them. *Where will Lady take me? Home? Not likely. Where?* She started to ask, but she was afraid it was all a dream and she didn't want to wake up.

Lady was now quiet after her previous animation. Jenny hoped she was not reconsidering. There had been no words spoken in what Jenny estimated to be a half hour since they left the house.

Jenny jumped when Lady said, "I'm going to take you to a pay phone. Here are several quarters. You should call your Mom and Dad. I have sunglasses and a hat I want you to put on over your blindfold. Please don't remove them until I am gone. Then you can make your call."

Jenny listened to the instructions. She found herself eager to obey whatever instructions Lady gave. She thought of something she learned in sociology class earlier this year. Psychologists had verified the existence of a strong natural tendency among hostages to bond with their captors. They called it the "Stockholm Syndrome" after an incident in Sweden in which it was first identified. It gained national attention in the United States in the Patti Hearst case. Was she experiencing that? She didn't know. She only knew she wanted to obey. She wanted to do exactly what Lady asked her to do.

Jenny heard heavy traffic and then the car came to a stop. She heard the clicking of the turn signal and then felt a right turn. There were two more stops that Jenny interpreted as stoplights, but no turns until the car slowed and made a sharp right turn and almost immediately stopped.

Lady said, "Here, put on your sunglasses and hat."

Lady left the engine running and the door open as she came around to Jenny's side of the car. She helped Jenny out, and with her hand on Jenny's arm, they moved forward on pavement. Jenny counted ten small steps before they stopped. Lady took Jenny's hand and placed it on the door of a telephone booth. She then moved close to Jenny and said into her ear, "Jenny, you are at the IGA Thriftway store on South Commercial in Branson. It is six-o-five P.M." She then pulled Jenny close in a strong embrace and said, "Please forgive me, Jenny." Then she was gone.

Jenny sat in the phone booth, gripping her handful of quarters, and sobbed. She could not have explained why. Finally, she removed the blindfold and recoiled at the glaring lights. But she quickly recovered and dialed home.

THE POLYGRAPH

"The wicked flee when no one pursues, but the righteous are bold as a lion."

—Proverbs 28:1

Special Agent John E. Reed was in his cubicle in the Oklahoma City Field office at 5:15 P.M. on Monday, April 6 when his boss, Special Agent in Charge Ralph Berger came in.

"Have you heard about the kidnapping over in Springfield, Missouri?"

Before Reed could answer, Berger went on, "They used a Ryder Truck that was rented in Tulsa by a guy using a stolen driver's license. Karlis and Kelley have been working it for the past couple of days. They think they have identified the guy who rented the truck. Actually, they don't have anything firm on him. Their suspicion is based mainly on a description of his automobile. They talked to him today and he denied knowing anything about it. The guy has agreed to take a polygraph examination regarding his knowledge of the kidnapping. Headquarters has approved. Our guys have tentatively set it for nine tomorrow morning. We're trying to expedite this thing. The victim, a sixteen-year-old girl, has not been released, even though the father paid a big ransom late last night. Does it sound like something you could work with?"

Reed checked his calendar, but he already knew he would go. "Sure, boss. I'll take a look at it. I have a couple of appointments I can cancel, but I'll pack up tonight and get over there early tomorrow morning. Did you say Joel Karlis is the case agent?"

"Yes. He's done a good job of running this guy down, but as I said, it's a mighty thin thread that ties him to the kidnapping. I think the polygraph is our best shot at resolving it."

"Right. I'll see what I can do."

"Okay, John. We're counting on you. This lead on the rental truck is about all they have going. They ran a fixed surveillance during the drop. Nothing too promising there. You're our best bet right now."

Reed was accustomed to being put on the spot. His boss, like most Bureau administrators, knew little about the polygraph but he knew that it sometimes got quick results. Under ideal conditions the polygraph could give him that. Bureau policy prevented the widespread use of the technique. It could never be used as a "fishing expedition" or as a substitute for a thorough investigation. But when the evidence pointed to one or two suspects, or, in a case like this one where going down the wrong path could be critical, the technique could in most instances point the investigation in the right direction.

Reed had been an FBI polygraph examiner for nearly ten years. In that time, he had conducted more than 350 examinations. The cases ranged from bank tellers stealing from the till to Soviet espionage agents trying to work a deal after getting caught spying.

John Reed had graduated from the University of Oklahoma with a degree in clinical psychology. He had helped pay his college expenses by joining the Army Reserve Officer Training Corps. To fulfill his military obligation, he had accepted a commission as a Second Lieutenant in the Army. He was assigned to the Criminal Investigation Command (formerly the Criminal Investigation Division, CID), the Army's internal investigative arm and a strong proponent of the use of the polygraph. Early in his army service, Reed attended the Army's Polygraph School at Fort McClellan, Alabama. During his four-year active-duty tour, he became the commanding officer of a CID unit and attained the rank of Captain. He'd also picked up the nickname "The Professor" because of his scholarly manner, receding hairline, glasses, and moustache.

Reed's CID unit had occasionally handled a case in which their investigation showed that the suspects were civilians. Since civilians were not subject to the Code of Military Justice, those cases were referred to the FBI. As a result, Reed had met and worked closely with several FBI agents.

The Professor learned two things during his Army tour that would greatly affect his future. One: very few people can deceive a capable polygraph examiner. And two: he wanted to be an FBI agent. His education, training, employment history and security clearance made him an ideal candidate. His selection for New Agents Training coincided perfectly with the completion of his military obligation.

After sixteen weeks of training at the FBI's Quantico, Virginia Academy, Captain Reed, CID, United States Army, became Special Agent Reed, FBI. His standing near the head of his class ensured the retention of his nickname.

Reed's first office was Cleveland. His early assignments, like those of all first office agents, were general criminal cases such as Interstate Transportation of Stolen Motor Vehicles, Interstate Transportation of Stolen Property, and Thefts From Interstate Shipments. Reed had slightly above average success in obtaining convictions in those simple cases. When Reed completed a year in the field, the Bureau sent him to a short polygraph refresher course at the John E. Reid school in Chicago. Reed began doing polygraph examinations in addition to his criminal caseload. After another year in Cleveland, Reed was transferred to Philadelphia. In the ensuing years his reputation as a polygraph examiner grew until he was considered the best in the Bureau. He conducted critical examinations in numerous field offices. His success rate in obtaining confessions was phenomenal.

The special assignments continued even after The Professor was transferred to his office of preference, Oklahoma City. He loved his work. He turned down administrative advancement, a move that would have meant promotion but assignment to Headquarters and giving up his polygraph work. He had never regretted that decision. Over the years he earned the respect and admiration of agents and supervisors throughout the FBI and, indeed, throughout the Federal Criminal Justice system because of his expertise as a polygraph examiner.

The FBI had started using the polygraph as an investigative tool on a very selective basis in the mid-1950s. The results of polygraph examinations are not admissible in Federal Court, although in a few instances, the results have been admitted by stipulation. The reluctance of the courts to admit the results has not been based on a question of the reliability of the evidence but upon other arguments. The arguments have included: the defendant's privilege against self-incrimination is violated; the defense's right to cross-examine the witness is taken away because the witness is a "machine"; and that the testimony of the examiner is hearsay.

The FBI's approach had never been toward having the results made admissible. The value of the technique was in interrogation of suspects and directing the course of investigations.

There is no question that in the hands of a capable examiner the polygraph is reliable in determining deception. In laboratory tests experienced examiners evaluated charts obtained by other examiners in actual cases: cases in which the innocence or guilt of the examinees was later verified by corroborated confessions. The experienced examiners were able to identify the truth-tellers and the deceivers with a combined success rate of more than ninety-one percent. Much admissible evidence, including eye-witness identification, has been shown in controlled experiments to have a lower rate of accuracy than the polygraph. But John E. Reed would emphatically tell you that the polygraph is not infallible and even the most reputable examiner will conduct some examinations in which the results are inconclusive.

Reed's experience verified the truth of a maxim he learned in his early training: the key to the reliability of the polygraph technique is in the design of the questions. The questions must be totally unambiguous so that the answer is clearly "yes" or "no" in the mind of the examinee. To ensure that there is no chance of misunderstanding, the questions are discussed in advance with the examinee and changed, if necessary, so that there is no doubt in his mind about their meaning. There are no surprise questions. In order to be found deceptive on the test, the examinee must lie in his response to the questions and know that he is lying. It is his attempt to deceive the examiner that causes the physiological changes that are measured by the instrument and recorded on the chart.

In addition to the questions that relate directly to the crime under investigation, the test includes two other types of questions. There are irrelevant questions; questions that are non-threatening and relate to a known fact. These questions establish a baseline for the examinee and return him to that baseline after he responds to other questions.

The third type, control questions, are the most difficult to design. These are questions about illegal or immoral acts other than the crime under investigation. The examinee will usually admit committing some such acts. The examiner must take note of these admissions and continue rephrasing the question to include the admissions. He finally has a question to which the examinee answers "no" even though he has not yet admitted all such transgressions, or at least he still has some concern about the validity of his answer.

On the test, the truth-teller will be concerned about the control questions. He knows he did not commit the act that is under investigation. He is not concerned about his answers to the relevant questions. His concern is the questions he did not fully answer or explain during the pre-test. He is afraid the examiner will think he is a liar and accuse him of the crime.

The guilty subject, on the other hand, will ignore the control questions. He is not concerned about a false or incomplete answer to a question about some minor misdeed. He is trying to control his reaction to the questions about the crime under investigation. Posing the proper questions, then, is critical to a successful polygraph examination.

Reed had explained many times that the polygraph itself is nothing more than a sensitive measuring device. The instrument precisely measures changes in blood pressure, pulse rate, respiratory pattern, and galvanic skin reflex (GSR). It records the measurements on a moving sheet of graph paper as the examiner asks a series of questions, usually ten. The resulting chart looks much like an electrocardiogram. The examiner marks the chart at the moment he asks each question and again at the point where the examinee answers. The instrument thus creates a permanent record of the examinee's physiological responses before, during and after the asking and answering of each question.

Blood pressure and pulse rate are measured by a cuff similar to that used to take blood pressure. The cuff is positioned over the brachial artery on the right arm. Changes in blood pressure and pulse rate are transmitted to the instrument through rubber tubes. Swiveling pens record the values on the moving graph.

Respiration patterns are measured by two pneumograph tubes; one fastened around the chest, the other around the abdomen. The tubes are of corrugated rubber. One end of each tube is sealed and the other attached to the instrument. Movement of the chest and abdomen, during breathing, changes the pressure inside the tube. The change in pressure is transmitted to a swiveling pen which records the changes on the graph paper.

The GSR is a measurement of the conductivity of the skin. A small current of electricity is introduced into two electrodes attached to the middle and index fingers of the left hand. The changes in conductivity are recorded on the moving graph.

Medical science has identified a myriad of stimuli that cause changes in blood pressure, pulse rate, respiration patterns and GSR. Among them is an attempt to deceive, to hide the truth. It is not the actual telling of the lie that stimulates but the fear of being found out. Tests have been given in which the guilty examinee was instructed to answer "yes" to all the questions, even the ones relevant to the crime. The resulting chart showed deception in the answers to the relevant questions even though later investigation proved that the "yes" answer was truthful. The same result was obtained when the guilty examinee was instructed not to answer any of the questions but to think about the answers as the questions were asked. It can't be known what the examinee thought about during his answers, but his attempt to deceive caused him to respond just as if he had verbally lied.

The writer of the book of Proverbs didn't know about the polygraph. But he knew human nature. When he wrote, "The wicked flee when no one pursues, but the righteous are bold as a lion," he described the reactions that are the basis of the polygraph technique. The person who is not involved in the crime has nothing to hide, or at least, nothing related to this crime. He, therefore, is not concerned with the relevant questions. His concern is the control questions.

The guilty man, on the other hand, fears he will be found out— that his body will respond to the relevant questions, regardless of his answers. His efforts to suppress those responses—to deceive the examiner—is the very thing that produces the response. The harder he tries to suppress his reaction to the question, the greater his response will be.

On Tuesday, April 7, at 7:30 A.M., Special Agent John Reed arrived at the Tulsa RA after the one-hour drive from Oklahoma City. Reed looked the part of the professional in his dark blue suit, white shirt, tie, shining shoes, rimless glasses and moustache. He carried his Lafayette portable polygraph and a briefcase.

SA Joel Karlis was waiting. "I appreciate your coming over on such short notice, John. This is a hot one as you know. Kansas City is pressuring us. The boss is pressuring us. The Bureau is pressuring us. We really hope to come up with something on this rental truck."

The Professor just smiled as he shook Karlis's hand. Last night it was the boss, now the case agent. He didn't mind being put on the spot. He thrived on it.

Karlis continued, "Here is a summary memorandum of what we know of the kidnapping case based on the original teletype and the investigation Kelley and I conducted in identifying and locating this guy Scott. There is also an account of our interview of Scott yesterday."

Reed took the papers, "How do you feel about him, Joel?"

"He makes a good impression. He seemed totally shocked when we told him we wanted to talk with him about a kidnapping. Otherwise he's cocky, confident, self-assured. No arrest record. He's a commercial pilot, flight instructor, works every day."

Reed responded, "A commercial pilot, huh? I don't think I've ever run a commercial pilot."

"Yeah," said Karlis, "and you know the odd thing about that? The father of the victim, Charles Kogan, runs an aviation business over in Springfield. His main suspect is a guy named Kline who also runs a flying service down toward Branson. Kogan and Kline are bitter rivals. Then this guy Scott turns up, and he is in the aviation business. Coincidence? It makes you wonder.

We do know Scott is not one of the kidnappers though. He has an airtight alibi for the period of the abduction: a lesson with a student that was arranged well in advance. We verified it with the student and the dispatcher at the flying school. Mr. Scott was right here in Tulsa at the time of the abduction. Also, he doesn't match the physical description of the kidnappers, what little we have.

"He became a little nervous when we got around to talking about the rental truck, but he absolutely denies renting it. The description the people at Ryder gave us matched him pretty close, but you know how that goes. They nailed his car perfectly, though, right down to the sticker on his rear window. There are quite a few cars like his but the sticker is pretty rare. Also the guy who rented the truck gave his address as 2880 Calhoun, which is nonexistent, and Scott's address is 2830 Calhoun.

"The people at Ryder haven't seen a photo line-up yet. We took his picture last night when we took the handwriting samples and..."

Reed interrupted, "Did you remember to hold out the name on the rental contract?"

"Yeah, we did that. The lab won't like it. His signature was the only cursive writing on the contract. Everything else was printed or typed. We went ahead and took a cursive alphabet along with a lot of printing but held out the name that was used on the rental contract. We can go back and get cursive samples of the signature later if we need to."

Reed looked at his watch, "What time is he due in?"

"Nine o'clock. I hope he shows."

"Did you have him sign the Miranda warning and the polygraph consent form?"

"Yeah, they are in the file jacket there."

"Okay. Give me about forty-five minutes to go over this material, make my peak-of-tension chart, and draw up some tentative questions, and I'll be ready for him."

"You want to go on into our polygraph lab?" Karlis grinned as they headed down the hall. "We've cleared out a small storage room back here. There are no windows and only one door."

Reed requested that any telephone that could be heard from the examination area room be disconnected and that any clerical personnel who had business in the area be instructed to be as quiet as possible. The only furniture in the room was a small table and two chairs.

Reed looked the room over. "This will be fine, Joel, just let me know when our man arrives."

Reed had a much more elaborate setup in his Oklahoma City office: a full-sized room with soundproofing on the walls and ceiling and a one-way mirror on one wall. The room was equipped with a special polygraph chair. The chair had curved wooden arm-rests for the comfort of the examinee and to minimize any tendency to move during the test. The chair cushion contained an inflated bladder which was attached by tubes to the polygraph. The bladder was designed to detect movements such as the flexing of muscles during the test, usually a sure sign of deception. The room also had a special table with a polygraph instrument permanently mounted flush with the surface. All the electrical connections were built into the table. There was a supply drawer in the end.

The special room was the ideal setup for administering a polygraph, but Reed wasn't bothered by having to use the storage room. He had conducted more examinations away from his special room than in it. He had done many tests in motel rooms. He had done several in prison visitation rooms. He had once done a successful test in the back of a trading post on an Indian reservation in South Dakota. The Professor had learned to adapt.

Reed took a QUIET, EXAMINATION IN PROGRESS sign from his briefcase and attached it to the outside of the door. He next went over all the material Karlis had provided. He was most interested in the write-up of yesterday's interview. He saw that Scott had two years of college. This was of special interest to him. It had been his observation that the more education a person had, the better polygraph subject they were; that is, the more likely they were to be good responders. As far as he knew there was no scientific proof of this theory, but it had held true in his experience, and other examiners had reported similar results.

Reed wrote down a group of preliminary questions. Based on what Karlis had told him and what he gathered from the summary memorandum, it was obvious that finding out if Scott had rented the truck was the key issue.

Reed took out a large poster board. At the top he printed the name Myron Gunter. Directly below that he printed the name Edwin Keith. Directly below that he printed the name William Patrick. Directly below that he printed the name Garth McBride and directly below that he printed the name Carl Keese. The names were meaningless in this investigation except for the name William Patrick which was the name on the Ryder rental agreement. He deliberately placed that name in the center position.

Reed put the poster out of sight and started a preliminary check of the instrument. He recalled when he was doing polygraphs in the Army, the filling of the ink wells and the cleaning of the capillaries that carried the ink to the pens was a time-consuming chore. His new portable Lafayette Courier used no ink. The heated pens left their tracings on heat sensitive graph paper: a welcome improvement. He turned the instrument on and checked the paper drive for alignment. The four stili were tracking straight and true. He gently flexed the two pneumograph tubes and noted the reaction of the stili. He slightly inflated the blood pressure cuff and flexed it gently. Its stilus painted a clear path on the moving graph. The GSR was last. Reed opened the Velcro straps on the electrodes and pressed his index and middle fingers onto the shining metal surfaces. The GSR stilus flexed wildly over the paper, leaving its mark as it went and making a scratching sound. He adjusted the sensitivity downward and removed the electrodes. Everything was in order.

The Professor started to feel the butterflies that were always there at this stage of an examination. He hoped they always would be. Giving a proper polygraph examination was a battle of wits between the examiner and the subject. He would need the butterflies and the extra energy they represented in the upcoming battle. Reed checked his watch. It was 9:06 A.M.

Taking a polygraph exam had to be voluntary. No one could conduct a polygraph examination against the will of the examinee. But once an investigation had narrowed the possible suspects down to one or two or three and they were asked to submit to an examination, there was some perceived pressure to take it. Each knew he would look bad if he didn't agree to take it. This was doubly true if one or two of the other suspects had already agreed to take it.

The examiner always learned a lot about his subject from his or her body language and demeanor during the pre-test. The truth-teller was anxious to please. It was in his best interest to be cooperative. He listened attentively to instructions. He trusted the examiner. He knew he didn't commit the crime under investigation, but he worried about a couple of those questions that he didn't quite get to finish explaining. He didn't want to do anything that would cause the instrument to make a mistake.

The guilty person, on the other hand, would not have agreed to take the exam but for the fact that other suspects agreed to. He felt pressured to do so. Or in a case such as this, the suspect denied any knowledge of the crime and was then caught by the "well then you don't have anything to hide" argument. Many in this group decided that since they could not avoid the test, they would beat the examiner and the instrument. But as the appointed time approached, their doubts increased. They sometimes failed to show up, or if they did, they were uncooperative during the pre-test. Some tried to manipulate the charts through subtle body movements or by thinking wild or exotic thoughts. To the experienced examiner, nothing was more indicative of deception. "The wicked flee when no one pursues…"

Reed's reverie ended when Karlis opened the door for a tall, slender, blond gentleman and said, "Mr. Scott is here."

It was 9:15 A.M. Scott was late. There was a feeling among examiners that guilty examinees were always late if they showed at all. Reed extended his hand and said, "Mr. Scott, I'm Special Agent John Reed." He noted that Scott had a firm handshake and a nice smile, but there was a slight quiver in his voice as he said, "Happy to meet you, I think."

Karlis was still standing by the door as Reed reached to close it. Reed said, "Thank you, Joel. We'll probably be a couple of hours."

"Come on over and have a seat, Mr. Scott." Reed gestured toward a straight-backed chair that was positioned at the left end and slightly ahead of the table on which the polygraph rested.

Scott didn't sit immediately but looked over at the polygraph.

"So that's what it looks like. Does it ring a bell or send up a flare if I tell a lie?" Scott asked with a smile.

Reed did not return the smile. "The polygraph is an extremely sensitive device that measures and records involuntary physiological changes produced by your autonomic nervous system. Please be seated." Reed again gestured toward the chair.

Scott sat, still looking over his right shoulder at the instrument.

Reed said, "I will go ahead and hook you up to the instrument as we talk so you can become accustomed to it. I will not turn the instrument on." Reed's manner was serious, professional, but he tried not to appear accusatory or judgmental. "I saw in the file that you have already signed the Miranda Warning and the Polygraph Consent Form."

"Yeah, I did that yesterday. I sure want to get this whole mess over with."

Reed proceeded with putting the blood pressure cuff on Scott's arm and asked, "Have you ever had a polygraph examination?"

Scott answered, "No…I probably shouldn't be taking this one."

"Why do you say that?" asked Reed.

"Well, I'm nervous about the whole thing."

Reed continued hooking up the pneumograph tubes and the GSR electrodes. "Everyone who takes an examination is nervous. I will adjust the instrument to account for that. You know, of course, we are investigating the kidnapping of a young girl from her home in Springfield, Missouri, on April second."

Scott replied, "Yes I know that, and I have told the other agents several times that I don't know anything about it."

Reed moved the other chair around the table and sat directly in front of Scott, pad and pen in hand. "I don't know if that is the truth or not…but you do. After I have run a series of tests, I will also know." Reed paused and studied Scott's reaction. He noted on his pad that Scott had poor eye contact, swallowed, and shifted in his chair during the pause after Reed's statement. Reed then asked, "Have you taken any medication during the past twenty-four hours?"

Scott seemed relieved at the break in the silence and answered, "No, none."

Reed checked his notebook and said, "I see that you were questioned at length yesterday by Special Agents Karlis and Kelley about the kidnapping of a young girl. Mr. Scott, did you have anything to do with that kidnapping?"

"No, I didn't."

Reed continued, "We're talking about a kidnapping in Springfield, Missouri, on April second. When I ask you that question that's what I'm talking about; understand?"

"Okay," replied Scott.

"I'm going to ask you this question on the test: 'Did you have anything to do with that kidnapping?'"

Looking at his notes, Reed continued, "I see from your interview that your full name is Eldred James Scott. Is that correct?"

"Yes, sir. But I hate that name."

"You are generally known as Jack. Is that correct?"

"Yes, sir."

"I'm going to ask you this question on the test: 'Do people call you Jack?'"

Scott responded, "Yes, sir."

"Please answer 'yes' or 'no' to all of these questions."

"Yes," said Scott.

Reed, looking directly at Scott, asked, "Did you ever steal anything?"

There was a pause and Scott answered, "No."

"Not in your whole life?"

After a pause, Scott said, "Well, when we were in junior high school we stole some watermelons."

"Did you steal the watermelons?"

"Well, yeah, I was in on it."

"How old were you when you stole the watermelons?"

"Fourteen, I think."

"Have you stolen anything since then?"

Scott paused, then said, "No."

"Okay," Reed went on, "I'm going to ask you this question on the test: 'Since you were fourteen, have you ever stolen anything?'"

When there was no answer, Reed asked, "And what will your answer be?"

"No."

Reed took notes and then asked, "Where are we right now?"

Scott looked up, smiled and said, "In the FBI building."

Reed didn't smile, "What city?"

Scott replied, "Oh, Tulsa."

"I'm going to ask you this question on the test: 'Are you in Tulsa, Oklahoma?'"

Scott replied, "Okay."

Reed with a trace of impatience said, "Yes or no. Are you in Tulsa, Oklahoma?"

"Yes."

Reed wrote on his pad and then looked directly into Scott's eyes and asked, "Did you rent that truck?"

Scott swallowed and his eyes shifted slightly to the right as he said, "I've told you all a dozen times…"

Reed softly interrupted, "Yes or no."

Scott said, "No."

Reed made notes and then said, "When I ask that question I'm talking about a Ryder Rental truck, a 1993 Ford, which was rented here in Tulsa on April third. That is the only truck I will be asking about. I'm going to ask you this question on the test: 'Did you rent that truck?'"

"No," Scott replied.

Reed wrote out a question and again looked directly into Scott's eyes and asked, "Do you know who kidnapped that girl?"

"No."

Reed went on, "I'm talking about the girl who was kidnapped on Thursday, April second in Springfield, Missouri. Do you know who kidnapped that girl?"

"No."

Reed said, "We must be careful with that question. If you *suspect* someone but don't actually *know* they did it you will react to that question just as you would if you knew who did it. Do you suspect anyone of kidnapping that girl?"

"No, I don't know anything about…uh, I mean no."

"I'm going to ask you this question on the test: 'Do you know who kidnapped that girl?'"

"No."

Reed then asked, "What girl are we talking about?"

Scott shifted in the chair, "That one you told me about in Springfield, uh…Missouri, is it?"

"Yes, the girl who was kidnapped in Springfield, Missouri, on Thursday, April second."

Reed wrote the question on his pad. When he looked up he

noticed that Scott was again looking back toward the polygraph. When Scott turned back Reed asked, "Did you ever steal anything from a place where you worked?"

Scott quickly said, "No."

Reed raised his eyebrows and asked, "Never?"

"Well, maybe some paper clips I took home or something like that."

Reed said, "Paper clips" and wrote it on his pad. He looked up and said, "Is that all?"

Scott seemed slightly annoyed and said, "Well maybe a pen or pencil I forgot to leave at work."

Reed said, "Pen and pencil," as he wrote. "Surely that's all."

Scott, seemingly relieved, quickly said, "Yeah, that's it."

"Okay, I'm going to ask you this question on the test: 'Other than what you told me, have you ever stolen anything from a place where you worked?'"

"No."

The Professor said, "We will have to go back and change that question about since you were fourteen. You have told me about stealing a watermelon when you were fourteen and you have told me about paper clips and a pen or a pencil from your work. I will change the question to read, 'Other than what you told me about, have you ever stolen anything?' and what will your answer be?"

"No."

"How old are you today?"

"Thirty-five."

"Then you are over twenty-one?"

Scott laughed, "Yeah, I'd say so."

"All right, I'm going to ask you this question on the test: 'Are you over twenty-one years old?'"

"Yes."

Reed quickly moved on, "Did you use someone's driver's license to rent that truck?"

"No."

Reed continued, "Someone did. We have interviewed the person whose driver's license was used. He can prove he was in another state when the truck was rented, and he had reported his driver's license stolen before the truck was rented."

Reed paused and watched Scott closely. Scott lowered his eyes and picked some lint from his shirt. Reed said, "I'm going to ask you this question on the test: 'Did you use someone's driver's license to rent that truck?'"

"No."

"What truck are we talking about?"

Scott showed a little weariness as he answered, "The 1993 Ford, Ryder Rental."

Reed filled in, "Rented last Friday here in Tulsa. That's the only truck we are talking about. Did you use someone's driver's license to rent that truck?"

"No."

"Now, I see from your interview that you are a high school graduate and have two years of college. Right?"

"Well, I didn't quite complete the second year."

Reed said, "Okay, I'm going to ask you this question on the test: 'Did you ever go to school?'"

"Sure, uh, I mean yes."

"Those are the questions I'm going to ask you on the test. Those are the only question I will ask you on this test. Would you like to discuss any of the questions before we begin?"

"No."

"Are you comfortable?"

Scott said, "I'm still nervous."

Reed said, "That's normal. Just relax and tell the truth. Please sit upright with your feet flat on the floor. Look straight ahead and do not move. I'm going to turn the instrument on and inflate the blood pressure cuff. You will feel some pressure on your arm for a few minutes while we go through the questions."

Reed got out of his chair and moved behind the polygraph table and out of Scott's line of sight. He used the rubber bulb to inflate the blood pressure cuff until the gauge on the face of the polygraph read 90mm of mercury. He quickly checked the blood pressure tracing on the chart. As the heart contracted, forcing blood into the aorta, the tracing pen moved upward on the chart. As the heart muscle relaxed, the pen moved downward until the aortic valve closed, stopping the flow of blood back into the heart. This closing caused a temporary reversal of blood flow. The recording pen showed this as a short horizontal line before the pen continued its downward movement in the diastolic stroke. This horizontal line was called the "dicrotic notch." Reed adjusted the pressure in the cuff to center the dicrotic notch between the top and the bottom of the tracing.

The two pneumograph needles were already tracing Scott's breathing pattern onto the graph paper. Reed adjusted the tightness of the tubes to obtain an amplitude of about one inch on the chart.

Reed adjusted the GSR pen to center its swing and adjusted the sensitivity downward until he observed no major pen swings. He made the adjustments quickly and with little conscious thought.

The Professor was now seated behind the table on which the polygraph rested. He said softly, "If you are telling the truth, the instrument will show it. If you are not, it will show that, too. Sit up straight, keep your feet flat on the floor, look straight ahead and answer 'yes' or 'no.'"

Reed marked the chart and asked, "Do people call you Jack?"

Scott answered, "Yes."

Reed marked the chart at the point Scott answered. He paused and then asked, "Are you over twenty-one years old?"

"Yes."

Reed marked the point of each answer and paused for fifteen to twenty seconds before asking the next question.

"Did you use someone's driver's license to rent that truck?"

"No."

Pause.

"Are you in Tulsa, Oklahoma?"

"Yes."

Pause.

"Did you rent that truck?"

"No."

Pause.

"Other than what you told me about, have you ever stolen anything?"

"No."

Pause.

"Did you ever go to school?"

"Yes."

Pause.

"Did you have anything to do with that kidnapping?"

"No."

Pause.

"Do you know who kidnapped that girl?"

"No."

Pause.

"Other than what you told me, have you ever stolen anything from a place where you worked?"

"No."

Reed paused for fifteen seconds after marking the last answer and then said, "Okay, you may relax now."

Reed made a cursory examination of the chart. There was a definite but weak response to question three, "Did you use someone's driver's license to rent that truck?" A response of this type sometimes occurs on the first relevant question, even among truthtellers.

The comparison of the response to relevant question five, "Did you rent that truck?" with the response to control question six, "Other than what you told me about, have you ever stolen anything?" showed a slightly greater response to the relevant question.

Scott's responses to the other relevant questions—eight, "Did you have anything to do with that kidnapping?" and nine, "Do you know who kidnapped that girl?"—were inconclusive when compared with his response to control question ten: "Other than what you told me about, have you ever stolen anything from a place where you worked?"

Reed often found that weak responses to both relevants and controls occurred when an examinee was either on some sort of sedative or was not convinced that the examiner could detect his deception. In this situation he used a stimulation test.

Reed walked around to face Scott, "This is another part of the test." He handed Scott a stack of seven numbered cards, all face down. "Take one of the cards, look at the number and then place it back into the stack."

Reed watched Scott to make sure he looked at the card.

"Be sure and remember what number you looked at. I'm going to ask you questions about the number on the card you picked. I want you to answer 'no' every time, even when I ask you about the number you did pick. Do you understand? You are to answer 'no' every time."

"Yes, I understand."

Reed returned to his chair and started the chart paper moving again. He marked the chart and asked, "Did you pick the number one?"

"No."

He paused for fifteen seconds and asked, "Did you pick the number two?"

"No."

Another pause and then, "Did you pick the number three?"

"No."

Another pause and then, "Did you pick the number four?"

"No."

Reed's pause was longer. There was complete silence except for the scratching of the pens on the moving graph paper. Scott swallowed. Reed noted that on the paper and then repeated, "Did you pick the number four?" The GSR pen swung wildly, the blood pressure base line rose and the pulse amplitude narrowed. The respiratory tracing showed a rising base line and increased amplitude. The needle made a "staircase" tracing on the exhalation stroke.

Reed turned off the paper transport and deflated the blood pressure cuff. He stated firmly. "You lied when you said 'no' to the question about the number four."

Scott said defensively, "Well, you told me to."

Reed said, "I now have the polygraph adjusted to your responses. I know exactly what it looks like when you do not tell the truth." Reed held up the list of questions from the first test and said, "I'm going to step out of the room for a few minutes and let your arm rest. Think of the questions I asked you on the first test. If there are any questions to which you did not tell the truth or any that you want to discuss, we will talk about it when I return. Otherwise, I will ask you the same questions on the next test."

Reed stepped out of the room but stayed near the door. It had been his experience that many times a truth-telling subject would make another small admission to one of the control questions after the number-card stimulation test. The guilty would usually not make any comment because his concern was with the relevant questions. He had already denied any knowledge in that area. He would not want to show any concern now.

Reed re-entered the room. Scott was slumped down in the chair. His chin was resting on his chest. He sat up as Reed approached.

"Do you have any comments about any of the questions?"

"No, but I'm still nervous."

Reed replied, "I have adjusted the instrument to account for that. We got a good chart on the last test. I will now go back and ask the same ten questions I asked on the first test. How does your arm feel?"

"Okay," Scott answered with little enthusiasm.

"Fine," said Reed. "I'm inflating the cuff. Just relax, don't move, look straight ahead, and keep your feet flat on the floor."

Reed made minor adjustments on the heart rate pen and re-centered the GSR pen. He then asked, "Do people call you Jack?"

"Yes."

Reed continued through the questions from the first test in the same order. After question ten he allowed the chart to run on for fifteen seconds before turning off the instrument and deflating the blood pressure cuff. He then said, "Okay, that's the end of that test. You may relax." The stim test had done its job. Scott's responses to relevant questions three and five, about using the driver's license and about renting the truck were clearly greater than the response to control question six.

Scott also showed tension in his responses to relevant questions eight and nine about his participation in or knowledge of the kid-napping. The responses clearly exceeded any response to control question ten.

Reed said, "I have just about reached my conclusion, but I want to run one more short test."

John Reed had found that the most reliable of all polygraph tests was the "peak of tension" test. If an examinee denied knowl-edge of a bit of information that the perpetrator would know but could know *only* if he was the perpetrator, it made an ideal test. The type of information needed for this test is not found in every case. Joel Karlis and Ed Kelley had been careful to preserve just such an item: the name used by the person who rented the truck.

Reed moved his chair around the table and again sat facing

Scott. He was careful to speak slowly and softly. He wanted to reason with Scott, not accuse him. "When you were interviewed yesterday, you denied any knowledge of the Ryder truck that was rented here in Tulsa last Friday. Is that right?"

"Yes, and that's the truth."

"I have asked you on this test if you rented the truck and if you used someone's driver's license to rent the truck. Is that right?"

"Yes."

"And you have denied any knowledge of who rented the truck."

"Yes."

"Did Special Agent Karlis or Special Agent Kelley tell you who rented the truck?"

"No."

"Did they show you the name of the person who rented the truck?"

"No, but I know it wasn't me."

"The person who did rent the truck would know what name he used, wouldn't he?"

Scott paused, swallowed and said, "Yes sir, I would think so."

"If you did know the name, it could only be because you did rent the truck. No one has told you the name; is that right?"

"I think we've been over that enough. I don't know anything about it."

"Fine," Reed said. "I have made a chart on which I have listed five names. One of the names is the name used by the person who rented the truck. The other four names are meaningless."

Reed removed the poster board and a small easel from his briefcase. He set the easel and chart up directly in front of Scott and only three feet from his eyes. When Scott looked ahead, he could not avoid seeing the names.

"I'm going to go down this list from top to bottom and then from bottom to top asking this question, 'Do you know if,' and I'll insert a name each time, 'rented that truck?' I want you to follow the names down the chart with your eyes as I ask each one. After you have answered each question, move your eyes down to the next name. Remember we will go down the list and then back up. Do you understand?"

Reed noticed that Scott scanned the list, blushed, and swallowed. He made a note of that. Scott answered, "Yes."

Reed moved his chair back behind the polygraph table, inflated the blood pressure cuff, and started the instrument. "Remember, sit up straight, feet flat on the floor, look at the chart, follow the names as I read them."

"Do you know if Myron Gunter rented that truck?"

Reed marked the chart as he asked the question and again as Scott answered, "No."

"Do you know if Edwin Keith rented that truck?"

"No."

During the pause after this answer, Reed saw a sharp rise in the blood pressure base line and suppression in the pneumograph tracing.

"Do you know if William Patrick rented that truck?"

"No."

There was an immediate wide swing in the GSR at the answer and a steep decline in blood pressure. The pneumograph showed a sharp increase in amplitude and a decrease in breathing rate; the proverbial "sigh of relief."

Reed continued, "Do you know if Garth McBride rented that truck?"

"No."

This answer was barely audible.

"Weak." Reed wrote on the chart.

"Do you know if Carl Keese rented that truck?"

"No."

Reed paused for fifteen seconds and now started reading the list from bottom to top. The tension again built as the questions neared the center name. There was another "sigh," though not as spectacular, after the answer to the William Patrick name.

After the final question and answer, Reed stopped the instrument and deflated the blood pressure cuff but said nothing while he moved his chair around to the front of the table. He moved the easel aside and set his chair as close to Scott as he could. His left knee was actually between Scott's knees.

Scott's face was flushed, and he was slumped down in the chair again. His eyes were downcast. He asked feebly, "How did I do?"

Reed said softly, "Why don't you tell me about it? You're too nice a guy to lie."

A tear sprang instantly to each of Scott's eyes and then eased slowly down his cheeks. His reply was almost inaudible, "Okay, I rented the goddamned truck. I did it for a friend who wanted to run out on his girlfriend. I swear I don't know anything about any kidnapping. He was supposed to bring the truck back here on Monday so I could turn it in. The next thing I know I'm being questioned by the FBI about a kidnapping I don't know a damned thing about…I guess this is the end of my flying career…No chance of ever getting on with an airline. How much trouble am I in?"

Reed asked, "Why did you rent the truck with someone else's driver's license?"

"That was all his idea. He said he was afraid his girlfriend would be able to trace him through the truck rental." Scott raised his hand defensively and said, "I know, I know, it doesn't make a lot of sense now, and I wondered about it at the time, but he furnished the money and the driver's license. He even gave me a cover story to use at the rental place. Something about moving my furniture from Illinois."

"Who is this friend?"

Scott slowly shook his head. His expression was pained. He mumbled, "His name is 'Wimp' Wilkins. I knew him in college. He's trying to make it in show business over in Branson."

"Wimp?"

"Aw, that's not his real name. His folks started calling him Wimpy, after some comic book character that loved hamburgers. This guy, my friend, loves hamburgers more than anybody. His folks called him Wimpy or Ronnie. We called him Wimp. His real name is Ron, Ronald, I guess."

"Do you know if Wimp was involved in the kidnapping? Your polygraph chart shows deception on the question about knowing who is involved."

"No, I don't know that he was involved, but after the mess he's gotten me into on the truck, I think he must be. I know something screwy is up. I'm really pissed off at him for getting me involved. I'm a commercial pilot. I don't need any legal problems on my record."

Reed said, "I want to get Karlis in here, and I want you to tell us the entire story of the truck rental and in particular everything you know about Wimp Wilkins. Maybe we can work something out where you can help us and we can help you. By the way, do you still have the driver's license you used to rent the truck?"

"Yeah, right here in my billfold. I kept it because I figured I would need it to turn the truck in and get my deposit back. But, man, when you put up that chart with the name on it, I thought it was going to burn a hole in my pants."

The Professor smiled for the first time today.

Scott didn't notice. He continued, "Here's the damn license. I want to get this thing cleared up. What do you want to know?"

Reed wanted Karlis to hear this but he was reluctant to interrupt a man who wanted to unburden himself. "Just tell me from the beginning how you got involved in this."

Scott, with no further prompting, went into a detailed account of his relationship with Wimp Wilkins. He traced their friendship from college days through the favors Wimp did for him in getting music show tickets in Branson.

He recounted Wilkins's recent telephone call and his plea for help in running out on his girlfriend; how Wilkins wanted him to rent a truck; how he set up the meeting, furnished the money, gave him the Illinois driver's licence, and even suggested a cover story to use in renting the truck. He told of delivering the truck to a rest stop as Wilkins had instructed. He concluded with another strong denial that he knew anything about a kidnapping, and then added some very uncomplimentary words about Wimp Wilkins.

Reed took copious notes and when Scott finished, he said, "What did you do with the truck after you rented it?"

"I did exactly what Wimp told me to. I took it to the first rest stop on I-44 east of Tulsa and left it there. I put the keys on top of the right rear tire just like he told me to, and I haven't seen or heard from him since."

"Did Wimp pay for the rental?"

"Yeah, he had the amount all figured out. He gave me nine hundred dollars; part of it was a deposit that I could keep when I took the truck back."

"Mr. Scott, I believe you are now telling the truth about your part in the kidnapping. We will want to get a signed statement setting out in detail what you have admitted to me."

"I'm not admitting anything about the kidnapping. I didn't have anything to do with it. I can't believe Wimp used me that way...Have y'all talked to him?"

"No, but I'm sure we will be talking with him soon. Let me get Agent Karlis in here."

THE DEAL

Every person who, with intent to cheat and defraud, shall obtain or attempt to obtain from any person, firm, or corporation any money, property or valuable thing, of a value of Five Hundred Dollars ($500.00) or more, by means or by use of any trick or deception, or false or fraudulent representation or statement or pretense...shall be guilty of a felony and upon conviction thereof shall be punished by imprisonment in the State Penitentiary, for a term not more than ten (10) years, or by a fine not to exceed Five Thousand Dollars ($5000.00) or by both such fine and imprisonment.

—Oklahoma Vehicle, Criminal, Alcohol, Tobacco & Drug and Boating Laws. Sections 1541.1 and 1541.2 (construed)

The Professor asked a clerk to have Joel Karlis report to the polygraph room. He also requested that two additional chairs be brought in. Reed was anxious to get back to Scott. It was not a good practice to leave an examinee alone, particularly one who had just made a serious admission. Most were in a state of depression although some experienced the euphoria of having a weight lifted from their shoulders. Scott was in the former category.

By the time Karlis arrived with Ed Kelley, Reed had arranged the chairs around the table that had held the polygraph.

When Karlis entered, he immediately noticed Scott's posture and thought, *The Professor has broken another one.*

Reed was careful to be considerate during this phase of an interrogation. The examinee had been through an exhausting mental battle and had reluctantly admitted his guilt. Any suggestion of gloating or a condescending remark by the examiner or one of the investigators could push him into silence, or worse, a refusal to cooperate or even a denial of the admissions he had made.

When the other two agents and Scott were seated, Reed began, "Mr. Scott has admitted that he did, in fact, rent the Ryder Truck that we questioned him about. He used this driver's license." Reed handed the Illinois driver's license to Karlis, careful to avoid a grandiose gesture.

The Professor proceeded to outline the story Scott had told him.

Reed, although speaking to the agents, looked directly at Jack Scott. He wanted Scott to approve of his version of what transpired. "Mr. Scott realizes he made a mistake and seems genuinely upset that a person he considered his friend got him involved in this crime. He has voiced concern about his professional future and he is willing to cooperate with us in identifying and locating Wilkins. Is that right, Mr. Scott?"

Scott nodded.

"Mr. Scott denies having any knowledge of the kidnapping prior to being questioned by the FBI. The polygraph confirmed his answers in that area."

Scott said, "I would never have agreed to take part in something like that. All I agreed to do was help a friend out of a bad situation with his girlfriend."

Reed continued, now addressing Karlis. "I did not go into great detail in my interview of Mr. Scott. I concentrated on his renting the truck. I did not get into who and where this Wimp Wilkins is. I think we should get a signed statement covering his admissions before we get too far into the next phase."

Karlis nodded his agreement. As much as he wanted to move ahead to looking for Wilkins, he knew the value of locking Scott into his confession. He did hedge slightly, however. "We don't want to overwhelm Mr. Scott with a three-on-one. Ed, how about starting to work on Wilkins's ID while I see what we can work out with Mr. Scott. While we're doing that, Professor, how about rough-drafting a statement covering Mr. Scott's admissions on the truck."

"Okay, Joel. I'll move over here out of the way and get going on that. I'll make it brief."

"Fine. Then, after Mr. Scott has checked it over, we will get it typed and signed and you can be on your way."

Karlis then turned to Ed Kelley, "Okay, Ed, if you will take notes, I will hit the high spots with Mr. Scott to get enough info to identify Wilkins."

"Okay. I'm ready to copy."

"Now, Mr. Scott, what is Wimp Wilkins's real name?"

"Like I told the lie detector guy there, I have always known him as Wimp, but I believe his real name is Ron. I know his folks called him Ronnie. I guess it could be Ronald."

"Any idea what his middle name or initial is?"

"No. No idea."

"How old is Ronald Wilkins?"

Scott shrugged and turned his hands outward, "He must be about my age. We started to college at Tahlequah the same year. He must be about 35, 36, something like that."

"Where does he live?"

"Somewhere in the Branson, Missouri, area. He was living with a woman down in Arkansas not too far from Branson, but he told me last week that he was running out on her and moving into Branson. That's why he needed the truck."

"You mentioned his folks. Where do they live?"

"They live in Wellston, just down the Interstate toward Oke City. I went bird hunting down there a couple of times when we were in college. His folks are good people. Wheat farmers. I was down there a few months ago trying to get in touch with Wimp. I was going to Branson with a group and was looking for some cheap tickets."

"Did you find him?"

"Yeah, well they gave me a number where I left a message, and he called me back. He got us some tickets. Then I talked with him while we were in Branson; that's when he told me he was living in Arkansas."

"Do you have the phone number?"

"Yeah, in my apartment. I tried to call him yesterday after you guys came down on me. I called it four or five times but never got an answer."

"Do you remember what the number was, what area code, any-way?"

"Oh, yeah, it's an Arkansas area code—501, I think—but I don't remember the number."

"How long has he been in the Branson area?"

"I don't know for sure. I lost track of him for a while after college, but I think he's been there, off and on, for five, maybe six years. He thinks he's gonna make it big, but from what I've seen and what he said, I think he's barely getting by." Scott smiled, "He's a hell of a fiddle player, but he can't sing a lick."

"What kind of car does he drive?"

Scott thought for a moment, "I don't know. When we met last week, when he gave me the driver's license, he was driving a dark blue Cadillac, Arkansas tag, but I doubt it was his. I didn't ask him. Could be, I guess.

"When I saw him in Branson a few months ago he told me his boss was working on something that should put both of them on easy street. He was still hoping to get on regular with a band though. He was doing spot substitutions. You know, if someone was sick or something."

"What about his height and weight?"

"He's a small guy. I'd say about 5'8", 145 or 150. He has real dark hair and eyes and a great tan. I think he might be part Indian. He used to wear a black western hat. We called him the Marlboro Man. He tried to reflect that image."

"A smoker then, I guess."

"Oh, yeah. True to his image all the way. But I always thought Wimp was a better nickname than 'Marlboro Man.'"

"Not too convincing as a tough guy, huh?"

"Well, it was his voice. He looked a little like the Marlboro Man, but he sounded like a wimp."

Karlis, anxious to get Wilkins identified but conscious of the need to get Scott locked into his story, said, "Okay, Ed, that ought to give you enough to check the DMVs in all three states."

Kelley said, "One more thing, Mr. Scott, has Wimp ever been arrested?"

"No, not to my knowledge. He was pretty straight in college. Course I haven't been close to him since."

As Kelley left to begin the records checks, he recalled what a rural sheriff once told him. *You don't know who a person is until you have his name and date of birth. If he has a common name, you don't know 'til you have his name, DOB and Social Security Number. If he's a con artist, you need his name, DOB, SSN, photograph, and finger-prints. And even then, you're not real sure.* For now Kelley would settle for a full name and address.

The Professor moved back to the table where Scott and Karlis were seated. "I have completed the draft of the statement. I will first read it to you, Mr. Scott. If we need to make changes, we can make them before having it typed."

SIGNED STATEMENT OF ELDRED JAMES SCOTT
Tulsa, Oklahoma

"I, Eldred James Scott, 2830 Calhoun Street, Apartment 420, Tulsa, Oklahoma, make the following voluntary statement to Special Agents Joel Karlis and J.R. Reed who have identified themselves to me as agents of the Federal Bureau of Investigation. No promises or threats of any kind have been made to influence me to make this statement. I have been advised verbally and in writing of my constitutional rights against self-incrimination and my rights to an attorney. I have waived those rights verbally and by signing a waiver.

"On Thursday, April 2, I received a telephone call at my residence from a person I know as Wimp Wilkins, who is also known as Ronnie Wilkins. He told me he was in a jam and needed my help in renting a truck so he could move out on his girlfriend. I figured he wanted to borrow money but he said he would furnish the money up front. He also said he would give me a driver's license to use to 'keep me out of it if she tried to trace the truck.'

"I owed Wimp a favor so I agreed to help him. He set up a meeting for the next day at the first rest stop east of Tulsa on I-44. He gave me an Illinois driver's license in the name of William A. Patrick. He said Patrick was a friend who let him borrow the license. He said I should tell the rental people I was moving from Illinois to Tulsa and would need the truck for three or four days. He said he had checked out the mileage, rental rate, and rental policy, and I wouldn't have any trouble. He gave me nine $100 bills which he said would cover everything including a deposit of around $250 which I could keep when I returned the truck. He said he had other business in the Tulsa area but needed the truck that day. He told me to bring the truck to the rest stop and leave it with the keys on top of the right rear inside tire.

"Wimp said he would call when he was done with the truck and we would work out the arrangements for me to return it.

"I drove back into Tulsa and went directly to the Ryder Truck Rental Agency at 16th and Clark in Tulsa and rented the truck. I used the Illinois driver's license in the name William A. Patrick. I gave the rental agency a fictitious Tulsa telephone number and address. I paid for the rental in advance with the money Wimp Wilkins gave me.

"I drove the truck back to the rest stop and left it there. The truck has not been returned to me, and I have not heard from Wimp Wilkins. I have been unable to contact him.

"This is the full extent of my knowledge of and involvement in this incident. I have no knowledge of a kidnapping involving the rental truck.

"Other than the $250 deposit which I was to keep when I returned the truck, I have not received, nor was I promised any money for renting the truck."

"I HAVE READ THIS STATEMENT CONSISTING OF THIS AND ONE OTHER PAGE. I HAVE INITIALED ANY CORRECTIONS AND EACH PAGE. I NOW SIGN IT BECAUSE IT IS TRUE."

Signed_____Date_____

Witnessed_____Date_____

Witnessed_____Date_____

After Reed read the statement he handed it to Scott. Scott took it but did not look at it. He turned to Karlis and asked, "Where does this leave me?"

"I will try and answer that fully, but first let's get it out to be typed. Are you satisfied with the statement? Is that the way it happened? We don't want to put anything in there that is not factual."

"That's fine. That's the way it happened."

"Okay, Professor. Have her make four copies. We'll wait for you before going on."

To cover the silence, Karlis asked Scott what kind of airplanes he flew. Scott immediately sat straight up in his chair and became more animated than Karlis had seen him in the two days he had known him. He spoke up and his blue eyes smiled as he talked about Cessna 310s and Piper Twin Comanches. He even told Karlis a couple of stories about bonehead tricks his students had pulled: feathering the wrong engine or lining up to land on the taxiway. Karlis saw a different Jack Scott as he talked about his profession. He was handsome, poised, articulate, likeable, funny—all-in-all a different person than the "hang-dog" victim of his friend's deception. *What a shame it would be to force this man out of his chosen profession, his dream.*

Reed's return with the typed document interrupted their pleasant interlude into the Oklahoma skies and returned them to the world of kidnappers, liars, criminals, and deals.

Karlis said as gently as he could, "Now, about your question a few minutes ago about where this leaves you. I want you to remember this moment. It is important to you, and it is important to us. Just like it says in the statement, we have not made any threats, nor have we made any promises to you.

"Mr. Reed and I are investigators. We do not have the power to prosecute, nor do we have the power to acquit. So we don't have much power to make deals. We report what we find to the prosecutors who do have that power. The prosecutors have great latitude, almost unlimited discretion in choosing the cases they prosecute and those they find unworthy.

"I am familiar with the federal law, but I don't have enough facts to know if you are involved as a conspirator or merely as an unwitting accomplice in this kidnapping. You have said you did not participate and had no knowledge of it until we questioned you. Mr. Reed has said that in his opinion the polygraph supports that contention. If those are *indeed* the facts, *all* of the facts, about your involvement, then I think you have been victimized by others and there is little chance you will be charged federally. But," Karlis paused and held his index finger in the air for emphasis, "that is not a promise. I am not the prosecutor.

"If what you have admitted is your total involvement, it seems to me that you would be anxious to assist us in getting to the bottom of this. You have already been of some assistance in providing information on Wilkins, but we still have a missing girl, a father out $300,000 in ransom money, and kidnappers on the loose. We need a lot of help. I believe you are in a position to provide it.

"Now for the bad news, as they say. I am not totally familiar with the laws of the state of Oklahoma. But all states have laws, criminal laws, covering the type of activity you participated in when you rented that truck. I looked at a couple of sections of the Oklahoma Criminal Code after we talked yesterday. I believe your false pretenses and deception in renting the truck puts you in serious violation. Even if there had never been a kidnapping, you perpetrated a fraud in the way you rented the truck. Even though you paid for the rental, you made a fraudulent representation when you used another's driver's license, and I'll bet that in that contract you signed, it specifies that you are the *only one* authorized to drive the truck. Then there is the matter of not returning it, which, although a civil matter, could be expensive. The truck has been recovered, by the way, and it is in good condition except for some modifications the kidnappers made. It will cost money to repair it."

Scott sank lower and lower into his chair.

Karlis continued, "I'm not enjoying this, Mr. Scott, but I don't want you to ever say I didn't spell it out for you. We need help, but I want you to be clear about what it entails and what is in it for you. Do you want to help us?"

"Yeah, I'll try to help you if it will help me."

"Have I made any threats to you?"

"No."

"Have I made any promises to you?"

"Hell, no!"

"Have you been truthful?"

"Yes, I have."

"Have you told us everything about renting and delivering the truck?"

"Yes, everything."

Karlis frowned, "How did you get back to Tulsa?"

"What?"

"How did you get back to Tulsa after you dropped the truck off?"

There was silence. Scott rose halfway out of his chair, his face turned toward the door. Then he flopped back down. He looked the part of a beaten man. "Well, shit, man. I don't know why she has to be brought into this. She doesn't know a damn thing about this. She followed me out to the rest stop and then took me back to get my car. That's *all* she did. We didn't even talk about the truck. She's just a girl I know. I haven't seen her or talked to her since that day. Why does she have to be brought into this?"

Karlis smiled, "Relax, Jack. We don't need to 'bring her into this,' but you should have told me about her. We must trust each other. Do you want to help us solve this kidnapping?"

"I told you I did, but I've told you all I know."

There was a knock on the door. Reed bounded over to meet the steno. He handed the typed copies to Karlis who passed one on to Scott, "Let's all read through this to make sure it is what Mr. Scott has said."

Scott read through the document quickly and reached for a pen. "This is all I had to do with it. I know I made a mistake, but I didn't have anything else to do with it." He signed two copies. Reed and Karlis came around to his chair and signed as witnesses.

Karlis put all four copies in his briefcase just as Ed Kelley came through the door with a wide grin. Kelley took his chair and with no introduction, started to read from a computer printout, "Ronald Gene Wilkins, White Male, DOB April 8, 1960, Wellston, Oklahoma, five foot seven, 140 pounds, Brown and Brown, large mole on right cheek. Home of record, Route 4, Box 275, Wellston, Oklahoma. Computerized Criminal History shows one arrest, Carrol County Arkansas, Burglary, last November, No disposition shown, FBI #346 485 D2."

Kelley paused long enough to look around the table at three smiling faces and then went on, "Oklahoma DMV records show a 1985 Pontiac Firebird registered to him last year, but the tag was not renewed in Oklahoma. It is not registered in Missouri or Arkansas. His DL shows the same Wellston address and is still valid. DMV is printing out a copy of his DL picture. There's probably a picture of him in Carrol County, Arkansas. I didn't want to contact them because the case could still be pending. Probably is. I called Branson PD and the Taney County, Missouri, Sheriff's Office, but they had nothing on him."

Reed said, "Hey, that was quick, Eddie. It sounds like you have your foot in the door."

"Yeah," said Karlis, "we know who he is; now we've got to find him."

Reed gathered up his belongings. He came over to Scott, who had been ignored in the excitement of identifying Wimp. He said, "Mr. Scott, I said it earlier, and I'll say it again: you are too nice a guy to be involved in this. Work with these fellows. I'll guarantee they will treat you right. Good luck."

Both Tulsa agents accompanied Reed to the door and thanked him for his assistance. He shrugged and said, "All in a day's work," and he was gone.

Karlis went back to Scott. "We were interrupted before, but I want to finish what I was saying about where this leaves you.

"We were talking about the state law. You could be in trouble there. It's serious; a felony. There could be a lot of evidence: photo line-up, handwriting, fingerprints, car description and, of course, your confession. I'm not trying to scare you or coerce you. I'm looking at the position you are in and the position we are in and frankly, I'm trying to make a deal. Here is what I propose.

"We want you to give us your assistance and maybe a couple of days of your time. I'm talking about canceling your students and being free to travel. To start, we want you to contact Wimp's parents and see if they know how to get in touch with him. You can come up with your own story about why you need him. Based on what they tell you, that is, whether it's a phone number or an address, we want you to follow through and force Wimp into a face-to-face meeting. If they give you an address, we want you to go there under our control and confront him; and we will want you to wear a wire. We'll get into that later. If they give you a phone number, we want you to arrange a meeting with him. You shouldn't have any trouble with that. You're madder than hell at him. You did him a favor and the next thing you know you're being questioned by the FBI, and you lied to cover for him. The truck hasn't been returned like he told you it would. Your flying career is in jeopardy, and you want some answers or you are going to the police, etc…He might be reluctant to talk on the phone, but if he isn't, tell him you are. You're afraid the FBI might have you tapped. We want to force a face to face. Your big stick is the threat of going to the police. Do you get the picture?"

"Oh, I get the picture. I don't have any problem with that because I think he owes me some answers. I take it you don't think he did this alone?"

"Not a chance! There are at least two besides him. Two entered the house. Wimp fits the description of one. The other was a big guy. We don't have a clue on him. Someone had to drop them off. That makes three."

Karlis checked his watch. "We can't cover all the possibilities, but that should give you an idea of what we want you to do. They might already be gone with the money, but they got away so clean they might see no reason to run. They don't know we have identified you. They didn't expect us to. We must push our edge. Do you think you can handle what I have outlined?"

Scott stood and smiled. He seemed taller than before, "Let's do it!"

"One other thing, Mr. Scott. It could be dangerous."

"Not any more dangerous than practicing single engine go-arounds with a weak student in a Piper Twin Comanche."

Karlis said, "I'll take your word for that, but you still don't have the answer to where it leaves you. Well, here it is. At the end of this investigation, if you have aided significantly in the solution and prosecution of this case, and if you are charged in the state court, the FBI will provide, in writing, an official statement to the local prosecutor, setting out the extent of your cooperation. And, that *is* a promise."

Lance Barron was preparing to go home for the first time since the case began. He had already called his wife. There were several agents still in the office finishing up dictation on leads, mostly from the fixed surveillance, when the night secretary said, "Urgent for you Mr. Barron."

Lance looked at the clock. It was 6:14 P.M. "Lance Barron."

A female voice whispered, "Mr. Barron, Jenny just called. Charles took the call, and he is getting ready to leave to go get her. He wasn't going to call you. I must go."

Lance was momentarily stunned, "What?...Who?...Oh, Mrs. Kogan, yes, where is she?"

"Here's his note. 'Phone booth, IGA Thrift, South Commercial, Branson.' That's all I know. Have to go. Bye."

Lance scribbled it down and yelled, "They've released Jenny!" He sat for a brief moment collecting his thoughts. He had anticipated her release and had done some planning. He wanted to have a female agent with him when he interviewed her. He had discussed it with Lucille Baldwin. She had just left. Lance yelled again, "See if you can reach Lucy Baldwin. Tell her the interview is on. Have her pick me up at the front door.

"Ben, do you recognize South Commercial in Branson?"

"Yeah, it's the main downtown artery. Runs north, south. It crosses Taneycomo to Hollister and points south."

"Jenny's dad just got a call. She's at a phone booth at an IGA Thriftway on South Commercial."

Castle came to Barron's desk, "Hey, I know that store; it's right across from the police station."

Lance was gathering up notes from his dictation, preparing to leave, "I hate to think of her standing out there for thirty or forty minutes. There's no telling what condition she's in. Ben, call the PD down there. Tell them where she is, and Ben, tell them this little girl could be in bad shape. Urge them to send a sensitive person, preferably a female, plainclothes officer over there and approach her gently. She could be in a fragile state of mind. We don't want some uniformed, macho, hotdog racing over there with lights and siren, scaring her half to death."

Lance was headed for the door with Castle in tow. "Ask them not to interrogate her, and, one more thing, Ben. Ask the PD to leave someone at the phone booth to tell her Dad where she is. He's already underway."

Special Agent Baldwin was waiting when Lance reached the ground floor. "You just caught me, Lance, tell me about it."

Lance gave her the meager information he had. "I don't have any idea what her physical or emotional state is, but she's alive."

They headed toward 65 Highway through the tail-end of the rush-hour traffic. Lucy Baldwin said, "I have thought about her so much in the past four days. I've caught myself looking for her in every teenager I saw, wondering what she's like."

"I've wondered, too. I've had the advantage of meeting and associating with her parents, but I still don't have a firm idea of what to expect. I'm sure it has been a devastating experience for her. Some hostages have been crippled mentally, for life, by the experience. One point I hope to make with her father is the necessity for a physical examination. I've found him difficult to deal with. He didn't want to let us know she called. Mrs. Kogan called me. Mr. Kogan told me once in anger that he wouldn't even let me talk to her. I'm not going to press that issue until she is cleared by the doctors, but at some point we have to find out everything she can remember if we're going to solve this thing.

"Of course, the information we got from Tulsa this afternoon is monumental. We can put Ronald Wilkins in the title. We don't know much about him yet, but we know he set up the truck rental. So he's a key player."

As they made the turn from Battlefield Road to South 65 Highway, Baldwin asked, "Do you want to go lights and siren, Lance?"

"No, there's no need to. The police should have Jenny well protected by now, and it looks like we missed the early Branson crowd."

In most places U.S Highways are referred to as Highway 1, or Highway 82, or Highway 67 with the number coming last. But Lance had noted that in Missouri, the natives always put the number first. It was "65 Highway" or "63 Highway" and he had finally given in to that practice. By either name, 65 Highway from Springfield to Branson was an impressive drive. Thirty-five miles of economic progress and mounting excitement as tourists read the billboards extolling the virtues of music shows and eating establishments awaiting them in Branson. Much of the route was four lane now, but there was still a two-lane bottleneck just south of Ozark. Lance was not surprised to see the traffic slowing to a crawl as they entered that stretch. But as they moved farther into it, the pace seemed even slower than the bottleneck would account for. Then he saw rotating blue lights on the right shoulder. As they crawled closer he saw two Missouri Highway Patrol vehicles, one in front and one behind a silver Cadillac. A highway patrolman was on the shoulder waving southbound cars by. As they went past the first patrol car, Lance saw Charles Kogan, flushed and fuming and waving his finger in a patrolman's face.

"Pull over, Lucy. That's Jenny's dad!"

Baldwin parked just past the second cruiser. Lance bailed out and headed back toward a scene he couldn't believe. A MHP officer Lance recognized, Orville Baines, was using the trunk lid of his cruiser as a desk, writing out a ticket. Charles Kogan was yelling and gesturing toward Baines. Another trooper, whom Lance did not recognize, was doing a two-step to stay between Kogan and Baines. Mrs. Kogan was standing just outside the Cadillac, wringing her hands and repeating, "Oh, Charles, Oh, Charles."

Baines didn't look up, but Lance got Kogan's attention. "What happened, Mr. Kogan?"

Kogan pointed to Baines and yelled, "Will you tell this asshole my daughter has been kidnapped, and I need to get to Branson?"

Baines looked up and with a calmness born of having seen and heard it all said, "Oh, hello, Lance. Do you know this gentleman?"

"Yeah. We're working a case involving his daughter." With a momentary glance toward Kogan, Lance continued, "I understand she has been released in Branson."

Baines went on writing. He calmly said, "I told this gentleman he would never have made it to Branson the way he was driving. I clocked him coming off the James River Bridge at ninety. I put the lights and siren on him, and he boosted it up to a hundred, passing everything he came to on the four lane. I radioed ahead, and Troy there was ahead of him and picked him up after he hit the two lane. He came very close to a head-on trying to get around Troy on the left. Troy slowed him down while trying to keep from getting rear ended. I was sandwiching him from behind. He tried to go around Troy on the right side and, well, you can see it there; he hit the guard rail and blew out both right side tires. He was lucky to stay on the roadbed. You can see the drop down there."

Kogan seemed to be subdued by the recounting of his exploits. He walked slowly back toward his car. He ignored his wife, who was crying, and inspected the damage to the side of his car. He showed no sense of urgency. He seemed to have forgotten the reason for his haste.

Officer Baines went back to his ticket book and quickly completed his work. "Mr. Kogan, I'm citing you for excessive speed, reckless driving, failure to stop, driving on the shoulder, and attempting to pass on the right. I'm sorry about your daughter, but that doesn't give you the right to kill yourself, your wife, and other drivers. You were a foot away from a head-on and a charge of murder with a motor vehicle...Now, do you want us to call a tow truck for your car?"

Kogan turned around. He was clenching and relaxing his fists and looking down. Lance saw the anger, damaged pride, and frustration welling up in Kogan. He had seen it before. Kogan didn't want any help from this government flunky who had lectured him in front of his wife.

Trooper Baines saw the danger, too. Lance knew Baines was battling to remain professional, and winning. He had pulled too many dead and mangled bodies from twisted steel not to feel disgust for anyone who would so recklessly ignore all the rules of safety for his own selfish reasons—but he wasn't going to show it.

Lance stepped between the two and said, "We'll give you and Mrs. Kogan a ride on down to Branson. What garage do you use? The trooper here can have a tow truck on the way quickly. They will take your car to wherever you want."

"Have them take it to Berman Cadillac on South Campbell." Kogan addressed this to Lance, not giving Baines the satisfaction of a direct answer.

"Tell me about the call, Mr. Kogan." This request broke an embarrassing silence that had lasted since Mr. and Mrs. Kogan entered the back seat of the Bucar and Lance had introduced them to Lucille Baldwin. A muffled "nice to meet you," from all three had been the only other words spoken so far.

"Not much to tell," said Kogan, still pouting. "She said she was at a phone booth in Branson."

Lance knew this was agonizing for Kogan. He must know his wife had tipped Lance off. Now here he was, dependent on the very person he tried to cut out; dependent on him for a ride, for christsake.

Lance turned to face Kogan, "Look, Mr. Kogan, I'm not going to play games with you. We are not in a contest. I hope we have the same objective. You chose not to call me when Jenny was released. You chose instead to leave her alone in a phone booth for thirty or forty minutes, much longer as it turned out, at a critical time for her, so you could rush to the rescue. Were you thinking of her, Mr. Kogan, or yourself, trying to win some imaginary contest?

"I asked the Branson Police Department to rescue your daughter. Yes sir, I said rescue. Rescue her from the loneliness and fear she was surely feeling out there in that parking lot. Think of her. Imagine how long that wait would have been for her."

Kogan didn't respond, but Lance thought he heard Mrs. Kogan, who was sitting directly behind him, say, "Bravo."

Lucy took the Highway 248 exit and headed down North Commercial into the center of Branson. Lance said, "One more thing I want to suggest. Regardless of your daughter's apparent physical and emotional condition, you should consider taking her immediately to a hospital for a physical examination and general observation by medical personnel. Some of the emotional problems that arise from these stressful situations do not surface right away. In addition, if the question of any physical abuse during her confinement should arise, it will be critical that she had been examined immediately upon her release. Past case histories have shown that many times victims will not admit such abuse to their parents out of a sense of embarrassment but will admit it to a medical professional."

There was no response from the Kogans as they covered the last four blocks to the Branson Police Department.

The receptionist met them at the door. "You must be here about the girl. We have been expecting you. Right this way." She led the four of them down a well-lighted hallway to a door at the end that read, ELEANOR GAMBLE, JUVENILE OFFICER. Lance and Lucy stood back as the receptionist tapped lightly on the door. A middle-aged man with half rim glasses and steel gray hair opened the door. The receptionist said, "Chief Knowles, the parents are here."

The Chief turned back toward the room and started to speak but was drowned out by a squeal and a blur as Jennifer Marie Kogan rushed by him and into her mother's arms. The Chief, grinning and shaking his head said to no one in particular, "That is a marvelous young lady."

He came past the embracing Kogans and into the hallway and introduced himself to Lucille and Lance. "Ben Castle called me and we found her right where he said we would. I took Eleanor with me, and we walked over there. The young lady was a little suspicious at first and said she was supposed to wait for her Dad. I told her the FBI sent us. She asked Eleanor if that was true and when Eleanor assured her it was, she agreed to come with us. She took to Eleanor right away and insisted on giving her all kinds of information. We understood that you didn't want her interviewed, and we had no intention of doing so but she insisted and asked Eleanor to take notes. She gave Eleanor all kinds of information: times, distances, turns, names, sounds, initials, numbers. I tell you, she is a marvel."

Lance and Lucille waited outside for ten minutes before knocking on the door. A neat, fifty-year-old woman answered the door and said, "You must be Agent Barron; I'm Eleanor Gamble. Won't you come in?"

Lance said, "Yes. This is Lucille Baldwin, FBI," as his eyes swept the room. Then he saw her! He was unprepared for his reaction. It was like seeing the president, or a movie star. You have seen pictures and read stories and seen them on TV and thought about them. You've formed a hundred mental images; then suddenly, you're face to face. It's no longer an image. It's a real person. And there she was, Jennifer Marie Kogan, a living, smiling, breathing, talking human being. Lance's eyes filled with tears. It had happened when he saw Ted Williams, but that was years ago. It had happened when he met George Bush, not so many years ago. It was happening again. He was not embarrassed on any of those occasions.

Introductions were made all around. Charles Kogan was smiling. His daughter was standing between him and his wife with her arms around both. Lance managed, "How are you feeling, Jenny?"

"Oh, I'm tired, and I need a bath, but I'm okay. My dad thinks I should get a check-up at the hospital so I guess I will, but I'm sure anxious to get home. Oh, Mom, how's Peaches?" Before her mom could answer she asked, "Has this been in the paper? I wondered how Jason was handling it?"

It was obvious to Lance that Jenny was on an adrenaline high. He did not want to add to her overload. He started to back away, but Jenny said, "You are with the FBI, right? I memorized a lot of things I don't want to forget. I gave all of it to that lady over there; Eleanor Gamble. She took notes."

Lance said, "That's great, Jenny. I know that will be very helpful. I will get the list from her, and you and I can go over it after you have gotten some rest. I'll look forward to that, maybe tomorrow morning. This lady is also with the FBI. This is Lucille Baldwin. She will be with me when we talk. Okay?"

"Yes, sir."

Lance noted that Jenny's smile had faded some just since he entered the room. Her high was subsiding. It was his guess that she would soon be a very tired young lady.

Lance sought out Mr. Kogan. "If you agree, I will ask Ms. Gamble to call the local hospital and arrange for an emergency admission. It is fairly routine for her, as juvenile officer. We five can ride over in the Bucar. The chief wants to give us an escort, just in case we should encounter one of those traffic jams Branson is famous for. As soon as Jenny is admitted, and you two feel comfortable about her, Lucy and I are going to head back to Springfield. Either of you or both are welcome to ride back with us."

Mrs. Kogan didn't even look toward her husband. She said firmly, "I'm going to stay."

There was a lengthy silence. Mr. Kogan finally said, "I think that's a good plan. We'll need a car down here. I'll ride back with these people and come back tomorrow to pick Jenny up."

Lance thought, *I hope that will include Mrs. Kogan.*

The trip to Skaggs Hospital was short and without incident. Mr. Kogan handled the check-in routine. Lance asked Lucille to go to the room with Jenny and explain to her and Mrs. Kogan that she would like to have all of Jenny's clothing for hair and fiber examination. "Suggest to Mrs. Kogan that she have her husband bring a change of clothes for Jenny."

It was 8:40 P.M. when Lance, Lucille, and Charles Kogan said their goodbyes and headed north. Lance could think of only one other task he had to complete tonight, and he could handle that by radio. He called the RA and asked for Tim Landry who was handling the 4:00 P.M.-to-midnight shift.

"I have a press release already approved by the SAC in the media folder on my desk. It sets out the highlights of the kidnapping up to today. Please add the following to the release: 'Jennifer was released today at approximately 6:00 P.M. in Branson and is confined at the Skaggs Hospital for routine observation. FBI sources said Jenny appeared to be in good condition and gave some preliminary information about her kidnappers before being hospitalized.

"'The FBI said they had not released information previously because of their concern for the safety of the victim. The FBI is pursuing numerous leads in the investigation.'

"That's it on the new material, Tim. The media list is in the folder. Make sure you get it to everyone on the list. They should be able to get it on their ten o'clock news programs. You'll probably be deluged with requests for additional information. Refer them to the media representative in Kansas City. Mr. Palmer will handle all future news releases. Thanks, Tim. It's been a long four days. I'm headed for home."

Lance stretched out and smiled. The safe recovery of Jenny Kogan was accomplished. The case was far from over, but the first critical step was complete. It gave Lance comfort to visualize Jenny in the hospital room with her mother. A small part of this crazy world was back in order.

Lucy would drop him at his car, and he would head for home where he would put another small part back together. He could rest, at least until tomorrow, in his own bed.

They followed the ribbon of tail lights moving up 65 Highway toward Springfield and the Interstate. Thoughts of his wife, his children, and his good fortune warmed his heart.

Patsy would bring him up to date on all the kids' activities. Not once would she mention the inconvenience to her plans that his unplanned four-day absence had caused. And this was only the latest in a long chain of broken or altered dinner dates. She could magically stretch a meal prepared for three into a feast for four when he came in early because he had to go back out. She could make him into a hero to his children when he didn't show up at all.

When he did make it home, she would ensure that he had private time with each of the children. And sometime during the evening, while he was catching up on the mail she so carefully sorted for him, she would slip into the bedroom and don the bright red, low-cut, short nightgown he bought for her and become his lover. What a woman!

THE WIRE

Small crimes always precede great ones. Never have we seen timid
innocence pass suddenly to extreme licentiousness.

—Jean Baptist Racine

Joel Karlis and Ed Kelley were parked on the shoulder of a farm
road a mile and a half outside the city limits of Wellston,
Oklahoma. From their position they could see Jack Scott's red
Corvette and hear him breathing into the hidden microphone as
he knocked on the door at the home of William "Wee Willie"
Wilkins and his wife Dora Mae. The Bureau automobile was only
a hundred yards away but the dense poplar wind break shielded
their car from the view of those in the house. There was little traffic on the farm road, and they didn't expect to be there long.
Kelley had a "Department of Agriculture checking the soil bank"
story ready if a passing neighbor should inquire. Ed dictated an
introduction into the tape recorder and then placed it next to the
radio speaker. The decision to have Scott wear the wire today was
not made because of any distrust of Scott nor any concern for his
safety. But Scott had to get used to wearing and operating the
transmitter in anticipation of the next step: a face-to-face meeting
with Wimp Wilkins. Karlis was concerned about that step. The
equipment had to work then.

The two agents listened as Scott made small talk with the
Wilkins. They first discussed the weather, a favorite subject of
wheat farmers, and then they turned to the beauty of Mrs.
Wilkins's garden.

Karlis, knowing the obligatory chat would go on for a while and that they were getting it all on tape said, "You know, Ed, it's going to be hard to convince Scott that Wimp is not the same weakling he knew in college. We've got to make him realize that Wimp, and whoever his partners are, have committed a serious crime, gotten away with a lot of money, and think they are home free. Oh, I'm sure Wimp figured Scott would squawk a little about him not bringing the truck back so he could collect his two-fifty. Wimp probably planned to give him that and maybe even a little bonus. He probably expects Scott to call, but, man, he's going to be shocked at what Scott tells him. They didn't think Scott would ever be identified. When Scott unloads on Wimp about our questioning him, things are going to happen. Just think about it; Scott is the only person who can connect them to that truck, the only one. Do you realize the position that puts Scott in? I doubt if Scott has thought about that. He's going to be a marked man."

Karlis stopped talking when he realized Scott's conversation had turned to Ronnie and Branson. Mr. Wilkins was talking, "Naw, that number we gave you before won't get him anymore. He's moved back into Branson. He said him and that lady didn't get along too good. Course we didn't go much for that arrangement anyway, but Ronnie's a grown man. We never did meet the woman. He never even told us her name."

"Did he hire on with a regular band yet? I know he was playing some at a place where he was working."

"No, I don't think so. Ronnie don't tell us much, and we don't ask him much. We just tell him once in a while that he is always welcome back here. I could use him on the farm, but he never did have much interest in farming."

Mrs. Wilkins added, "He hardly ever calls us, but he does let us know where we can reach him in an emergency. He's our only child, you know, and we'd like to have him closer by, but he's got that fiddle-playing in his blood…always did have."

"Well, he's good at it. Maybe I'll get a chance to hear him on my next trip. I was hoping to hit him up for some more of those wholesale tickets."

There was a pause. Karlis was anxious. He addressed the tape recorder, "Get the number dammit, Jack, you've got to ask them…" He realized Mr. Wilkins was speaking, "…idea what his address is, but he did give us a new number we can reach him at."

"Well, maybe he wouldn't mind getting another call from his old college buddy."

Karlis was squirming and pounding his palm with his fist. Kelley was trying to shield the Nagra from the extraneous noise.

"No, I don't think he would mind. Here…here it is. It's 417-335-9991."

Both Karlis and Kelley wrote down the number, then turned to face each other; both smiled and breathed a sigh of relief. Jack Scott, amateur actor, had passed his first test.

★ ★ ★

Lance Barron sat upright in bed. He checked the clock. 4:33 A.M. In a dream he had seen a note he wrote the previous day just before Mrs. Kogan called. Corporal Vickers had run Arkansas tag YYT-901 through the INLETS segment of NCIC. It was registered to a 1996 Cadillac, VIN 1G6KF52Y4SU8796543, blue. The registered owner was Jimmy Doyle Mahon, Route 2, Box 28, Lead Hill, Arkansas. Vickers's computer search had failed to show a driver's license for Mahon in either Arkansas or Missouri. Lance had written on the print-out, "Call LR, Urgent for Fayetteville RA."

"I wrote it down, but I never gave it to anyone." Lance felt compelled to get to the office and take care of it although reason told him that no one was going to cover the lead at that hour.

He kissed Patsy without waking her, dressed, and slipped out. As he made his way through the empty streets to the office, Lance thought back to the fixed surveillance. The Arkansas Cadillac was the remaining lead from among the six cars that survived Amos Trout's final sort. The other five, all seen at both key surveillance sites, had washed out, much to the chagrin of "Captain" Amos. One of them, the red Corvette with two guys, had proved to be an interesting investigation. DMV records showed the registered owner as Grant Turner, with a residence in the affluent Highland Springs development east of Springfield. The city directory showed Turner as Vice President, New Accounts, Commerce Bank. Not the profile of your average kidnapper. When Amos and Gretchen went to Turner's impressive home in mid-morning, Turner's wife reported that her husband had been out of town on business for the past two days and wasn't scheduled to return until midafternoon that day. *Oh, Yeah?* thought Trout, but he said, "Then I'll catch him at the bank this afternoon."

Amos made a pretext call to the bank and asked for Turner. He wanted to verify his absence since someone must have been using his car on the previous evening. To his surprise Amos found the vice-president on duty at the bank even though it was still only ten-thirty. Amos made up a quick story about being in the bank to open an account on the previous day. He feigned disappoint-ment that the banker didn't remember him. "I'll bet you weren't even there," Amos bluffed. Turner, who was under pressure from his boss because of the success of a new account campaign being waged by a rival, Empire Bank, took the bait, "Oh yes, sir, I was here all day. I do remember you, sir, and we would like to have your business." Amos decided to let him down easily. "Well, okay, but I expect you to recognize me the next time I'm in there."

Amos made an inquiry at the Springfield Police Department. He found that the vice squad had an extensive file on Turner. Their undercover squad was working the prostitution and homosexual beats in Phelps Grove Park and Park Central Square. They had observed Turner on numerous occasions. So far, there was nothing serious. Turner seemed to be just testing the water. He had never been arrested. Their surveillance log from the previous night showed Turner and his companion making verbal contact with two known prostitutes in Phelps Grove Park at the time the ransom package was lost. The PD's log covered Turner from before the ransom call until after the surveillance was discontinued. Turner's companion was identified by the police as Myron Maylock, a twenty-five year old homosexual and pimp who had a couple of drug arrests. The police department was in the process of compiling a confidential report on Turner to furnish to Commerce Bank Security. They said that based on Turner's current activities and associations, it was just a matter of time until he committed an illegal act. Amos reluctantly closed Turner as a suspect. He was guilty all right but not of kidnapping.

Lance reached the FBI office on East Sunshine at 5:30 A.M. He found the computer print-out on Jimmy Doyle Mahon still in his work basket. The note was just as he saw it in his dream. *I should have gotten someone on this before I left for Branson.* He had wanted to get a Little Rock agent up to Lead Hill to check out Mahon as soon as possible. It would be a long drive from Little Rock. Lead Hill was just south of the Missouri-Arkansas line. Little Rock would cover it from their Fayetteville RA, but it would still be quite a haul. It was too early to get anyone in Little Rock except the night clerk. It was much too early to check on Jenny's condition. Lance felt real frustration when he realized it had been more than twelve hours since Jenny was released, and he still didn't know how much help she was going to be. Still, he knew that the hospital stay and the examination were best for her.

Looking for something productive to do at this hour, Lance took out Eleanor Gamble's notes from her conversation with Jenny. He hoped to interview Jenny in great detail today. He scanned down the list of times, turns, names, initials, numbers, but he could find no pattern, no key to the meaning. *Wait a minute!* His heart leaped. *Is that "Ronnie"?* It looked like it, but Eleanor's writing was obviously hurried. So far they could only connect Ronnie Wilkins to the truck. Could Jenny connect him to the kidnapping? Lance fought becoming too excited. He knew this was a long way from being proof of anything, but he had butterflies in his empty stomach as he went down the list. Near the end he saw a group of digits that appeared to be a telephone number, Eleanor had written 725-1564 then added beside it, 800# and "jumping jacks." Lance decided to see if it was a telephone number. He dialed it as an 800 number. A recording came on line, "You have reached KinderCare Prosthetic and Research Center in Oklahoma City. Our office hours are Monday through Friday, eight A.M. to five P.M. and eight A.M. until noon on Saturday. Please call back during office hours, or you may leave a message at the tone."

Lance wrote down as much of the message as he could. He checked the number against Gamble's notes and redialed it. He copied the rest of the message but was still mystified as to the meaning. He hoped Jenny could remember the significance of those numbers.

In his mail folder, Lance found a copy of an Oklahoma City teletype to Little Rock setting out a lead for Little Rock to determine the subscriber to the telephone number 501-749-8922. This was the number where Jack Scott had been able to reach, or at least leave a message for, Wimp Wilkins before Scott's last visit to Branson several months ago. Oklahoma City pointed out that Scott had not been able to contact Wilkins at that number as recently as yesterday, and it might no longer be valid. Clipped to the Oklahoma City teletype was a teletype from Little Rock to Kansas City showing the subscriber to 501-749-8922 as J. Harris, Rt. 3, Box 48, Oak Grove, Arkansas, another address for Little Rock to check out.

Lance's attention went back to Vickers's computer printout of the Arkansas registration on the blue Cadillac. He leaned back in his swivel chair, propped his feet up on his desk, and folded his arms behind his head, a posture he rarely took at home and had never before taken in the office. On this dark morning in early April it seemed like the thing to do. He had spent hours during the past four days thinking about the kidnappers but always in general terms. In his mind they were still in their black coveralls and ski masks. One was big, the other small. That was about all he knew. He heard one of them say, "Okay." He didn't even know which one it was. Now he had a name to think about, two if he counted Eleanor's notes. Two names to think about. And that's what he did as he relaxed in this "thinking man's posture." *What was Jimmy Doyle Mahon of Lead Hill, Arkansas, doing driving the streets of Springfield, Missouri, on a Sunday night, before and after midnight, in his blue Cadillac? Who was with him? Those will be questions for Jimmy Doyle Mahon.*

Now, what was it Harold Sheffield told me about a blue Cadillac that first night at the Kogan's? Lance retrieved his write-up of that conversation. The story came back to him as he scanned the FD-302. Sheffield had been coming south toward Springfield on 65 Highway when he saw the blue automobile off on the left shoulder. He went on south but made a quick turn-around. He headed back north and saw the red Mustang, Jenny's car, also on the left shoulder and just a little way through the woods to the spot where the other car had been. Strange. But what else? The timing would have been right. Lance recalled how reluctant Harold had been to say the car was a Cadillac, but he did say it, and knowing Harold, that was almost a guarantee.

Lance returned to the file and found the Springfield, Illinois, teletype to Kansas City setting out the investigation of William A. Patrick. There it was, Patrick and his wife were robbed in Branson by two guys *in a blue Cadillac.*

Lance, like all other investigators, had seen cases in which eyewitness testimony—the testimony of good, honest, intelligent witnesses—had been so far off that it jeopardized the outcome of the case. The terrified bank teller who described the robber as "six foot four" when the bank camera film later showed him to be barely five foot eight, could create reasonable doubt in the jury's mind as to how she could have identified the robber in a line-up. You had to be careful relying too heavily on what witnesses thought they saw, particularly in stressful situations. Kogan's description of the kidnappers as black men was a good example. When he pinned Kogan down on how he had reached the conclusion they were black, Kogan had to admit he didn't have one shred of evidence to justify it. All he had was his racial prejudice. That sort of prejudice warped the judgment of a lot of people…about a lot of things.

As Lance went through the file, he argued the evidence to himself, *Here, your honor, here we have a seasoned Missouri State Trooper who was most careful in describing the car he saw near the victim's car as a blue Cadillac. And here, sir, we have a computer printout connecting an Arkansas tag to a blue Cadillac. That tag was seen on two occasions, each time by two FBI agents, in an area in which the kidnappers would have had an interest. The agents who reported the tag recorded in their notes that it was on a blue or dark-colored Cadillac.*

Then, your honor, we have the Illinois couple visiting in Branson. I will grant that their observation might be suspect, occurring as it did during a robbery. Yes, they were under some duress, but the gentleman thought the car was a Cadillac; he was certain it was blue. His wife was positive about the Arkansas tag.

I realize, sir, that none of this proves any crime, but taken overall, it seems to me that this is a trail we need to aggressively pursue.

When Lance finished his soliloquy he knew what he was going to do. He could not ignore the presence of a blue Cadillac at critical times in this case. He could not wait to have Jimmy Doyle Mahon interviewed by a Little Rock agent. Lead Hill, Arkansas was a small town just south of the Missouri-Arkansas line. He would call the supervisor in the Little Rock Division and request permission to cover a lead in their territory. This was a matter of courtesy and such requests were usually approved. When Lucille Baldwin got to the office they would leave for Branson and check on Jenny's condition. If she was still confined, they would continue on to Lead Hill and check out Mr. Jimmy Doyle Mahon. They could then check on Jenny on the return trip. It would be an interesting day. He could hardly wait!

Lance reviewed the rough drafts of reports of the investigation conducted by the other agents. The manufacturer of the garage door opener was cooperating fully in trying to follow the paper trail on that particular opener. They had determined that the lot containing the serial number of the questioned opener had been shipped last October to the Sears warehouse in Memphis for distribution to their retail stores in Missouri, Kansas, Arkansas, Mississippi, and Tennessee. The haystack containing their needle was still a large one.

The quizzing of welding shop owners was time-consuming and possibly futile. More than one shop owner had told the interviewing agents that a reputable shop would not have cut a hole in the bottom of a truck still bearing the Ryder logo because of the liability factor. Some shops also pointed out that the cutting would not have been a difficult job. There were a lot of unlicensed, untrained, and maybe unscrupulous welders out there who could use a cutting torch. Cutting wasn't really welding. It wasn't like making a delicate joint requiring a fine bead. Lance noticed that some agents were asking the shops to name some of the "bootleggers" who might do such a job and following those leads. It was a long, slow, tedious process, the kind upon which the FBI had built its reputation.

★ ★ ★

SA Joel Karlis rode back from Wellston with Jack Scott. He wanted Scott to place the call to Wilkins's new number as soon as possible. It was important that it be placed from Scott's home phone in the event of a quick call back.

Kelley was picking up pizza and would join them in Scott's apartment.

As Scott and Karlis entered the complex, they passed near the apartment manager's office. Karlis said, "Your apartment manager—Mr. Rose, isn't it?—he seems like a nice fellow."

Scott turned quickly to see if Karlis was serious.

Karlis, grinning, added, "He was most helpful to us when we were trying to locate you."

Scott said, "That asshole. He tried to get my car towed. He has about five parking slots designated as "management parking" and he's a one-man office. They're all poorly marked. I used one of them one day when I was in a hurry. I had a student pilot waiting, and I had to pick up his log book. There were open slots on both sides of me…He called the cops! Can you believe that? The police refused to tow my car and it ticked Rose off…at the police and at me."

Karlis, still grinning, said, "Well, he was sure helpful to us. I'll probably drop in and thank him one of these days." Scott could tell there was more to the story than that, but he wasn't sure he wanted to hear it.

In Scott's apartment, Karlis went right to work attaching the recording device to the phone. They discussed what Scott would say.

Scott said, "You understand this is not Wimp's number. From what his dad said, it is just a place where they can leave a message."

"Right, but you have to be prepared with your spiel on the chance Wimp answers or is nearby. Now remember, Jack, you're mad as hell. You have to get that across, but you're afraid the FBI is listening so you don't want to say much. Tell him the FBI thinks you're involved. You want to meet him so you can work out what to do. Let him figure out the details. You've got a problem; now he's got a problem. If he's reluctant to suggest anything, you might say something like, 'You better not leave me hanging out here, Ronnie. I'm not gonna let you ruin me.' We want to force a meeting. He will be more likely to talk face to face. And, by following him when it's over, we can find where he is living and maybe the identity of the other kidnappers.

"He'll probably ask for time. Try not to give him any. Make him make a decision. If he has to check with somebody, give him a short deadline. Tell him to call you back here. Mention losing your commercial pilot's license. You're not going to take a fall for him. He's got to tell you what's going on.

"I know that's a load, Jack, and you can never tell how the talk will go, but it helps to pre-plan what your attitude will be. Remember, you hold the key to his future. Use that position to make him do what you want. You want him to meet with you and discuss what he's done and what he is going to do for you."

Scott was still nervous in spite of his success in his matinee performance, "Do you think he'll set up something now or do you think he'll want to call back?"

"I think he'll be shocked that the FBI has located you. I doubt that he'll have any idea what to do. As I said, he'll probably ask for time. He might want to talk with someone. Push him for a quick decision. Remember what we want: the call back, the meeting, the surveillance."

Scott said, more from anxiety than from confidence, "Okay, I've got the picture. Let's do it."

Karlis rechecked the recording equipment and then carefully dialed the number. He handed the phone to Scott and picked up the extension.

A female answered, "Tarheel Theater, may I help you?"

Scott paused, then said, "I'm trying to reach Wim...I'd like to speak with Ronnie Wilkins."

"I'm sorry, sir, this is the office of The Tarheel Theater. I can take a message for Mr. Wilkins. He's one of our musicians."

"Well, okay, have him call Jack Scott in Tulsa. Tell him it's urgent."

"Does he have your number, Mr. Scott?"

"Yeah, well it's…it's 918-765-4631."

"Okay, sir, 918-765-4631 and you're Mr. Jack Scott, right? I'll see that he gets it."

"And, Miss, be sure and tell him it's urgent."

Kelley arrived with the pizza. Karlis brought him up to date as Scott broke out a round of beer. They got comfortable for the wait. There was little to talk about.

Karlis and Scott were watching the Atlanta Braves and Kelley was asleep on the couch at 11:15 when the phone rang. Karlis started the tape. Scott was on the phone quickly, "Yeah."

"Is that you, Scottie Boy?" It was the unmistakable squeak of Wimp Wilkins.

Scott turned toward Karlis, nodded and mouthed, "It's him."

Then, "Yeah, Wimp, you son-of-a-bitch."

"Hey, buddy, hold on there. I'm going to get the money to you. I appreciate what you did. I'll make it right."

"Wait a damn minute, Wimp." Scott's voice was firm and clear. "I'm only gonna say this once. I don't know what the hell you've done, but the FBI has come down on me hard about that truck. They know something, Wimp, and they're leaning on me. I haven't told them anything, but you better come up with some good answers, buddy. I'm not going to take the rap for something you did, and I don't know anything about…Do you hear me, Wimp?"

After waiting for a response and getting none, Scott said, "I'm not going to say any more on the phone. It's not safe, but I'm gonna have some answers from you or I'm gonna tell them exactly what happened. We better get together and get this straightened out and quick. Do you hear me, Wimp?"

"Yeah, but, Goddamn. I don't see how in hell…"

"Set something up, Wimp. I'll give you until noon tomorrow. It better be good. I'm looking at losing my job and my pilot's license. It better be real good, Wimp. Call me here." Scott slammed the phone down in real anger as he thought of the problems Wimp Wilkins had caused him.

Karlis said, "Hey, good job, Jack. I think you got his attention. His failure to even mouth some phony denial or even mention a reason for not returning the truck tells me he knew all along how it was going down. They just never figured you would be identified. But they know now that they have a problem."

Kelley asked, "How did he sound? Was he nervous?"

Scott said, "Oh, man. He froze up. He didn't say hardly anything after I told him I'd been questioned."

Kelley said, "It looks to me like they can do one of two things, Jack. One, they can meet with you and offer you money to keep quiet; or two, they can just run out on you. We ought to know which route they're gonna take by noon tomorrow."

Karlis, frowning, said, "They have one more choice, Ed, they can set him up for a meeting and then blow him away."

There was a lengthy silence. Scott looked from Joel to Ed and back again. Karlis finally said, "We'll work something out on that, Jack. I guarantee we won't leave you hanging out there."

★ ★ ★

Lucille Baldwin arrived at the office at 7:30 A.M. Lance was anxious to get to Branson and Lead Hill. He had written out several items for Tim Landry to take care of. Heading the list was getting a surveillance van and a couple of agents to Branson to set up near the Tarheel Theater. With the descriptive data Tulsa had developed on Ronnie Wilkins and the new knowledge that he was a musician there, it was possible they might spot him and put him under surveillance.

The second item was to stay in contact with Tulsa to learn what kind of response Wimp would make to Scott's ultimatum. Lance instructed, "If they set up a meeting for today, reach me through the Taney County Sheriff's Office. I'll check in there periodically. I'll drop the Lead Hill lead if I have to. I'm not going to miss the showdown between Scott and Wilkins."

★ ★ ★

Lance and Lucille arrived at Skaggs Hospital in Branson at 8:15 A.M. The parking lot was filled with television remote vehicles. TV reporters and their camera people were milling around the lobby. When Lance inquired at the nurse's station about Jennifer, he was told that Mrs. Kogan had called down earlier and instructed that Mr. Barron and Ms. Baldwin be admitted to her daughter's room upon their arrival.

Lance was surprised to find that Mr. Kogan was also there. Jennifer was standing by the window. She was wearing a long-sleeved white blouse and navy blue slacks. Her hair was longer than he realized, shining and pulled back in a pony tail: a very, very attractive young lady. Mr. and Mrs. Kogan were sitting on the edge of the bed, drinking coffee. Mrs. Kogan said brightly, "We waited for you. She's all checked out and ready to go home with a clean bill of health."

Lance's eyes went back to Jennifer. "So you're feeling well enough to give us a little time, are you?"

She smiled broadly, "Oh, yes, sir. I feel wonderful. I had a great night's sleep after they got through poking around on me. The breakfast this morning was delicious after my steady diet of hamburgers, fries and raisin biscuits."

"I know you're anxious to get home. I hope our interview won't take long. You made a great start with the lady from the Juvenile Office last night, and I have her notes."

Lance turned to Mr. Kogan for his approval, but Mrs. Kogan answered, "That will be fine, Mr. Barron. By the way, Ms. Baldwin, I bagged up her clothing as you requested, and I have it here for you. Charles brought down a change of clothes for her."

Lance realized that Mr. Kogan had not said a word. He felt compelled to include him in the conversation. "Are they taking care of your car for you, Mr. Kogan?" As soon as Lance asked about the car, he wished he hadn't. He knew that would be a sore subject for Kogan. He hoped Kogan wouldn't make a scene in front of his daughter.

Kogan's reply was curt, "It's being taken care of. Have you guys come up with anything on the kidnappers?"

"Yes, sir." Lance replied. "We have some promising work being done by one of the other field offices, and we have some good leads here in southwest Missouri."

Mr. Kogan said, "Jenny tells me one of the kidnappers—a woman—treated her very well."

"Well, we want to hear about that along with the other things she can tell us. So, if you will excuse us, Agent Baldwin and I will get started. We would like to talk with her here in this room."

Kogan, still sitting on the bed and drinking his coffee, did not take the hint. "What is your recommendation, Lance, on handling the media? They were all around the house when I left this morning. I just waved. Some followed me all the way down here."

Lance noted that Kogan was back on a first name basis. "Kidnappings are always big news, of course, and I don't think you can avoid the media. Maybe if you make some innocuous statement about the joy of having your daughter back and the 'clean bill of health' given by the excellent staff here at the hospital, or something of that nature, it would satisfy them for a while. Since the investigation is still pending, I hope that you will not go into any great detail about the ransom and what Jenny has told you about the people involved. Other than that, I'm sure your judgment is as good as mine. I do hope they don't start hounding Jenny everywhere she goes."

"I'm not going to allow that to happen. You can bet on it." A little of Kogan's fire was returning. "Mrs. Kogan and I will go on down and face them and let you get started with your work. We'll see you in a little while, Jenny."

As they left, Lance heard Kogan say to his wife, "For christsake try not to cry in front of these people."

The interview of Jennifer Marie Kogan was one of the most unforgettable events in Lance Barron's Bureau career. His amazement began when she remembered his first and last names, and Lucille's, from the previous evening. She also remembered Eleanor Gardner's name and the last name of the chief of police. She apologized for not remembering his first name.

Lance, working on the assumption that Jenny's clearest memory would be of the most recent events, suggested that she start with her release at the telephone booth at the IGA store and work backward to the place where she had been confined. This was a recommended technique and had worked well with other victims.

But this bright, energetic teenager spoke right up, "I've worked hard to remember as much as possible. I knew it would be important. Do you have the list I gave Ms. Gardner? I'd rather go right down that list because I memorized things in the order they occurred and that's the way I gave it to her."

Lance was amused and impressed by the intelligence and spunk of this girl. He produced the list, and they started off with her memory of the smell of the cloth that was pressed over her mouth. For forty-five minutes of almost uninterrupted monologue, Jenny recalled the walk between cars, she described the voices and demeanor of the people she named "Boss" and "Driver," and later, "Lady." She described the traffic, their speed, turns, times, gates, goats, gravel, dogs, steps, carpet, "the box," making the tapes, Lady's arm, wristwatch and ring, cheeseburgers, milkshakes, "genie," "Ronnie," J.D., the bite mark on J.D.'s arm, along with a possible head wound, the layout of the house, her toilet paper streamer, the medicine chest, lipstick, television, jumping-jacks, telephone numbers, and then the short drive to freedom.

Lance and Lucille took notes furiously and occasionally had a question, but mostly they marveled at this young lady. When she finished, Lance felt that he could drive to the general area of where she was held. He questioned her in detail about the 800 number, and she recounted "Lady's" side of the conversation. Some of her remarks fit with the information Lance had received from the answering machine in Oklahoma City.

Lance had never interviewed a witness who had as keen a feel for what was important as this young lady. He was sure that Jenny could have gone on for hours about her discomfort in the box, about her loneliness, and about her doubts and fears. Instead she had, in effect, said, *None of that is important. Here is what is important. Believe me. I was there and I memorized it.* Lance resisted an impulse to embrace Jenny and say, *God bless you, young lady. You are one in a million.* He settled for smiling and shaking his head in disbelief.

Lucille, excited, said, "Lance, she's put us in the general area. If we can verify a few of those things, like the gate and the drive..."

Lance broke in, "And the goats and the streamer; we've got enough for a search warrant. The place in Oklahoma can give us the phone number he called and the name of the person he spoke with. And with that we can determine the address, and with the address, we can verify the name of the person who lives there, and if it all checks out it spells 'Probable Cause.' We need to get going on the affidavit right away."

In their excitement Lance and Lucy momentarily forgot the source of all this information. Jenny was smiling at their animated exchange but became serious when they turned back to her. She said, "I want you to know that I would not have made it without the kindness of the lady who was there. I don't know her name, and I never saw her face, but she lives in that house where the box is. She has a son who lives some other place, I think in Harrison, with her mother. Lady is the one who released me. She made the decision on her own." As Jenny related this information, her elan faded and tears filled her eyes. "I don't know what would have happened to me if it hadn't been for her. When you find her, I want you to remember that. I intend to remind you."

Lucy went over and put her arm around Jenny. "We will remember, Jenny. I promise you we will."

Lance rang for a nurse and asked that she escort Jenny to the lobby and "put her directly in the care of her parents."

Lance checked in with the Taney County Sheriff's office before leaving the hospital. Tim Landry had just placed a stop for him to call the office.

Landry told him they had gotten the word from Tulsa. The meet was on for tomorrow at 3:00 P.M. Landry didn't want to give Lance the location over an unsecured line. "It's in our territory. Karlis wanted to make sure we realized the position his man Scott is in. We must set up protection for him."

"That's true. We have done some thinking on it. How about getting with Amos. We will use one of his units, but make sure he doesn't get carried away. I plan to be there in some capacity. We'll work out the details when I get back. Tell Amos to wait for me. I shouldn't be too late. Make sure we'll have an aircraft available."

"I've already handled that, Lance."

"We're headed for the address down south. Write this down, Tim. If Castle is not working on something critical, have him start working on an application for a search warrant. It will have to be filed in the Western District of Arkansas at Fort Smith. He can go ahead and outline the crime and the pertinent Title 18 Sections. I'll have the address and the probable cause information for him when we get back. Have Lambright or one of the other pilots stand by to fly Castle to Fort Smith."

"Ten-Four, Lance. I'll see that he gets started on it. He's been over at the PD all day, dismantling that plywood box he removed

WHEN NO ONE PURSUES   273

from the back of the truck. He said there are some good tool marks on it. I'll get some relief over there and get him going on the search warrant."

Lance and Lucille Baldwin took the hospital service elevator and left through a side door to avoid the media. It was a straight shot from Branson to the Arkansas line, but then the road started twisting some on the way to Omaha. Lead Hill, population 283, was twenty curving miles east of Omaha on Highway 14 and sat between two arms of sprawling Bull Shoals Lake. It was not difficult to determine which road was Postal Route 2 out of Lead Hill. There were only three possibilities, and they had come into town on one of them. They found the proper mailbox number sequence on Highway 7 going north from Lead Hill toward Diamond City, population 601. Based on what they saw as they drove north, they decided the odds were extremely high that the address they were seeking would be a mobile home. It was. They drove past it and checked the mailbox number. It was Rt. 2, Box 28, but there was no name on the box. The mobile home was parallel to the road and very close. Weeds were growing all around the base of the structure. A few were growing up through the boards that made up the small front porch. One of the two front picture windows was broken. Lance was speechless for a moment but finally said, "And this guy drives a Cadillac?"

Lance parked in the small front yard and walked over to check the mailbox up close. This was the place. When Lance returned to the car, Lucy said, "I see another mailbox down there about a quarter mile. Maybe someone is at home down there."

The distant mailbox marked the location of another mobile home set a little farther back and on the opposite side of the road. They parked in the yard. This one appeared to be occupied. There were dogs in the yard and a dirty Plymouth van. As they got out of the car, one of the hounds gave a lengthy howl to announce their arrival but didn't bother to get up. As they approached the front steps, a thin middle-aged man in overalls and no shirt came out. He smiled a toothless smile. "If you're selling, I'm not buying. If you're recruiting, I'm not joining. If you're preaching, I'm not listening." He was grinning as he said the latter, and he finished up by saying, "Now, how can I help you folks?"

Lance, in the spirit of the moment said, "I'm asking. Are you answering?"

The man said, "I will if I can. Don't make it too hard," and they all three laughed.

Lance pointed, "The man in the mobile home down there. How long has he been gone?"

The neighbor thought for a moment, scratching his head, "Pardner, he ain't never not been gone." The man laughed a little at his own phrase and then tried to top it. "He's been nothing but gone ever since he got there."

Neither Lance nor Lucy laughed this time.

"Aw, he came in here about a year ago. I don't know exactly when. We just saw his car down there one day and the For Sale sign was gone, but he never moved in. I don't know if he ever even went in. My wife said he was from North Carolina. She seen the tag on his car. He comes in there every two or three weeks and stays just a few minutes. I've never seen him go in the house. He just picks up his mail, and he's gone. I happened to be passing by one day while he was there. He was walking back toward his car. Big guy, had on nice clothes. He waved. I waved back. I remembered what my wife said so I checked his tag. It was Arkansas."

Lance asked, "What kind of car was it?"

"Oh, it was a Cadillac. Big and blue. No doubt about that."

Lucille joined in, "When did you last see him there?"

"Well, I don't keep tabs on him, but I'd say it's been within the past couple of weeks. He's about due again. I asked the mailman one time if the guy got much mail. He said they weren't supposed to give out that kind of information, but he went on to say the guy only wanted first class mail delivered, so he didn't get much." He laughed, "Heck, if I jest got first class, I wouldn't get any."

On the drive back to Springfield, Lance commented that the high he was on after the interview of Jenny was dashed a little by the failure to get anything on Jimmy Doyle Mahon.

Lucy said, "Oh, but we did, Lance. We found out he came here from North Carolina."

"Yeah, maybe. But where does he live now? What was he doing in Springfield, Missouri, on Sunday at midnight? And why does he keep a dump like that in Lead Hill, Arkansas just so he can get his mail there?"

Lucy said, "I think I know the answer to the last question. He's hiding from someone."

"I'm sure you're right, Lucy, but that only brings up new questions. Who is he hiding from and why?"

★ ★ ★

When Lance got back to Springfield, his first act was to call Joel Karlis in Tulsa. "You're doing a heck of a good job with your man Scott, Joel. Tell me about Wimp's call."

"He called at 10:37 this morning. He got right to the point. He said he had talked with the 'other people' and they pretty much told him that this was his problem and he better get it worked out. He started out sort of begging Scott to not ruin his big chance. He said 'Let's get together, Jack, and work out a deal.' Jack told him that was exactly what he wanted to do, but he warned Wimp again that it better be a good one.

"This part sort of worries me, Lance. Wimp already had a meeting place and time set up. He wanted to meet at that rest stop on I-44 just west of Joplin, the one on the north side, at 3:00 P.M. tomorrow. He emphasized that he didn't want anybody else involved. He asked Scott if he would be in the red Corvette. Scott told him he would be, but when he asked Wimp what he would be driving, Wimp said he didn't know. He would have to borrow something. We sure don't want to send him into a trap."

"I know, Joel. We will have enough manpower there to cover him, but he has to do his part. Make sure he gets there well ahead of time. Tell him to look over the setup and select a place where he can see the incoming cars, a place where Wimp will have to walk a long way in the open to get to him. Remind him that we will be monitoring his mike, and he should use it to tell us what's going on. He should tell us when he's in position and where. You will be able to tell us how he is dressed. We know his car. He should let us know as soon as he sees Wimp; tell us what Wimp is driving, what he's wearing, plus anything he sees that is suspicious."

"Yeah, we've been over most of that. He's a bright guy. I think he'll know what to do."

"Now, on the recording of the conversation. It will work better if you handle that since you will be wiring him up and checking out the equipment."

"Yes, Ed will handle that. I plan to walk around some with my dog and, you know, fake a few telephone calls. We'll be in a dark gray Bronco."

"Okay, we should be able to identify you. We will have two guys in an old white Chevy panel truck. They will park next to Wimp's car, once we identify it. The driver will do some walking around, use the vending machines, make some calls, the usual rest stop things. The man in the back will get a beeper installed on Wimp's car. We'll have the bird men, too. They will follow him when he leaves. We will also have one guy on a Harley. He will have a small mechanical problem that will keep him there 'adjusting things' for as long as he can fake it."

"What about you, Lance? You'll be there, won't you?"

"I wouldn't miss it. I'll be in my pickup, doing my contract work for the state, wearing my range grays, using my dust pan and broom to try and keep up with you 'littering tourists.' My noticeable limp is associated with the bulge on my right ankle. The holster there carries my trusty S & W snubby. I'll keep him covered."

Jack Scott was in position by 2:30 P.M. He had selected a picnic table that was more than a hundred paces from the center of rest stop activities, the restrooms. He had a clear view of the sidewalk that connected all the tables to the restroom area. He also had a clear view of the entry lanes to the CARS parking spaces. Although he had no idea what kind of vehicle Wimp would be driving, he presumed it would not be a truck.

Before leaving Tulsa, Joel Karlis had furnished Scott with a Kevlar vest which he was now wearing under his orange Oklahoma State sweat shirt. "Do you guys know something I don't know?" Scott had asked.

"We know you are all that stands between the kidnappers and a clean getaway."

"Aw, Wimp wouldn't be a part of anything like that."

"Oh, really? You didn't think he would lie to you about the truck, either, did you?"

Jack Scott now had plenty of time to think about this meeting. He had split up with Karlis before leaving Tulsa just in case Wimp might be checking on him. He had arrived at the rest stop at two-thirty. It was now after three. He had never spent a longer thirty minutes. He could not fight off the paranoia that told him some-one was slipping up on him. He had his back toward a thin stand of trees. He kept craning his neck in that direction although he could not see how anyone could leave the interstate and get into the trees without exposing themselves or taking a mighty long walk. Every man he saw looked like either an undercover FBI agent or a hit man, and he couldn't tell the difference. He made a few transmissions, but saw no reaction that would indicate he had been heard.

At ten minutes after three, he decided he was at the wrong rest stop. He must have misunderstood. He visualized Wimp and the FBI looking for him all over that stop on the other side of the interstate. Then he saw a man walking a large dog on a leash. As the man came closer, Scott realized it was Joel Karlis in truck driver clothes. "Boy am I glad to see you," he whispered into the mike. Karlis walked on without looking his way. Scott noticed that the FBI dog played his role by relieving himself on a nearby shrub. Scott was so relieved to find he wasn't alone, he couldn't resist another transmission. "Curb that dog, mister." Karlis was walking away, but Scott saw him nod and his shoulders were shaking.

Now that he knew he was in the right place and his handlers were nearby, Scott could devote all of his attention to the incoming cars. At eighteen minutes after three, he saw a silver Nissan Pathfinder with Missouri tags enter the parking area, continue well past the choice parking spaces near the restrooms and come to the end of the lot nearest his table. It parked beside his Corvette, and the unmistakable form of Wimp Wilkins left the vehicle and waved. Scott had plenty of time to describe the vehicle and Wimp's clothing—jeans, yellow sweater, black western hat and boots—long before Wimp reached hearing range.

"How are you, Scottie Boy?"

It always took Jack a few minutes to adjust to Wimp's voice. It reminded him of a young rooster, just learning to crow. He said, "You're late, Wimp."

Wimp was grinning from ear to ear and put out his hand to shake. When he saw Jack's expression, he dropped his hand and got serious.

"I'm sorry, Jack, about the truck. The people I was working with lied to me. They didn't tell me we would have to give up the truck in the deal. I thought I would be bringing it back to you, honest I did. Here's three hundred to cover what I told you you'd get, and a little more."

Jack had no trouble showing fury. "You still lied to me, Wimp.

You told me you were using the truck to move out on your girl-friend. But I don't even want to talk about that. I want to talk about now. I'll have to hire some powerful lawyers to try to get out of the mess you got me in, and you offer me three hundred dollars. It will cost me thousands if it can be done at all."

"I don't have that kind of money, Jack."

"The hell you don't! Look, Wimp, I know what you did. It's in all the papers. Somebody in the Branson Police Department leaked it. The man paid $300,000. There were three of you. The girl described you to a T with that squeaky voice."

Wimp, ignoring the insult and trying to keep things under control, said, "Yeah, but they don't have a clue who we are. She never saw a one of us."

"So you admit it. Do you think you're going to ruin my life and get off for three hundred damn dollars when you've got all that money?"

"No, I don't, Jack. I'll do what's right, but I'll tell you honestly, I haven't seen a cent of the money yet. My partner has it hidden away until the heat is off. He said the worst thing we could do is to start spending it and bring suspicion down on us."

"Oh, is that right? Where did you get the fancy car?"

"It's borrowed, Jack; I promise. I borrowed it from a girl." He grinned. "It's easy pickings in Branson, Jack, with all the young chicks trying to break into show business."

"Did you talk to your partners about what I told you?"

"There is only one partner. The other one dropped out."

"What did the one say?"

"He told me to talk with you and see if you would be reasonable."

"Oh yeah? You can tell him for me, Wimp, that I can be reasonable. Here's reasonable. I didn't kidnap anybody. I did a favor for a friend. Then I get accused by the FBI of renting a truck that was used in a kidnapping. I can be charged with a felony in

Oklahoma for using the fake ID you gave me. Reasonable you say? I can be reasonable. Ask him if he thinks it would be worth $100,000 of his ransom money to keep me quiet?"

"You can't do that, Jack."

"Yeah, you just watch me. You'd still have $100,000 each. Tell him if he doesn't want to deal, he'll wind up with nothing. Course, he won't need anything. They'll take care of him for free up there at Leavenworth. Tell him that, Wimp, and then ask him if he thinks I'm being reasonable."

Jack got up and started to walk away, then remembered Karlis's warning about exposing his back. He turned around, but Wimp was hanging his head and shaking it.

"It's not a hard decision, Wimp. I'll give you until this time tomorrow to let me know. I'll be waiting by the phone."

Scott walked away. He was a hundred feet from his car when he saw a man in coveralls slide from beneath the rear of Wimp's Pathfinder and across the three feet that separated it from a white panel truck. He remembered Karlis telling him to keep Wimp occupied for at least fifteen minutes. He had fallen way short, but when he looked back toward the bench, Wimp was still there, head down.

Jack Scott headed his Corvette toward Tulsa. He couldn't believe how tired he was. "If you read me, Agent Karlis, let's meet at the next rest stop going west. I need a rest." He removed the mike from his lapel and turned the transmitter off. He hoped like hell his acting career was over.

In Idaho Three they were tracking the silver Nissan visually, as well as making an occasional check of the OAR unit. Compared to some of their work, this was a piece of cake. It was mid-afternoon on a beautiful day. Visibility was unlimited. There was no air traffic and little ground traffic as Wimp left the Interstate at Joplin and took the scenic route on Highways 86 and 76 through, or near, such places as Neosho, Granby, Rocky Comfort, Cassville, Cape Fair, and Reeds Spring. The crew of Idaho Three flew their lazy circles, four thousand above and slightly behind Wimp as he made his way toward Branson. Pilot in Command Lewis McAllen and copilot Lanny Kapinski had flown the two-pilot operation for so many hours they felt comfortable with it even when the situation did not necessitate using it. Larry was flying the ailerons and talking with the ground units. He could widen or narrow the radius of his constant right turn and keep his eye on the Nissan. On the front side of the turn, he could look back down the highway and keep Lance Barron's pickup and Amos Trout's SUV in sight. If they threatened to close to a distance where Wimp might see them in his rear view mirror, he would alert them. He would occasionally call out a prominent land mark such as, "silo coming up on his left" or "he's turning left at the blinking light," so the ground units could gauge their own distance from the target and stay out of sight.

Wimp drove east on 76 Highway, or 76 Country Boulevard as it is known in Branson, to its intersection with Highway 165 where he turned right. The traffic was still light but it was picking up. Kapinski suggested that the ground units close the gap to a distance of four or five cars. They were still closing when Kapinski said, "He's turning into a condo complex on the left."

Lance said, "Let's go on past it, Amos, until he gets inside."

Idaho Three said, "He parked near the front. We have him out on foot. We're breaking off. What is that place, Lance?"

"It looks like a condominium development. The sign says Lakeview Manor. It's a classy looking place."

Amos said, "I'm turning around, Lance. I'll set up on his car."

"Okay, Amos, I'll cover the front door. He did go in the front didn't he, Idaho Three?"

"Yes, the front."

"Okay, I've got it covered. Amos, do you have the vehicle?"

"Yeah, I've got it. He parked in the Visitor Parking."

"Give the tag to Idaho Three. They can reach the office from their altitude. Maybe the owner lives here."

As Trout gave the tag number to Idaho Three, Lance got as comfortable as he could and readied himself for a wait. He thought back to the rest stop conversation. It seemed to lock Wimp into the kidnapping. *We have Wimp on tape admitting he's getting part of the ransom money. We are possibly at the residence of Wimp's partner, the guy Jenny called Boss. What is most likely to happen next? What should our response be? Maybe this is where Wimp lives, but he's in Visitor Parking and it looks expensive. Where does he live? He said he borrowed the car from a girl. If she doesn't live here, he will have to take it back, so we better be prepared for that.*

"Lance to Amos and Idaho Three. When our target leaves, you two work your magic on him. He's in a borrowed vehicle, so his first stop might not be his last. We want to know where he lives. I'm going inside and see if I can find out who he's talking to. How are you on fuel, Idaho Three?"

"We're in great shape. We've got a good two hours left and there's the airport right over there."

"That's the plan then. You and Amos take him when he leaves and I'll check inside here. Out."

Idaho Three, in its loitering configuration, was enjoying the sights of Branson from the best seat in the house; four thousand feet above the ridges where the trees were scraped away and replaced with automobiles. Traffic jams were a way of life here during the two hours before and after show time and a serious problem all the time. It was not surprising to Idaho Three's occupants to see a blue-lighted police car worming its way in and out of the traffic on 76 Highway. Then they noticed the ambulance a half mile behind. McAllen said, "I don't see how anyone gets up enough speed down there to have an injury accident."

Kapinski looked farther west out 76 and then under him on 165, but he saw no indication of a traffic accident. Maybe it was an accident at one of the amusement centers. Then the police car, now followed closely by the ambulance, turned left onto 165 and then left again right into the parking lot at the Lakeview Manor.

"What's going on down there, Lance?"

"I don't know, but we better sit tight for a few minutes and see if it flushes our man." After several agonizing minutes, Lance saw the ambulance crew bring a loaded stretcher out and depart. He reported it to the other units and then said, "Stay on Wimp's car, Amos. I'll see what I can find out."

Lance, in his range grays, had trouble at the front desk but his credentials and badge finally convinced the clerk, a young Asian man, to give him a few answers.

The nervous clerk said, "The resident in unit D-3 called the desk and told me he had just called the police after hearing gunshots in unit D-5, next door. I went down the hall to check on it just as the occupant of D-5 came running out carrying two suitcases. He almost knocked me down. He didn't even close the apartment door as he ran out the back entrance. I looked inside D-5 and saw a man on the floor covered with blood. I ran back here and called for an ambulance. I went back and closed the apartment door because other tenants were running around, asking questions.

"I told the police what I saw and gave them a key. They're still down there. The ambulance took the other man away."

"Did you know either of the men?"

Oh, yes, sir. I know the man in D-5. The one who lives there, I mean."

"And who is he?"

"Mr. Jim Doyle. He likes for people to call him J.D."

"Is he the one who ran out?"

"Yes, sir."

"Any idea who the other man is?"

"No, sir, but I didn't get a good look at him."

Lance was afraid he knew the answer as he headed down the hall to D-5 where two Branson Police Officers were starting a crime scene investigation. He didn't recognize either of the officers so he had to go through his identification routine again before asking, "Who was the victim here?"

The Corporal checked his clipboard and said, "He had an Oklahoma driver's license in the name Ronald Gene Wilkins, Route 4, Box 275, Wellston, Oklahoma."

"What was his condition?"

The crusty old Corporal said, "He was seriously dead. He had at least four bullet holes in him. We recovered the gun. It was empty."

"What about the other guy, the one who lives here?"

"The desk said he is Jim Doyle. Our dispatcher found a Missouri driver's license in that name showing this address, but there are no cars registered to him in Missouri. One of the neighbors said he owns a theater here. He didn't know which one."

Lance thought, *I'll bet I do.*

THE SEARCH

A warrant may be issued under this rule to search for and seize any (1) property that constitutes evidence of the commission of a criminal offense; or (2) contraband, the fruits of crime, or things otherwise criminally possessed; or (3) property designed or intended for use or which is or has been used as the means of committing a criminal offense; or (4) person for whose arrest there is probable cause, or who is unlawfully restrained.

—Title 18, United States Code
Rule 41(b) Search and Seizure

The Federal Rules of Criminal Procedure state that a search warrant authorized under Rule 41(b) may be issued by a federal magistrate within the district wherein the property or person sought is located, upon request of a federal law enforcement officer. The application for a Search and Seizure Warrant must be supported by a sworn affidavit establishing the grounds for issuing the warrant.

If the magistrate is satisfied that there is probable cause to believe that the necessary grounds exist, he issues a warrant identifying the property or person to be seized and naming or describing the person or place to be searched. The finding of probable cause may be based in whole or in part upon hearsay evidence. The warrant *commands* the officer of the United States, i.e., the FBI, to search within a specified period of time not to exceed ten days, the person or place named, for the property or person specified. The warrant can only be served in the daytime.

With the murder of Ronnie Wilkins in Branson, Lance Barron decided to devote all his effort toward determining the true identity and location of the man who called himself Jim Doyle. He had asked Ben Castle to replace him as the affiant on the application for a Search and Seizure Warrant at the residence in Oak Grove, Arkansas, where Jennifer Kogan had been held.

Castle had access to all the reports that had any bearing on the location of the house and the identity of the woman who resided there. He started the affidavit with a brief statement about the abduction. He quoted Lance Barron on the receipt of the ransom demand and the delivery of $300,000 in response to the kidnappers' instructions.

The affidavit leaned heavily on Jennifer Kogan's mental pictures of the place where she was held: the box, the bathroom, the lipstick message, the streamer, the chain link gate, the gravel drive and the goats. It included her meager description of the two men, one called Ronnie, the other J.D., and the woman she knew as Lady, who lived in the house where she was held.

Castle's statement linked Ronnie Wilkins to a rental truck used in the kidnapping through the statement of Jack Scott of Tulsa, Oklahoma. Scott knew Wilkins well and had once reached him at telephone number 501-749-8922, a number subscribed to by Jamilla Harris, Rt.3, Box 48, Oak Grove, Arkansas. Castle told of an 800 number furnished to the female kidnapper and memorized by Jenny on the day before her release. The subscriber to the 800 number was identified as a clinic in Oklahoma City. The owner's records showed that on Monday, April sixth, he made a call to a client, Mrs. Jamilla Harris, after she cancelled an appointment. Her address: Route 3, Box 48, Oak Grove, Arkansas, telephone 501-749-8922.

The affidavit reported the observations of Special Agent Leland Fain during a driveby at the Harris residence in Oak Grove, Arkansas, on the previous day. Fain reported that there was a chain link fence and gate and a long gravel drive.

Finally, Castle reported the observations of Special Agent Loyal Lambright during an aerial surveillance of Jamilla Harris's residence on the previous day at three thousand feet in which he observed a white streamer flying from a window on the south side of the residence and a herd of some twenty goats gathered in the shade in the northeast corner of the pasture.

Ben Castle's affidavit totaled seven double-spaced, type-written pages. United States Magistrate James Germany, Western District of Arkansas, Fort Smith, placed Castle under oath and had him read the affidavit. Judge Germany questioned Castle about the lack of descriptive data on Jamilla Harris. Ben Castle read from the interview of Jennifer Kogan that to the best of her knowledge there were only three other people in the house during her four-day confinement there: the man called J.D., the man called Ronnie, and the woman she had called Lady.

The court reporter was present and made a complete record of the proceedings so that the magistrate's questions and Castle's responses became a part of the affidavit.

Judge Germany found there was probable cause to believe that certain evidence of the crime of kidnapping would be found at the residence of Jamilla Harris. He issued a Search and Seizure Warrant for the residence commanding, "that Agents of the Federal Bureau of Investigation search the premises for evidence of the crime of kidnapping and further that such evidence and the person of Jamilla Harris be seized and brought before the United States Magistrate, Western District of Missouri, Springfield."

Castle took the signed warrant back to the airport where Loyal Lambright was waiting in Idaho Five. The Harris residence was not far off their return course to Springfield. Castle requested a flyover at five thousand feet. He noted that there was a small, older model, maroon automobile in the drive. "If Jamilla Harris is the only resident, she must be home," Castle commented. He checked his watch and the sinking sun. There was no way he could get the search party organized and transported back here before dark. He started making plans to serve the warrant on the following day. Maybe Lance would be available by then.

In Branson, Lance Barron returned to his car and advised Amos and the Idaho Three Crew by radio that Ronnie Wilkins had been involved in a shooting. Lance did not want to put out an unsubstantiated death report so he didn't mention the victim's name or fate. "We need to concentrate all of our efforts here. Idaho Three, how about putting down at Point Lookout. Amos will pick you up. Before you descend, contact the RA and tell Landry what has happened. Have him send a couple of people down to report to me at the condo. Amos, bring the Idaho Three crew here, and we will work out a plan of action. I'll be in suite D-5."

Lance returned to D-5 where the man in charge of the two-man police investigation introduced himself, "I'm Al Weistart, Branson PD. If I might be so bold, what is the FBI's interest here?"

Lance knew from Weistart's accent he was not a native. He shook the proffered hand as he answered, "The man who was shot, Ronnie Wilkins, was involved in a kidnapping. We had him under surveillance when he arrived here a little over an hour ago. We hoped he would lead us to the people involved with him and maybe to the money."

Weistart said, "Oh, yeah, I heard down at the station about the young girl who was in there for a while the other night. Was this guy involved in that?"

"Wilkins was. We don't know about the other man. We know the other kidnapper was a big guy sometimes called J.D. There was a woman involved. What have you come up with here?"

"Well, for starters, it was Wilkins's unlucky day. From what the desk clerk told us, Wilkins had come in only a few minutes before the tenant in D-3 reported hearing shots. From the looks of things, if Wilkins had arrived five or ten minutes later, the guy here, Jim Doyle, would have been gone. Look here." Weistart, wearing rubber gloves, walked through the apartment, opening drawers and closets. "All empty. This guy was packed and ready. The desk clerk saw him leave, and he only had two bags with him. He had already moved everything else out. The only things we found besides the gun were a couple of paper items stuck onto the inside of the wastebasket. Weistart showed Lance an evidence envelope with a legal-size white business envelope inside. The envelope bore a return address of the North Carolina State Bank, Post Office Box 3454, Concord, North Carolina. The postmark was April 2. The typewritten address read Jimmy Doyle Mahon, Rt. 2, Box 28, Lead Hill, Arkansas.

Lance said, "We were down there yesterday. We must have just missed him."

Weistart was surprised. "You knew about the guy down there?"

"Very little. We spotted his car while covering the ransom drop. It was registered down there, but he didn't live there. We didn't know about this place. You mentioned a Missouri driver's license. How does it describe this guy, Jim Doyle?"

Weistart checked his clipboard. "He's thirty-eight, six feet two inches, 240, dark brown hair, brown eyes. The desk clerk here gave pretty much the same description; said he's a flashy dresser, drives a Cadillac."

"Let me guess. It's blue with Arkansas tags."

"Yeah, he said it was blue. He didn't mention the tags."

"Corporal Weistart, do you fellows have a contact at the telephone company?"

"Hey, call me Al," he laughed. "You Southern guys are so damned formal, it breaks me up…About the contact, I haven't been around here long, but the guy with me knows everybody. He went out to the car to get the other dusting kit just before you came in." Checking his watch he laughed, "Christ, he must have stopped for coffee and donuts. Well, anyway, what's with the phone folks?"

"I'd like to find out what calls—toll calls—he made in the last week or so right up through today. That could give us a lead on Doyle and maybe the others. Course we know about one of them."

"If the phone company needs a subpoena we'll get one, but I can't imagine any of it ever becoming testimony…unless they made a ransom call from here."

"I'm pretty sure old Sam can get that for you if he ever gets back, for christsake," checking his watch again. "I know I could get it in a New York minute if I was back in Chicago."

"Chicago, huh? I knew you weren't from around here. You have New York minutes in Chicago, too?"

Weistart smiled, "Yeah. I had plenty of them. I retired from the force up there, and me and the wife moved down here. We'd been here several times and enjoyed the shows, but I've found out being here on vacation is one thing and being retired here is something else. I couldn't stand the long days. I don't fish or golf or nothing, so I applied for a job. Can you believe they didn't have a man on the force who had ever worked a murder? They've been growing so fast they didn't have anyone with much experience so they made me a corporal. How about that?"

"That's great. I like to meet people who enjoy their work...You mentioned a couple of things from the trash. What else besides the envelope?"

"I don't know what to make of this, but there were several pages from last Sunday's *News-Leader* and, well, it looked like someone had been cutting out paper dolls or something. It was cut up in an unusual way; a little bit from here and a little bit from there, you know."

Lance showed his excitement. "You kept that, didn't you?"

"Oh, yeah. Sam sealed that and the gun up while I was working with the medics. Here's Sam now."

Al rolled his eyes at Lance and smiled as Sam, lugging the dusting kit, came through the door and closed it behind him. "Did you find some good-looking babe out there, Sam? Here, let me have that kit and I'll start dusting. Meet Vance Barton. He's with the 'feebies.' Who do you know at the phone company?"

Sam and Lance waited for the barrage to end; Lance extended his hand, "It's Barron, Lance Barron, FBI; good to meet you, Sam."

"Sam Lynch. Nice to meet you, Lance. What was that about the phone company?"

Lance said, "I want to get information about the recent use of this phone. You know, who this fellow has been calling, maybe figure out where he went."

Sam reached for the phone, "I can get that for you. No sweat."

"Have you dusted it already?" Lance knew the answer; Sam had just returned with the kit.

"No, by George, we haven't. Thanks for the reminder. The phone is usually a pretty good place."

Sam found a couple of good-looking latent prints, probably palms based on where they were located. When he finished, Lance said, "I hope it's still working. Let me call my office before you call your source."

"Sure, go ahead. We haven't had any incoming calls, but I'm getting a dial tone." Sam wiped off most of the dusting powder and handed it over to Lance just as Al called out from the bathroom, "Boy, we're in luck. I've lifted some great latents from the mirror and the commode handle."

Lance dialed the Springfield RA. "Tim, things are really popping down here. Did you get some people headed this way?…Great. I need a couple of things done right away. Run an NCIC check on Jimmy Doyle Mahon. We had him before on the blue Caddy with Arkansas tags, but we didn't have a date of birth. Run a Missouri driver's license check on Jim Doyle. You'll get a hit. Then use Doyle's date of birth with the Jimmy Doyle Mahon name and see what you get. It looks like it's one guy using a Missouri driver's license and an Arkansas car registration.

"The next thing, Tim, is to call Security at Springfield Regional Airport and ask them to discreetly canvass the airlines for a departing passenger using the name Jimmy Doyle Mahon or Jim Doyle. He couldn't have departed more than thirty minutes ago. He might still be around. If there's anyone left in the office, send them out to assist airport security. They won't be able to help us if they're busy screening departures. We also need to search the airport parking lots for that blue Cadillac with Arkansas tag YYT-901.

"If Doyle or Mahon purchased a ticket, get all the flight information. If he purchased the ticket today and paid for it with cash, check all the twenty-dollar bills against the ransom list.

"I'm going to be here for a while. You can reach me at this number: 336-4916. Keep me posted. By the way, have you heard from Castle?"

"He called me from the Fort Smith airport about forty-five minutes ago. He had the warrant in hand. He wanted an Arkansas DMV check on Jamilla Harris. Vickers is working on it. They're doing a flyover of the place on the way back.

"Oh, and one more thing. Sears called. The retail stores don't list items by serial number anymore. They…"

"Let me interrupt you there, Tim. I want to hear that, but I think you better get the word out to the airport first. We also need that NCIC check as soon as you can get to it. Call me here if you hit on anything. And one more thing, Tim, call Joel Karlis in the Tulsa RA and tell him about Wimp Wilkins. He will probably want to let Jack Scott know. Tell him it looks like Wimp couldn't talk the man into being reasonable. He'll know what you mean."

Landry said, "I take it then that Wimp was the loser in the shooting down there."

"Yeah, he was the loser all right. It wasn't even close. I need to get off this phone. Thanks, Tim."

Sam Lynch had joined Al Weistart in laying fingerprint powder over nearly every square inch of the apartment. They had lifted some high quality latent prints. Maybe Wimp's early arrival had served one good purpose. It had flushed Jim Doyle out before he had a chance to wipe the place down.

"The phone is yours now, Sam; you can try your source."

"Okay, let me clean my hands, and I'll give her a call."

There was a knock at the door. Lance opened it and greeted Amos and the Idaho Three crew, McAllen and Kapinski. Lynch was on the phone. Lance made whispered introductions to Corporal Weistart and then led the three agents back out into the hall. No one would have ever guessed the four were FBI Agents. With Lance in his range grays, McAllen and Kapinski in their flying suits, and Amos in his LA Gear casuals, they were hard to label. Lance led them to a secluded corner of a patio near the pool.

"You probably guessed it already. The victim in the shooting was Wimp. The shooter was apparently the tenant, Jim Doyle. He fled the scene. We have two guys on their way from Springfield. They should be here soon. I hope they'll be in their 'interview suits.'

"Amos, I'm going to put you in charge so I can finish up in there with the Branson PD. I hope to get some lead info from the phone company. If Tim gets the information from NCIC that I think he will, I'll be heading back to Springfield to file a complaint. I hope to catch the magistrate before he goes home.

"Here is what needs to be done down here. I'll leave it up to you, Amos, to parcel it out among you three and the two 'suits' who are on the way." Lance spelled out the suggested leads as Amos, pleased that his leadership skills were being recognized, took cryptic notes:

1) Determine owner Nissan Pathfinder Wimp using, locate keys (check in vehicle, w/police here, possibly morgue), return vehicle to owner. Get all she (presumably, she) knows about Wimp. Living with her? Where? Did he talk about kidnapping? Ransom money? Other people involved?

2) Jim Doyle. Start here. Condominium application. How long here? How much paid? Close friends, other tenants? Vehicle description. Where employed? Check dumpster.

3) Credit and Criminal on Doyle. Financial problems? Branson Chamber of Commerce: Doyle, Tarheel.

4) At Tarheel Theater. Owner? Financial status. Who's in charge?

Where is Doyle? Where from? Where would he go? Car? Wimp's employment.

"If you can get that done, Amos, we ought to know enough about Doyle to find him and maybe enough to indict him."

Lance was answering questions from the pilots about the murder when Sam Lynch interrupted. "Sorry, Lance. There's a Tim Landry on the phone for you. He said it was important. I reached my lady at the phone company. She's getting the info."

"Thanks, Sam. I was just heading back in. Good luck, fellows. I'll see you back in Springfield. We might need some of you on the search tomorrow. I'll let you know."

Lance took the phone, "Go ahead, Tim."

It was hard to get Tim Landry excited, but as soon as Lance heard his first words, he knew Landry had struck pay dirt. "NCIC shows an arrest warrant for Jimmy Doyle Mahon, a k a J.D. Mahon, Jimmy Doyle, Mack Mahan, DOB 8/12/60, for bank fraud out of the District of North Carolina. I called our Charlotte office. They verified the warrant. He falsified a loan application on a music hall in Concord, North Carolina, and left with the proceeds. Left his partners and the bank holding the bag. He's a white male, six feet three inches, 250 pounds. Brown and Brown. Tattoo of a dagger on right upper arm."

"That's him, Tim! It's a tenuous thread, but it ties Jim Doyle, true name Jimmy Doyle Mahon, killer of Ronnie the kidnapper, to the car we saw twice during the ransom drop. He's got to be the second kidnapper. Anything from the airport?"

"No, nothing positive. I sent a couple of guys out there to assist, but they're just getting started. They're having problems finding anyone at some of the feeder airline desks. You know how that is. The same person sells tickets, checks baggage, issues boarding passes, loads baggage, waves the incoming plane in, unloads baggage, and waves the outgoing plane out. They are a little hard to pin down, but our guys are working on it."

"Okay, Tim. That's great news on the NCIC hit. I don't have to scramble to get a complaint filed. If we can find him, we can arrest him on Charlotte's warrant. I think Taney County will have a murder warrant out for him soon. By the way, Tim, I interrupted you earlier on the Sears lead. Did you get something on that?"

"Yeah. It's sort of anticlimactic now, but here's what happened. You know we had traced the garage door opener from the manufacturer to the Sears warehouse in Memphis. That warehouse serves several states, one being Missouri. A Memphis agent went out there to see if he could determine by serial number which Sears retail store our particular opener went to. He found out that the Sears warehouse and Sears retail stores use what they call 'assumed receiving.' When they get a lot shipment of, say, garage door openers, they scan one item in the lot into their computer and *assume* the others are there. So they couldn't tell us which retail store our opener went to.

"Gretchen was working on that. After she got the bad news from Memphis, she decided to go over to the Sears store here in the Battlefield Mall and see if they might *remember* someone they sold a garage door opener to. It was a longshot, but she hated to turn it loose. She talked to the three clerks in the department that sold that type of equipment. She only had a description of Wimp Wilkins to go on. She didn't get anywhere. She was about to leave when a supervisor from the Sears Accounting Department happened by and heard a little of their conversation. She offered her help. Gretchen lamented the fact she could not trace a garage door opener by serial number and explained why that was important.

"The young lady told Gretchen that Sears accounting uses a point-of-sale extract system. When they sell an item, they not only extract it from inventory, but they show the name of the customer who purchased it. They can then access the information in one of two ways. They can use the customer's name and tell what items he purchased within a specific time frame, or they can describe, by make and model, any item in their inventory and set search parameters for any time period they desire. The result is a report not only of the number of those items sold during the chosen period but the *names* of the customers who purchased those items. The fallacy in the system involves the customer who pays cash. Sears asks for their name for warranty purposes but does not attempt to verify it. Most customers pay with a Sears Card, another credit card or personal check, so most of the names are accurate.

"Gretchen gave the supervisor the exact make and model of the recovered opener and asked her to search for the past three weeks. Sears at Battlefield Mall had sold seven of the openers during that period. Gretchen got those names, but none were in our case index. It just gave her seven new suspects to check out. Not exactly what she needed. Gretchen came back to the office a little down, but she had started to run record checks on the seven when the Sears lady called her. She said she had asked the Joplin store, the second largest store in the area, to run the same check she had run. Joplin had sold three of the openers; one of them, a week ago, to a customer named Ronald G. Wilkins. He paid for the opener with a second party check. Sears had a picture of the check. It was drawn on the account of the Tarheel Theater, Branson. The check was payable to Wilkins and endorsed by him but signed on its face by Jim Doyle."

"Tim, that is great news! We now have one kidnapper's name and another one's alias on the same document. True, we can't prove the garage door opener they purchased is the one we recovered, but Doyle, a k a Mahon, doesn't have a garage and poor Wimp didn't even have a car. Tell Gretchen she did a great job of hanging in there. And make a note to have the SAC send a letter to the Sears store manager commending that young lady in accounting."

Lance was feeling the euphoria of success. The police officers were preparing to close up the crime scene. Lance asked Sam if his source might have tried to call while he had the phone tied up.

"No, I told her I would call back."

Lance was anxious to get back to Springfield and plan for tomorrow's search. He wouldn't have to file a complaint now. The Charlotte warrant would be adequate to hold Jimmy Doyle Mahon until the kidnapping charges were filed. The Taney County prosecutor would probably have a murder warrant on file by then. They would set a high bond on that one. The problem now was not holding Mahon, but finding him.

While waiting for Sam to reach his source, Lance asked Corporal Weistart if he could reconstruct the shooting.

"Well, I worked a lot of these in Chicago and I believe I know about how it happened. Like I used to say, 'who's gonna prove me wrong?' The dead man ain't and the accused sure ain't gonna jump up in court and say, 'naw, that's not the way it happened; let me show you.' But, seriously, based on the position of the body, the wounds inflicted, and the trajectory of the bullets, I can make a pretty good guess.

"It looks to me like the victim, Wilkins, was about here," Weistart pointed to a spot on the living room floor about eight feet from the entrance door, "when the first bullet hit him…in the back. We found an entry wound for that bullet just below his right shoulder blade. There was no exit wound. I'm not the coroner, but I believe that injury alone would have been fatal.

"That first bullet spun Wilkins around, and he went to his knees. The other three wounds were in front. I could not tell the order of those three shots. One entered the palm of his left hand and exited the back of the hand. We found a bullet, almost certainly that one, lightly imbedded in the right door facing, right here." He pointed to a scarred area twenty-four inches from the floor. "You can see the downward trajectory of that one; and if you extend your line back, you can see that the shooter, holding the gun at his waist, would have been standing right here by the desk.

"The other two bullets, probably the last two, left entry wounds very close together in the victim's throat. One of those grazed the victim's chin before entering, probably as he pitched forward from his knees toward the shooter. There was no exit wound for either of those bullets. We recovered the bullet from the door facing, and we anticipate recovering three more from the coroner. Incidentally, there was no evidence of any gunshot residue on the victim's skin or clothing. With that and the trajectory of the shots, I think the shooter was standing right here by the desk. He probably had the gun in the desk."

"What about the gun? Where did you find it?"

"You know, it looked like it could have been a last minute decision, to not take it with him, I mean. It was right over here in this corner, here on the chair in plain view, like he just tossed it over there as he went out the door."

"What kind of gun was it?"

"A real 'Saturday night special.' A piece of junk. Let's see," checking his clipboard, "a .38 caliber Tartar Revolver, manufactured by M.I.F. It had six empty cases in the cylinder."

"But you think only four shots were fired?"

"We only found evidence of four wounds. No evidence of any misses, and the guy next door on his 911 call and in his statement to Sam said there were four shots; one shot, a pause, and then three more shots. He was adamant about it. By the way, do you know if these guys knew each other?"

"Well, yes. We believe they committed a well-planned kidnapping together. Why?"

"We had a theory in Chicago that proved to be right most of the time. If the first shot was in the back, it was someone the shooter knew."

The phone interrupted Al's discourse on that theory. Lynch took the call and said, "Hold it, Marie, let me get my pad...Okay, go ahead. April 5, Springfield, Missouri, 417-865-1232, 6:10 P.M.,

1 minute; April 5, Springfield 417-433-7300, 6:16 P.M., 17 minutes; April 5, Concord, North Carolina 704-923-6572, 6:37 P.M., 6 minutes. That's it, huh? Only three long distance calls in this cycle? Okay, Marie, I've got it. Thanks, Hon."

Sam read the information from his pad. Lance had gotten most of it as Lynch wrote it down. Lance studied the information. Only three long distance calls in the two weeks of this billing period and all of those in succession on the same day—two days ago.

Lance decided that the one minute call was possibly not significant so he would chance a pretext call. He had never considered himself as skilled at making pretext calls as many agents were. Some thoroughly enjoyed it and were experts at passing themselves off as any one of a number of personae they had developed. Lance always felt the person he called could see right through the facade and might even identify him and call him by name. In spite of these doubts, he decided to dial the first Springfield number. It was answered on the first ring, "TWA Express."

"Pardon me."

"TWA Express; may I help you?"

"Yes, did you say TWA?"

"Yes, sir, TWA Express. How may I help you?"

Lance paused, then recovered. No need for a pretext here.

"Yes, my name is Lance Barron with the FBI. I'm interested in a passenger who might have boarded or perhaps is waiting to board one of your flights."

"Which flight, sir?"

"Well…I don't know which flight, we just…"

"What was his destination, sir?"

"I'm sorry, I don't know that either." Lance realized he was not making sense. He decided to try a different tack. "Ma'am, we are attempting to locate a man named Jim Doyle or Jimmy Doyle Mahon. Will you check your passenger list for that name?"

There was a pause. Lance could hear the TWA clerk talking with someone. "I'm sorry, sir, we can't give you that information over the phone."

"I understand. Thank you." Lance had a better idea. If Mahon talked to TWA Express for only one minute, then the sixteen minute call must be to another airline where he had success. Lance immediately dialed the second Springfield number.

"American Eagle."

"When is your next departure?"

"I'm sorry, sir, we have no other departures today. Our next departure will be tomorrow morning at 9:00 A.M., arriving at DFW at 10:15 A.M."

"When was your last departure?"

"Today?"

"Yes."

"Our Flight 3212 departed SGF at 4:45 P.M. and, let's see, it should be arriving at DFW just about now."

"Thank you very much."

Lance immediately called the RA for Tim Landry, "Tim, have your people at the airport contact the American Eagle desk immediately. I think it is very likely our man is on their Flight 3212 for Dallas-Fort Worth."

"We're way ahead of you, Lance. Our guys found his car in the long term parking. We impounded it. We finally tracked down the ticket agent. Jim Doyle made reservations two days ago for Auckland, New Zealand, and departed today on American Eagle Flight 3212 for DFW. We called Dallas and they transferred me directly to the RA at the airport. We briefed them on Mahon's fugitive status. They tried to intercept him. Unfortunately the American Eagle flight arrived early. Mahon had transferred to an American Airlines flight to Los Angeles and was taxiing before our people got the word. We have Los Angeles fully briefed and ready. He is scheduled to arrive at LAX at 9:30 our time, 7:30 their time. He is ticketed on Quantas Flight QF-100, non-stop LAX to

Auckland, New Zealand, scheduled to depart LAX at 9:30 their time. LA has assured me he would not be on it. American Eagle told us he has one carry-on bag and one checked bag which he has to claim and re-check for the Quantas flight. LA plans to grab him when he claims the bag."

"How about the ticket, Tim? Did he pay cash, by chance?"

"No. We can't get all the breaks. He paid with an American Express card in the name Tarheel Theater, Jim Doyle."

After Lance read Ben Castle's affidavit for the Search and Seizure Warrant, he reduced the size of the search team to six agents beside himself. From Jenny's description of the house, there would not be much area to search, and it seemed likely there would be only one person there.

Corporal Vickers had determined through INLETS that Jamilla Harris, Rt. 3, Box 48, Oak Grove, Arkansas, owned a 1985 Ford Escort, Arkansas Tag SAU-090. Idaho Five had been dispatched to the Harris residence early. They reported a maroon automobile in the drive.

The team, in two automobiles and a pickup truck, arrived at Harris residence at 8:05 A.M. Leland Fain, who had been designated as the photographer, began his log with photos of the chainlink fence, gate, and the long gravel driveway to the house.

The three vehicles moved slowly up the drive. While Lance's lead vehicle, with Fain in the passenger seat, was still fifty yards from the porch, the front door opened and a tall female in a dark business suit with a white open-collar blouse stepped onto the porch. She stood motionless until Lance, in the lead vehicle, reached the parking area behind the ten-year-old maroon Ford. When Lance opened his door, the woman slowly raised her hands until they were high above her head. Lance and Fain relaxed a little as they started for the porch. The woman said softly, "I'm Jamilla Harris. I've been expecting you."

As unique as this scene was in Lance's experience, he still felt himself slip into the normal arrest routine. "Jamilla Harris, you are under arrest for the crime of kidnapping in violation of Title 18, United States Code, Section 1201. I also have a search warrant for your residence. We will be searching for evidence of the crime of kidnapping.

"For our safety and yours, please lean against the wall there while Agent Baldwin pats you down for weapons." As Lucy did the perfunctory pat-down, Lance thought back to Jenny's statement about this woman, how she had saved Jenny from abuse and how she had performed several acts of kindness. He could believe it. She displayed a serenity that Lance found difficult to associate with an arrest.

The next step in the routine was handcuffing. It was the rule. It was always done. Lance had his cuffs in his hand, but decided he could not do it. He could recall only one other time he had made an exception to the rule. Several years ago, he was to arrest a diminutive seventy-seven-year-old labor leader who had his rival for the presidency of the union killed. FBI headquarters knew that news of the indictment had been leaked and there would be much media coverage of the arrest. In deference to the union leader's age and failing health, FBIHQ ordered that he not be handcuffed. That was Lance's first exception to the rule. He decided to make this the second. He had started to put the handcuffs away when the woman held out her hands, back to back and said, "Go ahead. I understand. You're doing your job."

Lance and Lucy took the woman, in handcuffs, to the Bucar and put her in the rear seat, right side—the place for prisoners. Lucy closed and locked the door. Lucy then guarded the prisoner while Lance went around the back of the car and entered the driver's side front door. Lance then guarded the prisoner as Lucy went around the back of the car, entered the rear seat on the driver's side, closed and locked that door. By the book. That routine had always seemed so right to Lance, so official, so efficient. Why did he now have the agonizing feeling that he was doing something wrong? He almost felt shame. It was not that she was a woman. He had arrested many women: revolutionaries, prostitutes, embezzlers, the wife of a porno king who had a purple mohawk hairdo. No, it was this woman's dignity that set her apart. Dignity? Lance would have been hard pressed to define it, but he knew it when he encountered it.

I must be getting soft or maybe I'm just tired, but I've got to shape up, Lance admonished himself. He forced himself to think back to yesterday, to the bloody floor in Suite D-5, the door facing scarred by a bullet. A bullet that had passed through the hand of a simple man pleading for his life. Then he thought back to two days ago when he saw Jenny Kogan at the police station with bloodshot eyes and tape in her hair. A sixteen-year-old girl forced to face up to the real possibility of death or insanity much too early in her life, but who still fought to remember all she could. A girl standing proud in her cheerleading uniform in spite of urine stains on her skirt, hamburger stains on her sweater, and scrapes on her knuckles. Stains and scrapes from having to live locked in a box for four days right there in that house. And the woman in the back seat had been a part of it. *Lord, forgive our inhumanity.*

Lucy Baldwin was reading the advice of rights. Lance thought, *I've got to remember she's a kidnapper. I've got to quit thinking of her as "the lady." She's Jamilla Harris, criminal.*

When Lance didn't take over the interview after Jamilla Harris signed the waiver and agreed to answer questions, Lucy Baldwin went into the background and descriptive data and soon Jamilla Harris was telling her story. There was no reason to ask questions. Jamilla Harris was making her statement. She told of growing up in poverty, working in the fields, working her way through high school and community college. She had married an Army Sergeant and was divinely happy until he went to Vietnam and came back broken in body and spirit. They used his mustering-out pay and the G.I. Bill to buy this place because he had always wanted to farm and raise chickens and goats. They didn't know he would die.

She told with pride about the accomplishments of her son who was born with a crippled leg but still lettered in basketball in junior high school. After her husband died, she had to let her son go to live with her mother in Harrison because of her long and irregular hours as a paralegal for an attorney in Berryville. She told of meeting Ronnie Wilkins, a client her boss was representing on a burglary charge; how Wilkins took an interest in her son. He told them of a clinic in Oklahoma that had done wonders for youngsters by fitting them with a new kind of prosthetic device. She and her son became obsessed with the idea. Then they learned the price, almost $20,000. Ronnie even had an answer for that. He told her of a friend who was working on a plan to make some real money. He said his friend would cut her into the project in exchange for the use of her house for a few days. The plan also called for Ronnie to live at her place for a while so he could use her workshop during his off-work hours.

Jamilla Harris said that by the time she realized what the plan was, her son had become so excited about the possibilities the new leg offered that she could not bear to disappoint him. She agreed to be a part of the kidnapping only on the condition that no harm would be done to the girl. Once she met J.D. and sensed his cruelty, she became concerned not only for the girl but for her own safety.

Jamilla Harris described in detail the notification system she set up through her minister and her mother so that if anything happened to her, the authorities would be notified and the whole scheme exposed.

Jamilla Harris provided all the information she had on the identity of Ronnie Wilkins, which was considerable since she had a file on him in the office. She had little information on the man she knew as J.D., but she had learned that he ran a music hall in Branson and Ronnie Wilkins worked for him.

On the day of the abduction, she had driven her car and followed Ronnie and J.D., who were in J.D.'s Cadillac, to a spot on 65 Highway north of Springfield. They parked on the shoulder and left the car there. When Ronnie and J.D. got into her car, they both carried gym bags and Ronnie had a gun—a rifle of some sort.

They told her to drive south on 65 Highway. Ronnie and J.D. put on black coveralls, ski masks, and gloves, and sat low in the seats as they directed her to a high school in southeast Springfield. They spotted a red Mustang and had her park nearby. When they saw a girl in a cheerleader outfit hurry toward the Mustang and drive away, J.D., who gave all the orders, had her follow at a distance. He was able to predict each turn the Mustang made. As it entered a residential area and pulled into a driveway, J.D. yelled, "Stop!" Both men jumped out. She last saw them running up the driveway past the Mustang and into a garage.

Jamilla Harris told the whole story with little emotion. When she finished, she paused and gazed out the window and across her land. "I know what I did was terribly wrong. I confess to my part in it, and I will sign a statement to that effect." Then slowly and with heavy emphasis on each word she said, "But I want you to know, and I want the girl to know, and I want her parents to know, and I want the judge to know, a truth that Almighty God already knows. I would never have done any of it for myself. Until you have seen your own flesh and blood suffer and in need you don't know what you would do." With that, she buried her face in her handcuffed hands and sobbed.

Lance headed for Springfield with his prisoner and pondered the fine line of fate that had put him in the front seat and Jamilla Harris in the back.

JUSTICE

In the State of Missouri, First Degree Murder is a Class A Felony
(Penalty shall be death or life imprisonment without probation or
parole). A person commits the crime of first degree murder if (s)he:
1. knowingly, 2.causes the death of another, 3.after deliberation upon
the matter. Deliberation is defined as cool reflection for any length of
time no matter how brief.

—Section 565.020 Revised Statutes of Missouri

FBI agents awaiting the arrival of Jimmy Doyle Mahon's flight at
the Los Angeles International Airport had no photograph. They had
the description received in the phone call and follow-up teletype:
name, aliases, age, height, weight, color hair, color eyes, a tattoo
which was concealed by clothing and the comment, "flashy
dresser."

Three of the passengers who arrived on American Airlines Flight
372 fit the general description of Mahon. All three went to the
baggage carousel. The agents feared that once the bags arrived all
three suspects, including Mahon if he became suspicious, could be
out the door quickly and gone. They would have to detain all
three, and they were short-handed.

One of the agents, a veteran who had been assigned to the LAX
RA for nine years, called airport security where he was well-
known. He asked security to page Quantas passenger Doyle and
instruct him to pick up the nearest service phone for a "flight
scheduling" message. The agents surreptitiously watched their
"possibles" as the announcement was made. None went to the service phone, but one began a pattern of looking first over one
shoulder, then the other. He continued the exercise at an acceler-
ating rate until the bags arrived. There was little doubt he was the
man. He was the only one with tassels on his shoes.

When Mahon claimed his bag, the agents claimed Mahon and

the bag. During the search incident to his arrest, the agents found twenty-five twenty-dollar bills in his billfold. All twenty-five were on the ransom list. They impounded the checked bag, a large gray canvas-sided bag with rollers and a pull strap. It weighed forty-six pounds. The following day they obtained a search warrant for the bag based on probable cause information furnished by Kansas City and supplemented by their finding of ransom money on his person. The suitcase contained twenty-two used, hardcover books. The books were placed neatly around the edges of the suitcase. The space in the center held a plastic garbage bag containing $289,880 in strapped twenty-dollar bills. All 14,494 bills were on the ransom list.

The search of Jamilla Harris's house in Oak Grove, Arkansas, produced a wealth of evidence that Jenny Kogan had been held there. Agents recovered her toilet paper banner from the bathroom window. In the garage they found the plywood box exactly as Jenny had described it. The four agents stood reverently beside it, resembling pallbearers as they imagined Jenny's ordeal and thought of their own children. They carefully removed the box, intact, for shipment to the FBI lab. Hair samples later found inside were identified as Jenny's, and fiber samples matched those from Jenny's skirt and sweater.

The lipstick message on the inside of the box and on the banner was identical in all respects to lipstick from a tube found in the bathroom. The tube bore Jennifer Marie Kogan's left thumb print. The metal hasp securing the lid on the plywood box bore the left index and left thumb prints of Jimmy Doyle Mahon. Tool marks on the box were made by a hammer found in Jamilla Harris's workshop. The hammer bore the right index fingerprint of Ronald G. Wilkins.

A metal chair found near the plywood box had a small blood smear on it. When Jimmy Doyle Mahon was returned from

Los Angeles, court-ordered blood and hair samples were taken. The FBI laboratory matched the DNA in Mahon's sample with the DNA in the smear found on the chair.

The agents in Los Angeles wondered how Mahon expected to get through New Zealand customs with the cache of ransom bills. In Branson Amos Trout thought he had the answer. He had assigned the two pilots the task of searching the trash dumpster at Lakeview Manor. They struck gold. The dumpster must have been dumped just before Mahon cleaned out his room. Almost every item they found came from his apartment. A warm personal letter to Mahon from an Angie Riddle in North Carolina indicated she would be arriving in Auckland just hours before him. There were numerous newspaper clippings about Charles Kogan, Kogan Airways, and the contract fight between Kogan and Kline. There was a series of letters from a Daniel McCall of Auckland, apparently an old Marine Corps buddy of Mahon. McCall's assurance to Mahon that he would, "meet your flight and personally handle the baggage matter," led Trout to believe that McCall either worked for New Zealand Customs or had paid off someone who did.

Amos furnished the Daniel McCall information to Tim Landry by telephone for relay through FBI Headquarters to the State Department. New Zealand Customs needed to know about Daniel McCall.

Amos's team also learned from the local Chamber of Commerce that the Tarheel Theater was in dire financial straits. Jim Doyle had purchased the theater with a cash down payment. He financed the major portion through a local bank. The loan was set up with low monthly payments for the first year with a large balloon due in May. Rumor among the bankers was that Mahon would not be able to make the balloon payment.

Amos's team found a dispirited group of employees at the

Tarheel. Attendance was down. No one had received a raise since Mahon, known to them as Doyle, took over. Rumors were that Doyle was "messing with the books." A week ago, Doyle had had a heated argument with the bookkeeper, Jerry Bates, who doubled as rhythm guitarist in the band. Doyle fired Bates on the spot. The band had been without a rhythm guitarist since.

★ ★ ★

Two days after the murder of Ronnie Wilkins, Lance was in the office preparing an affidavit in support of a complaint charging Jimmy Doyle Mahon with kidnapping in the Western District of Missouri. The kidnapping warrant was to be used in the removal hearing in California to bring Mahon back to Missouri.

"Phone call for you, Lance." Millie, the secretary, smiled, covered the phone and said, "I guess he wants you. He asked for agent 'Vance Barrow.' It's a Corporal Al Weistart, Branson PD."

Lance laughed, "Hello, Corporal Al. Have things slowed down any in Branson?"

"Not a helluva lot. Remember the two extra shell casings in the Saturday night special? We've found the bullets that were fired from them."

"Don't tell me the coroner found…"

"No, nothing like that. A fisherman in Lake Taneycomo thought he'd hooked a world champion trout until he realized it wasn't moving. He had hooked into a body floating right beneath the surface. It was a young man who had worked for Doyle at his theater, a Jerry Bates. His wife had reported him missing two days ago. The coroner found two slugs in the body. I'm taking those two, Doyle's gun, and the slugs from the other job to the crime lab. I'm sure from eye-balling them that they all went through the same gun."

Lance was momentarily speechless. Amos had just briefed him on Mahon's problem with his bookkeeper; now he was dead. "Any idea when he did it?"

"The coroner thinks it was just hours before Wilkins. Do you guys still have Doyle's car?"

"We have it impounded, but we haven't processed it. Get us a set of prints on Bates. We'll send them in with any latents we lift. Our guys talked to some people at the Tarheel who heard the argument when Mahon fired him. It was ugly."

"Right, and with the ballistics, if we could put Bates in Doyle's car, that would be the clincher."

"Have you talked with your prosecutor, Al? I think you've got a strong death penalty case. That could affect the thinking of our federal prosecutor."

"Oh, yeah. I talked to him. He's gung ho. He's young and wants to make a name for himself. You know, all these young lawyers stay in the prosecutor's job a couple of years, make a name, and then go over to the other side where the money is. A death penalty case would be worth about a million dollars in advertising to him."

"Keep me up to date on that, Al, and I'll keep our AUSA posted. We can't get ready for both trials at the same time. We'll be using many of the same witnesses."

"Sure thing, Buddy. I'll let you know as soon as we file."

"Say, Al, as a matter of interest, did your theory hold up in this one?"

"What's that?"

"You know, your theory about where the entry wounds are?"

"Oh, Yeah. I'm batting a thousand. Doyle shot this one in the back, too."

"Doyle?…If you're going to put this guy Mahon to death, Al, you've got to start calling him by his real name."

"Okay, okay, G-Man, I'm not much for names."

"Yeah, Al, I've noticed that." They both laughed.

It had been three months since Ronnie Wilkins's funeral. Jack Scott had attended the graveside services, but he stayed in the background and made no effort to speak to Wimp's grieving parents. Not that he felt any guilt over what had happened. In fact, he still felt anger toward Wimp every two weeks when he wrote his check to the county court paying off his fine and when he went to the Ryder Agency to make his court-ordered restitution for the cutting torch damage to their truck. The FBI had come through in advising the county prosecutor of his assistance in the kidnapping case. No criminal charges had been filed. The incident had been handled as a civil offense. There would be nothing on his record that would affect his pilot's license.

As Jack drove from Wellston toward the Wilkins farm he felt better than he had in months. He hoped this visit would help him shed that last bit of anger. He also had someone he wanted them to meet.

Jack was saddened to see how much the Wilkinses had aged. Mr. Wilkins didn't even remember him. Dora Mae tried to help, "Don't you remember, Willie? This is the young man that was going to Branson to see Ronald."

Mr. Wilkins scratched his head, "We always said we were going over there to see him play, but we never did. The policeman that called said Ronald was breaking up a kidnapping over there. That's what happened to him."

Jack said, "I stopped by to see how you were getting along, and I wanted you to meet my fiancé, Miss Gloria Benson."

Mrs. Wilkins said, "It's so nice to meet you, Gloria. My, aren't you a pretty thing?"

Miss Gloria Benson blushed, "Why thank you, Mrs. Wilkins. Jack has told me about you and your pretty flowers, and I can see what he meant."

As the two women talked about flowers and walked toward the flower bed on the side of the house, Mr. Wilkins said, "Did you ever get over to Branson to hear my boy play? They tell me he was good at it. We always said we were going to get over there to hear him, but we never did."

"No, sir, I didn't make it this time. Course I heard him a lot in college." The conversation was awkward for Jack. More so than he thought it would be.

Mr. Wilkins scratched his head again and headed inside. He stopped near the porch, turned and said once more, "We always said we were going over there to see him play, but we never did."

He didn't even mention the weather.

In Springfield it was one of those sparkling October days that brings people flocking to the Ozarks to see the foliage and visit the Bass Pro Shop. Lance ran into Charles Kogan in the parking lot as they headed for a scheduled meeting with the AUSA. Kogan was in a foul mood because the trial of the kidnappers had not yet been scheduled. Lance knew that after today's meeting with Paul Trammel, Kogan's mood would be worse. Trammel had decided not to have the Federal Grand Jury indict Jimmy Doyle Mahon during this session. The reason was simple and sound. The Federal Speedy Trial Act required that a trial begin within sixty days after indictment. The Taney County prosecutor was ready to go with his two-count first-degree murder case. He had announced he would seek the death penalty. The evidence was overwhelming against Mahon in the Wilkins case. The Bates case was equally strong on ballistics. It had become even stronger when Lance found a cuff link in the back seat of Mahon's car that was identical to one still in Bates's shirt when they pulled his body from the lake. Lance also found Bates's guitar in the trunk of Mahon's car with Mahon's palm print on the neck.

If Taney County failed to convict Mahon of first-degree murder, he could still be indicted and tried for kidnapping in the federal system. He would probably plead guilty. With the solid physical evidence plus the testimony of both Jenny Kogan and Jamilla Harris, a trial would seem to be futile.

The decision had been made. AUSA Trammel was going to defer the indictment of Jimmy Doyle Mahon until the State of Missouri completed its trial on the two counts of Murder in the First Degree. As a courtesy, Trammel wanted to explain his decision to Mr. Kogan before he made it public.

Jenny Kogan was taking advantage of the schedule to introduce Jamilla Harris and her son Kevin to her father. Jenny had visited Mrs. Harris several times while she was still in jail. She had met Kevin on two occasions when she traveled to Harrison to meet Jamilla's mother. Jamilla's mother had made the arrangements for getting Kevin to Oklahoma City for the fitting of his new prosthetic device. Charles Kogan had put up the money. Today was to be the first chance Mrs. Harris and Kevin had to meet and thank Mr. Kogan for his generosity.

The release of his daughter and the recovery of most of the ransom money had put Charles Kogan in a generous mood. He had decided that his daughter needed a new car. Without consulting Jenny or his wife, he surprised her with a gleaming new Cadillac Catera convertible. Jenny tried to be gracious but could not hide her true feelings. "Daddy, I love you and I appreciate your generosity, but I don't *need* any more things. I now realize there is so much more to life than that. When I was in that box I made a list of what I wanted most. Do you know what, Daddy, not a one of them could be purchased. Jamilla Harris gave me something I could never have bought: hope. She saved my life and showed great courage in doing it. I now know she wanted nothing for herself. Her total motivation was to do something for her son.

"I know you grew up poor, but you overcame it. Your pride should not be in the things you have *bought* but in what you have accomplished. I want you to do something now that few people have the power to do. I want you to give someone a chance to lead a normal life." Her father looked perplexed. She went on, "This is more important to me than anything else you could do. Please listen to me, Daddy. I want you to take the money you spent on that car and give it to Jamilla Harris. To lead a normal life, her son needs an artificial leg. Can you imagine, Daddy, having the power to give someone a chance at a normal life? That's what it would mean to Kevin. That's awesome, Daddy. Giving someone a chance. That's real power. Not many people have that kind of power."

Jenny's magic had worked again. Her dad had checked with his CPA about the tax implications of such a gift, but it was Jenny who had won him over. Today was the Harrises' chance to thank him.

As Lance and Kogan walked together toward the elevators in the Federal Court House, Lance recalled a mannerism of Kogan's he had observed several times. He had noticed that when anyone on the elevator punched the button for their floor, Kogan would invariably follow up by punching the same button himself. Lance at first thought it was a one- or two-time thing, but after several trips with Kogan—to the bank when they returned the recovered ransom money, to the hospital the night Jenny was released, and now several trips to the Federal Court House—Kogan had never failed to follow the same strange routine.

Lance had not seen Kogan for a few weeks. He wondered if Kogan would continue the harmless but bizarre behavior.

AUSA Trammel's office was on the sixth floor of the Federal Building. They entered the elevator, and Lance punched button number six. Before the elevator moved, Kogan reached over and punched button number six. A late arrival barely made it through the door. He punched the button for the fourth floor. Kogan reached partway around Lance to re-punch button four. When the late arrival left the elevator on the fourth floor, Lance punched the CLOSE DOOR button. Kogan followed suit even though the door was already starting to close. Lance chuckled to himself as he watched Kogan go through the routine like a trained seal, unaware of how ridiculous his actions appeared to others. *Maybe I'm the only one who notices such things,* Lance thought.

AUSA Trammel congratulated Kogan on an article that had appeared in the Sunday edition of the *News-Leader,* crediting Kogan with the phenomenal growth of Kogan Aviation and pointing out the favorable impact his company had on the local economy.

Kogan had a hard time accepting compliments. He said, "All it means to me is I have to send more to Washington every month. Now, what is this I hear about you not charging anyone with my daughter's kidnapping?"

AUSA Trammel had dealt with Kogan enough to know he was not one for friendly conversation, but he kept trying. After receiving this latest rebuff he explained to Kogan that he was recommending that the indictment of Jimmy Doyle Mahon be held in abeyance until after the Taney County trial. The State had charged Mahon with two counts of Murder in the First Degree, each one of which could result in the death penalty, and one count of kidnapping. Trammel patiently explained the federal government's speedy trial act and how Mahon could still be tried for kidnapping after the state trial whether or not he was convicted of murder.

AUSA Trammel also explained the government's decision to recommend Jamilla Harris for pre-trial diversion, a form of probation before trial. Trammel said Harris was a perfect candidate. She had been totally cooperative with the government in preparing the case for prosecution, bringing out facts about Mahon and Wilkins that the government would not have otherwise known. She had no previous record. She was gainfully employed. She was supporting a dependent son and helping support her mother. She had agreed to testify at Mahon's trial (federal or state) and, finally, she had been instrumental in ensuring Jenny's safety during her ordeal and had actually taken the initiative in releasing her from that confinement.

Lance said the FBI had no objection to the State of Missouri getting the first shot at Mahon.

Kogan said, "I just hope no one gets the idea they can kidnap Charles Kogan's daughter and not even go to trial for it."

AUSA Trammel said, "No one will think that, Mr. Kogan. If Missouri doesn't convict Mahon, he will be indicted and if he doesn't plead guilty, we will go to trial. He will probably jump at the chance to plead guilty in federal court to get into the federal prison system. It doesn't take a con long to learn that the federal pen is the place to do time."

Trammel's intercom came to life, "Sir, Miss Kogan and her guests are here."

"Okay, Margie, send them in."

Kogan couldn't take a chance that the AUSA didn't know of his benevolence. He leaned over and said, "They're here to thank me for what I did for them."

Jenny Kogan was grinning broadly as she came through the door. She had one arm around the waist of a tall, striking black woman. They were followed by a young black man wearing a high school letter jacket and a strapping young man Lance and Trammel recognized from the sports pages as football star Jason Yeager. Lance noticed that the black youth had an almost imperceptible limp.

Kogan's mouth was still agape when Jenny, beaming, said, "Daddy, this is Jamilla Harris and her son Kevin. Mrs. Harris—Lady—I'd like for you and Kevin to meet my dad."

Kogan put out his hand toward Mrs. Harris but quickly pulled it back. His face was flushed, and perspiration popped out on his upper lip. He made a couple of efforts at speaking and finally came out with, "Well, I'm, uh, happy to meet you folks." He almost choked on the words.

Lance watched Jenny as her father sputtered. She was oblivious to his impaired state. He thought, *The unbiased mind is a beautiful thing.*

There was some obligatory small talk about the Harrises' trip up from Oak Grove, the traffic around Branson, and then Kevin made a well-rehearsed but still nervous speech about the blessing of getting a chance to lead a normal life. Mrs. Harris made a brief but eloquent statement of her own gratitude. She told of reading an article in the Sunday newspaper more than a year ago about a young man from Texas who had been fitted with a new kind of prosthetic device made by a company in Oklahoma City. The new device enabled the young man not only to lead a normal life but to play basketball for a small college. From that moment on, getting such a device for her son had become her consuming desire. "Mr. Kogan, you have made it all come true." She again extended her hand toward Kogan and said, "We will never forget what you have done for us."

This time Kogan took her hand and said, "Well, you've got to know how stubborn Jenny is. She is the one you should thank."

After more small talk Jenny said, "I'm taking them out to see Bass Pro Shop. I'll see you later, Dad, and you too, Mr. Barron. Nice to see you again, Mr. Trammel."

Smiles and goodbyes were exchanged all around, but as soon as they cleared the door an irate Charles Kogan turned to Lance, "Goddamn you, Barron, you didn't tell me they were black."

Lance knew this was coming. He let Kogan rant on about being deceived by Lance and his own daughter. Lance finally moved around to get squarely in front of Kogan. He looked directly into Kogan's eyes and slowly, emphasizing each word with his finger, asked, "Does it really make a difference?"

Kogan stopped his ranting. He seemed to examine the question as though he had never considered it before. Lance allowed himself to hope that Kogan was coming to some great moral awakening. Instead Kogan said, "Well, I'll still get my tax break."

Kogan made a final admonishment to AUSA Trammel to make

it clear in his press release that Mahon was also being charged with the kidnapping of Charles Kogan's daughter. After receiving that assurance, Kogan and Barron bid farewell and headed for the elevator. Lance deliberately stood near the control panel. He punched the button for the ground floor. Sure enough, Kogan started to reach around him to make his punch. Lance gently intercepted his arm and said, "Let's see if it'll work if you don't punch any buttons."

Kogan pulled his arm back, gave Lance an angry look as the elevator started down. "What the hell do you mean by that, Barron?"

Lance smiled, "Oh, it's just a little test I wanted to run. I thought I knew the answer. I just wanted to make sure."

Kogan shook his head and muttered something about "frigging college boys."

Kogan was still pouting when they reached the parking lot. He headed for his car without so much as a goodbye. But as Lance neared his car Kogan called out across the lot, "Hey, Lance!"

When Lance looked up, Kogan continued, "I guess you college boys are all right."

Lance Barron smiled and nodded. As he entered his car he said aloud. "Considering the source, that's the best compliment I have ever received."

Give the gift of

WHEN NO ONE PURSUES

to your friends and colleagues

☐ Yes, I want _____ copies of *When No One Pursues*
at $19.95 each, plus $2 shipping per book.
Please allow 15 days for delivery.

My check or money order for $_____ is enclosed, or
please charge my ☐ Visa ☐ MasterCard

Name _____

Address_____

City / State / Zip _____

Phone _____

Credit card number_____exp. date _____

Signature _____

Please make your check payable and return to:

Golden Shield Press
Post Office Box 8115
Hot Springs, AR 71910-8115

Or

Call credit card orders to (800) 451-1214. Code 03.

11/21 Eleanor